PICTURE WORD BOOK is reprinted by permission of Western Publishing
Company, Inc, by:

THE RIGGS INSTITUTE PRESS
4185 SW 102ND AVENUE
BEAVERTON, OREGON, 97005

This special edition was edited by Myrna McCulloch and Sharon Madsen for The
Riggs Institute for use with *America's Spelling & Reading with Riggs* curriculum
materials and *The Writing Road to Reading,* November, 1991.

ISBN 0-924277-04-1

THIS BOOK BELONGS TO
Kayla

A B  C  D E

Z

A Basic
and Usage

Y

Edited for special use by

Myrna McCulloch & Sharon Madsen

X

THE RIGGS INSTITUTE PRESS
Beaverton, Oregon

W  V  U  T  S

F G H I J

Spelling Dictionary

K

L

Formerly published as

PICTURE WORD BOOK - A Child's Dictionary

by Garnette Watters & S.A. Courtis

M

WHITMAN PUBLISHING COMPANY
Racine, Wisconsin

R

Q

P

O

N

A WORD FROM THE PUBLISHERS

This PICTURE WORD BOOK was first planned and published as "A Children's Picture Dictionary," and it is as a Picture Dictionary that it has become known and accepted by tens of thousands of parents, teachers, and children. It is now published under the main title of PICTURE WORD BOOK with the sub-title A Child's Dictionary to emphasize that it is useful to children of all ages, from the tot first learning to read to the older child beginning to understand the changing forms of words.

Parents and teachers are urged to refer to "Explanation of a Picture Word Book" on pages 467–468, and "A Word to Teachers" on pages 469–470. However, the child can use this book alone, without aid, simply as a child's dictionary.

The authors wish to acknowledge that the development of this PICTURE WORD BOOK was made possible through the co-operation and diligent efforts of teachers, principals, and supervisors of the elementary grades of the public schools of Hamtramck, Michigan. To all those persons who participated in or contributed to the development of this book, the authors extend gratitude and appreciation.

PRESENT PUBLISHER'S INTRODUCTION
TO
A BASIC SPELLING & USAGE DICTIONARY

The primary-level *Picture Word Book*, subtitled "A Child's Dictionary" by Garnette Watters and S.A. Courtis, originally published by Whitman Publishing Company of Racine, Wisconsin, is now republished by The Riggs Institute with permission of the current copyright holder, Western Publishing, Inc.

As originally intended, it is still appropriate for use by any primary student. It should also prove useful for E.S.L and bilingual students, and it has now been edited for special use with the multi-sensory, intensive phonetic, and unified language arts program taught by The Riggs Institute in their curriculum materials entitled, *America's Spelling & Reading with Riggs*. These direct instruction and non-consumable teacher aids are recommended by the non-profit Riggs Institute to be taught in conjunction with the original text by Romalda & Walter Spalding, *The Writing Road to Reading*, William Morrow and Co., New York. The methodology in the Spalding text is based on the learning and teaching theories of Dr. Samuel T. Orton, a neuropathologist who researched the functioning of the brain in learning language.

The Riggs Institute conducted a search for several years for a primary-level dictionary which did not suggest pronunciations of words as dictionaries generally do. According to researchers, Drs. Robert Seashore, Rudolph Flesch and Jeanne Chall, children already have speaking, pronunciation and comprehensive vocabularies ranging from 4,000 to 24,000 words when they enter grade one. It follows that the first task of teaching reading is not one of teaching pronunciation. Spelling is the more important task in beginning instruction whether with the primary student or with an older, but new, speaker of English.

The language method taught through *The Writing Road to Reading* and the Riggs' materials recognizes this, and begins its instruction at that exact point - the primary-level *speech* capability. Obviously, children already know how to say the 45 sounds of English speech (all that are needed to say over one-half million English words) which they use in conversation. During the first eight weeks of instruction, primary students are taught to "isolate" these sounds - in both print and speech - as they also learn manuscript printing skills such as is shown, with markings for each word, in the dictionary.

Students then apply these newly learned 70 "phonograms" (see listing and illustrative "key" words for these phonograms on pages v. & vi.) which are the most commonly-used correct spelling patterns of the 45 speech sounds of English, through written, dictated spelling lessons. 28 spelling rules are taught, not by rote memorization, but by application in the 1700 most commonly used English words. A special, memory-aid marking system is also used. Its key is on page iii.

Generally, when there is a difference between what one hears or pronounces in the rhythm of English speech (regional pronunciations considered) and correct spelling, this system first stresses what one must "think" to spell correctly. For instance, in the U.S.A., we say, "*ugenst*" but think, to write and spell, "*ā gāinst*" - more like our British friends still pronounce it. We say "*butn*" but think, write and spell, "*but tŏn,*" sounding both t's for spelling. Which ah? The letter "**o**" which we have taught as "**ah**" - "**ō**" - "**o͞o**." If we relied on pronunciation alone, we could easily misspell it using an **a**, **u**, **e**, or **i** for the vowel in the last syllable. Since we very often use a "schwa" pronunciation in speech, Romalda Spalding employs mnemonic memory aids and rules to teach correct spellings to those students who cannot simply memorize the shape and form of words. We say, "*Wenzday*," but write, spell, and think, "*Wed nes day*."

This method teaches around the "schwa" which is shown by an upside-down ə which indicates the "uh" sound for the vowels a, e, i, and o in unstressed syllables. The schwa was included in most American dictionaries by the 1940's, and, probably, has been a major contributing factor in the general deterioration of both speech and spelling skills. Correct spelling is stressed in this method to eliminate some of these problems, and because most good spellers are also good readers while the reverse is not true. The marking system shown on the following page will assist young students to recall correct spelling patterns which can, in turn, very often be explained through etymology, a study of word origins.

Of course, we recognize that the illustrations in this book are dated, but we elect to leave them intact. We think them charming, and hope that they will form the basis for many interesting classroom discussions.

MARKING KEY FOR SPELLING

This dictionary has been edited by The Riggs Institute to include these markings which indicate the spelling structure of each word as follows:

1) Vowels are underlined when they say their names in a given word (belong - name - old).

2) Phonograms of two or more letters are underlined to show that the letters in these combinations are not pronounced separately but form one sound in each word as they are shown (fault, sight, eight, nation, badge). The multiple letters in consonant "blends" are not underlined since they each retain their own sound value even as they are blended.

3) All silent letters (limb, naughty, raspberry) and those which use a different sound, in an individual word, from those taught in the 70 phonograms (onion, dwarf, friend) are double underlined. This includes five kinds of silent final e's (time, have₂, blue₂, chance₃, charge₃, little₄, are₅).

4) If a phonogram has more than one sound, small numerals are placed above it to indicate its sound in the order in which it has been taught if . . .

    * it is not the first sound taught. First sounds are understood (am, not, though, receive).

    * it is not an underlined vowel which says its name and,

    * a spelling rule does not first explain its use. Spelling rules supersede marking rules.

(do, low, you, cough, pie, has, vein)

PHONETICS - FOR CORRECT SPELLING

These consonant phonograms[1] are taught in most reading methods though usually not "explicitly" as federal research[2] now recommends. In this method, two sounds for the letters c, g and s are taught immediately and q is taught with u with which it is always used. Only the sound(s) are dictated as the letters (or symbols) for them are written; the key word is for the teacher to determine the correct pronunciation only.

b (bat)	**c** (cat, cent)	**d** (dog)	**f** (fed)	**g** (got, gentle)
h (hot)	**j** (jog)	**k** (keg)	**l** (lid)	**m** (mop)
n (no)	**p** (put)	**qu** (quit)	**r** (run)	**s** (sit, days)
t (top)	**v** (vase)	**w** (wag)	**x** (box)	**y** (yet) **z** (zip)

Next are the vowels. The multiple sounds are not taught soon enough in most methods. Vowels are taught in the order of frequency of their use in words as shown in the sample words. The third sounds of a, o and u are needed early for both spelling and reading of simple words.

a (at,ate,want)   **e** (end,we)   **i** (it,like)   **o** (dot,open,do)
u (up,music,put)   **y** (myth, my)   Note: y takes the place of i for spelling and is used as both a vowel and a consonant.

These common combinations are not consistently taught in most methods though they are needed for spelling. Very often, the letter, r, is taught as "er" which is incorrect. Spelling errors and students with poor sound discrimination abilities are the result. "Key words" are taught with this grouping. For practice, children make lists of words with these spellings to aid their memory.

er [the er of] (her)   **ir** (first)   **ur** (nurse)   **or** (works)
ear (early)   **oa** (boat)   **oe** (toe)

This grouping is taught in pairs to illustrate their use in spelling:

ay (pay)   **oy** (boy)   **aw** (law)   **ew** (grew,few)
[used - for spelling - at the end of words]
ai (paid)   **oi** (boil)   **au** (fault)   **ui** (fruit)
[spellings not used at the end of words]

iv

The common spellings of the sounds - "sh" and "zh" - are taught early:

sh [used at the beginning of a word (shut), at the end of a syllable (push) but not at the beginning of any syllable after the first one (na tion) except for the ending "ship." (friendship)].

ti (nation) **si** (session, vision) **ci** (special) [all used to spell "sh" or "zh" (session, equation) at the beginning of any syllable after the first one]

The next group are 2, 3 and 4-letter spellings of sounds more commonly represented by one letter. Children can fail to learn to read or spell because they don't know these spellings for common speech sounds.

ck (neck) 2-letter "k" **dge** (badge) 3-letter "j" **tch** (catch) 3-letter "ch" [all used after a single vowel which says ă, ĕ, ĭ, ŏ, ŭ.]

kn (knee) 2-letter "n" [used to begin a word] **gn** 2-letter "n" (reign, gnaw) [used to begin & end word] **ee** (feel) double e always says "ē"

igh (high) 3-letter "ī" **eigh** (eight) 4-letter "ā" **wr** (write) 2-letter "r"

ph (phone) 2-letter "f" **gh** (ghost) 2-letter "g"

These phonograms are rarely taught in most methods but are essential phonetic information for accurate spelling and fluent reading. The sounds are taught in the order of their frequency of use in English words just as they are given here.

ow (now, low)	**ou** (out, four, you, country)	**ch** (chin, school, chef)
ng (ring)	**ea** (eat, head, break)	**ei** (seize, veil, forfeit)
wh (when)	**ed** (started, loved, missed)	**ie** (field, pie, lilies)
ar (far)	**oo** (boot, foot, floor)	**ey** (they, key, valley)
or (for)	**th** (think, this)	
ough (though, through, rough, cough, thought, bough)		

TEACHING HINTS: Teach the sounds as they are given in the key words, in the order shown and with any instructions. It is not necessary to teach letter names since they are not <u>heard</u> in English speech except for - sometimes - the vowels. At first, you are trying to establish the unknown symbols (letters) for the known sounds. We say, "k" "ă" "t" for "cat," not "see-a-tee.

1. A phonogram is a letter or group of letters which represents one voiced sound in a given word.
2. Anderson, et al. *Becoming a Nation of Readers*, Center for the Study of Reading, University of Illinois, Champaign, Illinois, pg. 43.

28 RULES FOR ENGLISH SPELLING

1. The letter q is always written with u and we say, "kw." The letter u is not a vowel here. (quiet)
2. /c/ before e, i, or y says, "s." (cent, city, cycle)
3. /g/ before e, i, or y <u>may</u> say, "j." (gentle, get)
4. Vowels a, e, o, u usually say, "ā" - "ē" - "ō" - "ū" at the end of a syllable. (be long, pro tect, fu tile)
5. Vowels i and y may say, "ī" at the end of a syllable but usually say "ĭ." (fi nal, my - Indian, baby) [for spelling]
6. Vowel y, not i, is used at the end of an English word. (my)
7. There are five kinds of silent final e's. The first rule (as in time) is one of the three ways a vowel says its name.
8. o-r may say "er" when w comes before the o-r. (works)
9. We use e-i after c ... if we say, "ā" ... and in some exceptions. (receive, vein) Exceptions: neither, foreign, sovereign, seize, counterfeit, forfeit, leisure, either, weird, heifer, protein)
10. s-h is used at the beginning of a word, at the end of a syllable but not at the beginning of any syllable after the first one, except for the ending, "ship." (shut, fish, na tion)
11. t-i, s-i and c-i are used to say "sh" at the beginning of any syllable after the first one. c-h says, "sh" in a word of French origin. (nation, session, special, chic)
12. s-i is used to say, "sh" when the syllable before it ends in s (session) and when the base word has an s where the word changes. (tense/tension)
13. Only s-i can say, "zh" except for t-i in "equation." (vision)
14. When a one-syllable word ends with one short vowel and one consonant, double the final consonant before adding a vowel suffix. (hop, hopping/hopped)
15. When a two-syllable word ends with a vowel and a consonant, double the final consonant when adding a vowel suffix, *if* the accent is on the last syllable. (admit, admitted, admitting)
16. Silent final e words are written without the e when adding an ending beginning with a vowel. (have, having)
17. We often double l, f, s, after a single vowel, at the end of a one-syllable word. (full, puff, pass)
18. Base words do not end with the letter a saying, "ā" except for the article a; a-y is used most often. (may, pay, say)
19. Vowels i and o <u>may</u> say, "ī" and "ō" when followed by two consonants. (find, bold - gift, bond)

20. s never follows x. (box, boxes)
21. All is written with one l when added to another syllable. (almost,also)
22. Till and full added to another syllable are written with one l. (until)
23. 3-letter "ĭ" (dge) may be used after a single vowel which says, "ă" - "ĕ" - "ĭ" - "ŏ" - "ŭ." (badge, edge, ridge, lodge, fudge)
24. When adding an ending to a word that ends with y, that has a sound alone, change the y to i unless the ending is i-n-g. (fry,fried - cry,crying)
25. 2-letter "k" (ck) may be used <u>only</u> after a single vowel which says, "ă" - "ĕ" - "ĭ" - "ŏ" - "ŭ." (pack, peck, pick, pock, puck)
26. The letter z, never s is used to say, "z" at the beginning of a base word. (zero, zipper)
27. The letters e-d say, "d" and "t" as the past tense ending of any base word which does not end in the sound, "d" or "t." (loved,wrapped) When e-d says "ed" after words ending with "d" or "t," they form another syllable. (word,word ed / part,part ed)
28. Double consonants within words of more than one syllable should both be sounded for spelling. (lit tle, but ton)

PRONOUNCING SPELLING RULES: Pronounce all sounds of letters written with virgules /o/. Pronounce the names of letters written alone (x) or with dashes between (s-i). Pronounce the sound of all letters written with quotations and dictionary markings as shown ("sh" "ă" "er"). Word examples in parentheses are not taught as part of the rule but are shown as illustrations only and for use in teaching. The rules are most effectively taught when the phonograms are applied, sound by sound, in written, dictated spelling lessons - not by rote memorization only.

MULTI-SENSORY INSTRUCTION: A very effective way to present any factual information which should be "over-learned" - for automatic response later - is to have the student SEE the print (teacher shows a visual of the letter(s) as he HEARS the teacher SAY the sound(s) which he repeats (SAYS) aloud as he WRITES the correct letter(s) which show the sound(s) in print. Teach a few at a time, then test. The student has mastered them when he can write the correct letter(s) as they are dictated without seeing a visual of the phonogram. This is multi-sensory instruction which, when used at the primary level, allows few language failures.

APPLICATIONS FOR SPELLING: Study the spelling rules and teach them by application only as you dictate words. Ask the student to write the words, sound-by-sound, from the phonograms he has learned. Spelling is harder than reading but it is also more easily taught using the rules and multi-sensory teaching for all students.

Additional information, research findings and a catalog of professional materials are available from the present publisher, The Riggs Institute, 4185 SW 102nd Avenue, Beaverton, Oregon, 97005, (503) 646-9459.

Notes:

How to Find Words in This Book

1. Look at the first letter in the word you want to find.

2. Put your right thumb on the A at the side of this page and the rest of your fingers at the back of the book.

3. Move your thumb down the page. Stop when you find the letter that is just like the first letter in your word.

4. Keep your right thumb on the letter.

5. Let the pages fly past your thumb until you find the letter you are looking for. It will be the top letter.

6. Move your fingers down the pages until you find the word you are looking for.

7. Look at the picture if there is one.

8. Read what it says.

9. Sometimes boxes are made around words like this:

Mother said it was | bedtime.
time to go to bed.

The words in the second line tell what the word with a line under it means.

10. If you cannot find the word you are looking for at the side, find the word that looks nearly like your word. Then find the words opposite it that have these marks around them. ( ) These words will help you build big words from little words.

11. If you want to learn to write or print the word, try to copy it like the written or printed word.

Dear Girls and Boys:

In this book we have hidden many words. They are like gold, for they will help you when you need them. You will want them for your word friends. Hunt for them.

> They will help you to read;
> They will help you to spell;
> They will help you to write
> And to say things well.

You will have fun hunting for new words.

You will like the pictures.

You will enjoy reading the stories.

You will enjoy finding, all by yourself, words that will help you to read, to write, and to spell.

We hope you will like this "Picture Word Book" we have made for you.

The Authors

John has <u>a</u> dog.

I saw <u>a</u> bird.

a

a

ɑ

Baby | is not <u>able</u> to / cannot | walk alone.

able
a-ble

able

<u>ɑ</u> b l <u>e</u> ₄

I will tell you a story

| <u>about</u> / of | "The Little Red Hen."

about
a-bout

about

<u>ɑ</u> b <u>ɑ</u> u t

The picture is | <u>above</u> / over | the table.

above
a-bove

above

<u>ɑ</u> b o v <u>e</u> ₂

The car ran
into a post.

It was an <u>accident</u>.

(accidents)

accident
ac-ci-dent

accident

ɑ c c i d e n t

7

B
C
D
E
F
G
H
I
J
K
L
M
N
O
P
Q
R
S
T
U
V
W
X
Y
Z

ache *ache* a c̱ẖ e̱	The boy was sick. He had │an ache / a pain all the time│ in his stomach. (aches ached aching)
acorn a-corn *acorn* a c o̱ r n	This is an acorn. It grows on an oak tree. (acorns)
across a-cross *across* a̱ c r o s s	Bob threw the ball │across / to the other side of│ the room.
act *act* a c t	Mother told the children │to act / to do│ well. (actor actors) (acts acted acting)
add *add* a d d	If you │add / put together│ 2 apples and 2 more apples, you have 4 apples. This sign + means to add or put together. (adds adding added)

Do you $\boxed{\dfrac{\text{admire}}{\text{like}}}$ good stories? (admires admired admiring)	**admire** ad-mire *admire* a d m i̲r̲e̲	**A** B C D
I could not make the kite. Father gave me some good $\boxed{\dfrac{\text{advice}}{\text{suggestions}}}$ about making it.	**advice** ad-vice *advice* a d v i̲c̲e̲	E F G H I
  The cat is not $\boxed{\dfrac{\text{afraid}}{\text{scared}}}$ of the dog.	**afraid** a-fraid *afraid* a fra̲i̲d	J K L M N
Africa is a far-away land. Many people live in Africa.	**Africa** Af-ri-ca *Africa* Africå	O P Q R S T
  The cat ran after the mouse.	**after** aft-er *after* afte̲r̲	U V W X Y Z

A		
B	**afternoon** aft-er-noon *afternoon* afternoon	We eat lunch at 12 o'clock noon. After 12 o'clock noon, it is <u>afternoon.</u> (afternoons)
C **D** **E**	**afterward** aft-er-ward *afterward* afterward	We work first. We play │ afterward. │ at a later time.
F **G** **H** **I**	**again** a-gain *again* again	The girl jumped the rope │ <u>again</u> │ and │ <u>again.</u> │ │ another time │ │ another time. │
J **K** **L** **M**	**against** a-gainst *against* against	The ladder │ is <u>against</u> │ │ touches │ the wall.
N **O** **P** **Q**	**age** age *age* age	What is your │ <u>age?</u> │ How many │ years old │ are you?
R **S** **T** **U** **V** **W** **X** **Y** **Z**	**ago** a-go *ago* ago	Father went to work a long time <u>ago.</u>

The boys could not | agree. / think alike.

(agrees   agreed   agreeing)

agree
a-gree
agree
a g r e e

The girl is | ahead / in front |
of the boy.

ahead
a-head
ahead
a h e a d

We | aim / try | to do our best.

The boy | aimed / pointed |

the arrow at the tree.

(aims   aimed   aiming)

aim
aim
a i m

Father is putting air
in the tire.

Bob put up
the window.

Fresh | air / gentle wind | came in.
A

air
air
a i r

A
B
C
D
E
F
G
H
I
J
K
L
M
N
O
P
Q
R
S
T
U
V
W
X
Y
Z

airplane air-plane *airplane* <u>airpl</u><u>a</u><u>n</u><u>e</u>		This is an <u>airplane</u>. (airplanes)
airport air-port *airport* <u>a</u><u>i</u><u>rp</u><u>o</u><u>r</u>t		This is an <u>airport</u>. Airplanes come down at and start from an <u>airport</u>. (airports)
airship air-ship *airship* <u>a</u><u>i</u><u>r</u><u>sh</u><u>i</u><u>p</u>		This is an <u>airship</u>. It is like a long balloon. (airships)
alarm a-larm *alarm* <u>a</u><u>l</u><u>a</u><u>r</u>m	An <u>alarm</u> clock A fire <u>alarm</u> box When the fire <u>alarm</u> sounds, the firemen go to put out the fire. (alarms alarmed alarming)	
alike a-like *alike* <u>a</u><u>l</u><u>i</u><u>k</u><u>e</u>	These trees are <u>alike</u>. / the same.	

An auto ran over my dog but he is $\boxed{\begin{array}{c}\text{alive.}\\\hline\text{not dead.}\end{array}}$	**alive** a-live *alive* <u>a l i v e</u>	A
"Someone has been eating my porridge, too, and she ate it $\boxed{\begin{array}{c}\text{all}\\\hline\text{every bit}\end{array}}$ up," said the wee little bear.	**all** *all* all	B C D E F G H I
This is an <u>alligator.</u> Alligators live in water. (alligators)	**alligator** al-li-ga-tor *alligator* alligator	J K L M
Mother will not $\boxed{\text{allow}}$ me to go. Mother will not $\boxed{\text{let}}$ me go. (allows allowed allowing)	**allow** al-low *allow* allow	N O P Q R
It is $\boxed{\begin{array}{c}\text{almost}\\\hline\text{nearly}\end{array}}$ time to go home.	**almost** al-most *almost* almost	S T U
See baby stand $\boxed{\begin{array}{c}\text{alone.}\\\hline\text{by herself.}\end{array}}$	**alone** a-lone *alone* <u>a l o n e</u>	V W X Y Z

A
B
C
D
E
F
G
H
I
J
K
L
M
N
O
P
Q
R
S
T
U
V
W
X
Y
Z

along a-long *along* along	Little Miss Muffet sat on a tuffet, Eating her curds and whey. <u>Along</u> came a spider and sat down beside her, And frightened Miss Muffet away.
already al-read-y *already* already	The boys have come <u>already.</u> / by this time.
also al-so *also* also	John has a ball. I have a ball <u>also.</u> / too.
always al-ways *always* always	Father is good to us <u>always.</u> / at all times.
am *am* am	He put in his thumb and pulled out a plum, And said, "What a good boy <u>am</u> I!" I <u>am</u> a good boy, too.

The land in which we live is called <u>America</u>.	**America** A-mer-i-ca *America* <u>A</u>méric̀a	A B
I live in America. I am an <u>American.</u> (Americans)	**American** A-mer-i-can *American* <u>A</u>mérican	C D E F G
Grass is found <u>among</u> / mixed with the daisies. He divided the cake <u>among</u> six boys.	**among** a-mong *among* <u>a</u>mon<u>g</u>	H I J K L
I have <u>an</u> apple. I have <u>an</u> orange.	an *an* an	M N O
This house is <u>ancient.</u> / old.	**ancient** an-cient *ancient* <u>a</u>n<u>c</u>ient	P Q R S
Jack fell down <u>and</u> broke his crown, <u>And</u> Jill came tumbling after.	and *and* and	T U V W X Y Z

15

A
B
C
D
E
F
G
H
I
J
K
L
M
N
O
P
Q
R
S
T
U
V
W
X
Y
Z

angry an-gry *angry* angry	I wanted to go to the picnic. Father would not let me go. This made me <u>angry</u>. <div align="center">(angrier angriest anger)</div>
animal an-i-mal *animal* animal	See these <u>animals</u>. A pony or one <u>animal</u> Two cows or two <u>animals</u> <div align="center">(animals)</div>
announcer an-nounc-er *announcer* announcer	The <u>announcer</u> tells who will sing on the program. <div align="center">(announce announced announcing)</div>
another an-oth-er *another* another	The boy lost his ball. Mother said, "Do not cry. I will buy you <u>another</u> ball."
answer an-swer *answer* answer	Mother called to Bob but he did not <u>answer.</u> call back. Our teacher asked a question. We did not know the <u>answer</u>. <div align="center">(answers answered answering)</div>

This is a big <u>ant.</u> (ants)		*ant* *ant* a n t
Baa, baa, black sheep, Have you <u>any</u> / some wool?		any an-y *any* a n y
I heard the doorbell ring. I did not see <u>anybody.</u> / a person.		anybody an-y-bod-y *anybody* a n y b o d y
I did not see <u>anyone</u> / a person coming.		anyone an-y-one *anyone* a n y o n e
The teacher said, "Do not write <u>anything</u> / one thing on the board."		anything an-y-thing *anything* a n y t h i n g
Mary cannot go to the party but I will go <u>anyway.</u>		anyway an-y-way *anyway* a n y w a y
You may sit <u>anywhere</u> / in any place you like.		anywhere an-y-where *anywhere* a n y w h e r e

A
B
C
D
E
F
G
H
I
J
K
L
M
N
O
P
Q
R
S
T
U
V
W
X
Y
Z

apart
a-part
apart
ap̲a̲rt

Mary stood | apart / away |

from the other children.

ape
ape
a̲p̲e̲

This is an ape.
He is a kind of monkey.
He has no tail
like some monkeys.

(apes)

appear
ap-pear
appear
appe̲a̲r

Soon the stars will | appear / come out | in the sky.

(appears   appeared   appearing)

apple
ap-ple
apple
apple̲₊

This is an apple.
Apples are good to eat.

(apples)

April
A-pril
April
A̲pril

April showers bring May flowers.

April is the fourth month
of the year.

apron
a-pron
apron
a̲pron

This is my mother's apron.

(aprons)

These fish are in | an aquarium. / a bowl of water.

aquarium
a-quar-i-um

aquarium
aquȧrium

(aquariums)

Grapes grow on | an arbor. / a frame.

This is | an arbor. / a shady place.

arbor
ar-bor

arbor
arbor

(arbors)

are
are
are_s

The boys <u>are</u> running.
The girls <u>are</u> running.
The children <u>are</u> running.

The children | aren't / are not | at home.

aren't
aren't
aren't

This is an <u>arm</u>.
We have two <u>arms</u>.

(arms)

arm
arm
arm

A
B
C
D
E
F
G
H
I
J
K
L
M
N
O
P
Q
R
S
T
U
V
W
X
Y
Z

19

A
B
C
D
E
F
G
H
I
J
K
L
M
N
O
P
Q
R
S
T
U
V
W
X
Y
Z

armchair arm-chair *armchair* armchair	This chair is an <u>armchair</u>. You can rest your arms on the sides. (armchairs)
army ar-my *army* army	Bob's father is in the <u>army</u>. He fights for his country. (armies)
around a-round *around* around	The train goes <u>around</u> and <u>around</u> on the track.
arrive ar-rive *arrive* arrive	I $\boxed{\begin{array}{c}\underline{\text{arrive}}\\ \text{reach}\end{array}}$ home early every day. (arrives arrived arriving)
arrow ar-row *arrow* arrow	This is an <u>arrow</u>. Bob has a bow and <u>arrow</u>. (arrows)
art *art* art	We draw pictures in $\boxed{\begin{array}{c}\underline{\text{art}}\\ \text{drawing}\end{array}}$ class. Sewing, like music, is an <u>art</u>. (arts)

The boy is not <u>as</u> big <u>as</u> the girl.		as *as* a͞s
Sometimes children act badly. Afterwards they feel <u>ashamed</u>.		ashamed a-shamed *ashamed* <u>a</u>sh<u>a</u>m<u>e</u>d
Bob put his pencils	aside. / away.	aside a-side *aside* <u>a</u>s<u>i</u>d<u>e</u>
Can you go with me? I do not know but I will <u>ask</u> my mother. (asks asked asking)		ask *ask* a s k
Baby has gone to bed. She is sound <u>asleep</u>.		asleep a-sleep *asleep* <u>a</u>sl<u>ee</u>p
This flower is an <u>aster</u>. <u>Asters</u> are pink, purple and white. They bloom in the autumn. (asters)		aster as-ter *aster* <u>a</u>st<u>er</u>

A
B
C
D
E
F
G
H
I
J
K
L
M
N
O
P
Q
R
S
T
U
V
W
X
Y
Z

21

A		
at *at* at	Where is your mother? She is <u>at</u> home.	
ate *ate* a t e		Baby is at the table. She <u>ate</u> her bread and milk. (eat eats eating)
Atlantic At-lan-tic *Atlantic* Atlantic	The Pilgrims came to America in a boat. They crossed the <u>Atlantic</u> Ocean.	
attention at-ten-tion *attention* atten<u>ti</u>on	Mother called the children. They were playing. They did not pay any <u>attention</u> to her.	
August Au-gust *August* <u>Au</u>gust	<u>August</u> is the eighth month of the year.	
aunt *aunt* <u>au</u>nt	My father's sister is here. She is my <u>aunt.</u> My mother's sister is coming. She is my <u>aunt,</u> too. (aunts auntie)	

We ride in our <u>automobile</u>. (automobiles auto)		automobile au-to-mo-bile *automobile* <u>automobile</u>s
Leaves come on the trees in the spring. Leaves fall off the trees in the <u>autumn</u>.		autumn au-tumn *autumn* <u>autumn</u>
This man is an <u>aviator</u>. He flies an airplane. (aviators)		aviator a-vi-a-tor *aviator* <u>aviator</u>
Baby is awake. She is not sleeping. (awakes awakened awoke awakening)		awake a-wake *awake* <u>awake</u>
Bob threw the ball to me. I threw the ball away. from me.		away a-way *away* <u>away</u>
This is an <u>axe</u>. This man is cutting down the tree with an <u>axe</u>. (axes)		axe *axe* <u>axe</u>s

A
B
C
D
E
F
G
H
I
J
K
L
M
N
O
P
Q
R
S
T
U
V
W
X
Y
Z

B b 𝓑 𝓫 B b

B
C
D
E
F
G
H
I
J
K
L
M
N
O
P
Q
R
S
T
U
V
W
X
Y
Z

baby ba-by *baby* baby	Our <u>baby</u> cannot walk yet. (babies)
back *back* ba<u>ck</u>	The boy is riding on the horse's <u>back</u>. The boy sits <u>back of</u> / behind the girl. See father <u>back</u> the car out of the garage. (backs backed backing)
bacon ba-con *bacon* b<u>a</u>con	This meat is <u>bacon</u>. I like <u>bacon</u> and eggs.
bad *bad* bad	Bob is a good boy. He is not a <u>bad</u> boy. (badly)
bag *bag* bag	We carry things in <u>bags</u>. A hand<u>bag</u> (bags) A paper <u>bag</u>

24

The porter put the | baggage / trunks and bags | on the train.

baggage
bag-gage
baggage
baggage

Mother made a cake.
She put it in the oven.
to | bake. / cook. |

(bakes   baked   baking)

bake
bake
bake

This man makes bread and cake to sell.
He is a baker.

(bakers   bakery)

baker
bak-er
baker
baker

These boxes | balance. / weigh the same. |

(balances   balanced   balancing)

balance
bal-ance
balance
balance₃

This is a | bale / big bundle | of cotton.

(bales)

bale
bale
bale

B
C
D
E
F
G
H
I
J
K
L
M
N
O
P
Q
R
S
T
U
V
W
X
Y
Z

B
C
D
E
F
G
H
I
J
K
L
M
N
O
P
Q
R
S
T
U
V
W
X
Y
Z

ball *ball* ball̊	Children like to play with a <u>ball</u>. (balls)
balloon bal-loon *balloon* båll<u>oo</u>n	Mary has a <u>balloon</u>. The air in the <u>balloon</u> keeps it from coming down. (balloons)
banana ba-nan-a *banana* bånanå	One <u>banana</u> A bunch of <u>bananas</u> (bananas)
band *band* band	This is our <u>band</u>. We play music to march by. (bands)
bang *bang* ba<u>ng</u>	Bob shut the door with a loud <u>bang.</u> / noise. (bangs banged banging)

A toy <u>bank</u> A city <u>bank</u> We put money in a <u>bank</u>. (banks)	bank *bank* bɑnk
This is a <u>bar</u> of soap. This window has <u>bars</u>. (bars)	bar *bar* bɑr
The <u>barber</u> is cutting father's hair. (barbers)	barber bar-ber *barber* bɑrbɐr
The cupboard was <u>bare.</u> empty. This hand has a This hand is glove on it. <u>bare.</u>	bare *bare* bɑrɐ
The dog <u>barks</u> at the cat. (barks barked barking)	bark *bark* bɑrk

B
C
D
E
F
G
H
I
J
K
L
M
N
O
P
Q
R
S
T
U
V
W
X
Y
Z

| barn *barn* b**a**rn | The farmer put the horse in the barn. He keeps hay in the barn, too. (barns) |

| barnyard barn-yard *barnyard* b**a**rny**a**rd | The barn stands in the barnyard. (barnyards) |

| barrel bar-rel *barrel* b**á**rrel | This is a barrel. We put apples in barrels. (barrels) |

| baseball base-ball *baseball* b**a**s**e**b**à**ll | The boys like to play baseball. They bat the ball and run around the bases. They play this game with a baseball. (baseballs) |

| basket bas-ket *basket* b**a**sket | This is a basket filled with apples. (baskets) |

| bat *bat* b**a**t | This is a ball bat. We $\frac{\text{bat}}{\text{hit}}$ the ball with the bat. (bats   batted   batting) |

This is a <u>bat.</u>
It looks like
   a mouse with wings.
    (bats)
		bat
		bat
		bat

Mother is giving
   the baby a <u>bath.</u>
    (baths)
		bath
		bath
		ba<u>th</u>

This is a <u>bathroom.</u>
It is the room in
   which we bathe.
   (bathrooms)
		bathroom
		bath-room
		bathroom
		ba<u>th</u>r<u>oo</u>m

This is a <u>bathtub.</u> (bathtubs)		bathtub bath-tub *bathtub* ba<u>th</u>tub
A <u>bay</u> is part of a sea. It is a big body of water. Boats sail on the <u>bay.</u> (bays)		bay *bay* b<u>ay</u>
Jack said, "I will <u>be</u> a good boy."		be *be* b<u>e</u>

The children are
   playing on the <u>beach.</u>
They like to play in
   the sand on the <u>beach.</u>
   (beaches)
		beach
		beach
		b<u>ea</u><u>ch</u>

B
C
D
E
F
G
H
I
J
K
L
M
N
O
P
Q
R
S
T
U
V
W
X
Y
Z

B
C
D
E
F
G
H
I
J
K
L
M
N
O
P
Q
R
S
T
U
V
W
X
Y
Z

bead		This is a string of beads.
bead		
b<u>ea</u>d		(beads)

bean		These are beans.
bean		Beans are good to eat.
b<u>ea</u>n		(beans)

bear		
bear		
b<u>ea</u>r		This is a bear.
		Bears are white, brown, or black.
		(bears)

beard		This man has a beard on his chin.
beard		This man does not have a beard on his chin.
b<u>ea</u>rd		(beards)

beast		A beast is an animal.
beast		A lion is a beast.
b<u>ea</u>st		(beasts)

Did you ever <u>beat</u> a drum?

Mother <u>beats</u> the eggs
with the egg beater.

The bad boy | <u>beats</u> / whips | his dog.

(beats   beating   beaten   beater)

beat

beat

be̲a̲t

The flowers are | <u>beautiful.</u> / pretty. |

beautiful
beau-ti-ful

beautiful

be̲a̲utifûl

This animal is a <u>beaver</u>.

He lives in the water
and on the land, too.

A <u>beaver's</u> fur is used
on coats.

(beavers)

beaver
bea-ver

beaver

be̲a̲ve̲r̲

It is warm <u>because</u>
the sun is shining.

<u>Because</u> tells why.

because
be-cause

because

be̲cau̇s̲e̲s

If you drink milk, you will

| <u>become</u> / grow to be | strong and healthy.

(becomes   became   becoming)

become
be-come

become

be̲come̲s

B
C
D
E
F
G
H
I
J
K
L
M
N
O
P
Q
R
S
T
U
V
W
X
Y
Z

B
C
D
E
F
G
H
I
J
K
L
M
N
O
P
Q
R
S
T
U
V
W
X
Y
Z

bed *bed* bed	We sleep in a <u>bed</u>. (beds)
bedroom bed-room *bedroom* bed<u>roo</u>m	The room in which we sleep is a <u>bedroom</u>. My bed is in my <u>bedroom</u>. (bedrooms)
bedtime bed-time *bedtime* bed<u>time</u>	Mother said it was <u>bedtime</u>. time to go to bed.
bee *bee* b<u>ee</u>	This is a <u>bee</u>. <u>Bees</u> make honey. (bees)
been *been* b<u>ee</u>n	"Someone has <u>been</u> sleeping in my bed," said the father bear.
beet *beet* b<u>ee</u>t	This is a big red <u>beet</u>. Mother cooked some <u>beets</u> for dinner. (beets)

I wash my hands <u>before</u> I eat. I wash my hands after I eat, too.	**before** be-fore *before* b<u>e</u>f<u>o</u>r<u>e</u>

This dog wants something
    to eat.
 	
See him $\boxed{\begin{array}{c}\text{beg}\\\hline\text{ask}\end{array}}$ for it.
 	
    (begs   begged   begging)
	beg
	
	beg
	beg

The sky grew black and it $\boxed{\begin{array}{c}\text{began}\\\hline\text{started}\end{array}}$ to rain. (begin begins beginning)	**began** be-gan *began* b<u>e</u>gan

The teacher said,
 	
"Mary may $\boxed{\begin{array}{c}\text{begin}\\\hline\text{start}\end{array}}$ the story."
 	
    (begins   began   beginning)
	begin
	be-gin
	
	begin
	b<u>e</u>gin

The boy sits $\boxed{\begin{array}{c}\text{behind}\\\hline\text{back\ of}\end{array}}$ the girl.	**behind** be-hind *behind* b<u>e</u>h<u>i</u>nd

B
C
D
E
F
G
H
I
J
K
L
M
N
O
P
Q
R
S
T
U
V
W
X
Y
Z

B
C
D
E
F
G
H
I
J
K
L
M
N
O
P
Q
R
S
T
U
V
W
X
Y
Z

being be-ing *being* being	Mother gave baby an apple for <u>being</u> good. (be been)
believe be-lieve *believe* believe,	I do not $\boxed{\dfrac{\text{believe}}{\text{think}}}$ it is snowing. (believes believed believing)
bell *bell* bell	Hear the <u>bell</u> ring. (bells)
belong be-long *belong* belong	The book is not mine. It <u>belongs</u> to Bob. (belongs belonged belonging)
below be-low *below* below	The sun is high above. The ground is down <u>below</u>.
belt *belt* belt	This is father's <u>belt</u>. He wears it around his waist. (belts)

Father's work <u>bench</u> A <u>bench</u> to sit on (benches)	bench *bench* ben<u>ch</u>
The wire was not straight. Bob tried to <u>bend</u> it so it would be straight. (bends bent bending)	bend *bend* bend
The stool is | beneath / below | the window.	beneath be-neath *beneath* b<u>e</u>n<u>ea</u><u>th</u>
strawb<u>erry</u> rasp<u>berry</u> black<u>berry</u> <u>Berries</u> are good to eat. (berries)	berry ber-ry *berry* bérry
Along came a spider and sat down | beside / by the side of | her, And frightened Miss Muffet away. (besides)	beside be-side *beside* b<u>e</u>si<u>de</u>

B
C
D
E
F
G
H
I
J
K
L
M
N
O
P
Q
R
S
T
U
V
W
X
Y
Z

best *best* best	Mary reads well. Bob reads better than Mary. Jack reads <u>best</u> of all.
better bet-ter *better* bett<u>er</u>	Bob reads <u>better</u> than Mary.
between be-tween *between* b<u>e</u>tw<u>ee</u>n	 Mary walked <u>between</u> her mother and father.
beyond be-yond *beyond* b<u>e</u>yond	I stopped at the first store, Bob went beyond. farther on.
bicycle bi-cy-cle *bicycle* b<u>i</u>cycl<u>e</u>	Bob is riding his <u>bicycle</u>. (bicycles)
bid *bid* bid	I bid tell my mother good night.

Baby is not little. She is <u>big</u>. (bigger biggest)		big *big* big

The bird eats
   with its <u>bill</u>.
Mother paid
   our gas <u>bill</u>.
This is money.
It is a dollar <u>bill</u>.
(bills)
		bill
		bill
		bill

This <u>bird</u> can fly high. (birds)		bird *bird* bird
See the bird in the <u>bird cage</u>. (bird cages)		bird cage *bird cage* bird cage

Bob made
   this <u>birdhouse</u>.
Some birds build
   their nests
   in <u>birdhouses</u>.
(birdhouses)
		birdhouse
		bird-house
		birdhouse
		birdhouses

B
C
D
E
F
G
H
I
J
K
L
M
N
O
P
Q
R
S
T
U
V
W
X
Y
Z

B
C
D
E
F
G
H
I
J
K
L
M
N
O
P
Q
R
S
T
U
V
W
X
Y
Z

birthday birth-day *birthday* b<u>ir</u>th d<u>ay</u>	This is my <u>birthday</u> cake. I am six years old today. (birthdays)
bit *bit* bit	He gave me a $\boxed{\begin{array}{c}\underline{bit}\\ \text{small piece}\end{array}}$ of candy. The cat <u>bit</u> off the mouse's tail.
bite *bite* b<u>i</u>t<u>e</u>	Baby has two teeth but she cannot <u>bite</u> you. (bit bitten bites biting)
bitter bit-ter *bitter* bitt<u>er</u>	The doctor left some medicine for Bob. Bob did not like it because it was <u>bitter.</u>
black *black* bla<u>ck</u>	We burn coal in our furnace. Coal is <u>black</u> and hard.
blackberry black-ber-ry *blackberry* bla<u>ck</u>bérry	This is a <u>blackberry.</u> <u>Blackberries</u> grow on bushes. They are good to eat. (blackberries)

See the <u>blackbird</u>
in the tree.

Some <u>blackbirds</u> have
red wings.

(blackbirds)

blackbird
black-bird

blackbird

bla<u>ck</u>b<u>ir</u>d

The teacher writes
on the <u>blackboard</u> with chalk.

The <u>blackboard</u> is black.

(blackboards)

cat ran

blackboard
black-board

blackboard

bla<u>ck</u>b<u>oa</u>rd

The <u>blade</u> of the knife is sharp.

We cut with the <u>blade</u>
of a knife.

This is a $\boxed{\dfrac{\text{blade}}{\text{leaf}}}$ of grass.

(blades)

blade

blade

bl<u>a</u>d<u>e</u>

The man did not drive well.

He was $\boxed{\dfrac{\text{to blame}}{\text{at fault}}}$ for the accident.

(blames   blamed   blaming)

blame

blame

bl<u>a</u>m<u>e</u>

The $\boxed{\dfrac{\text{blanket}}{\text{cover}}}$ on your bed

keeps you warm.

<u>Blankets</u> are made
of wool or cotton.

(blankets)

blanket
blan-ket

blanket

bl<u>a</u>nket

B
C
D
E
F
G
H
I
J
K
L
M
N
O
P
Q
R
S
T
U
V
W
X
Y
Z

B
C
D
E
F
G
H
I
J
K
L
M
N
O
P
Q
R
S
T
U
V
W
X
Y
Z

blaze *blaze* bl**a**z**e**	The Indians are watching the ⬚ blaze bright light ⬚ of the fire. The fire ⬚ blazes burns ⬚ high into the air. (blazes blazed blazing)
blew *blew* bl**ew**	The wind <u>blew</u> the leaves off the trees. Bob <u>blew</u> the whistle for the men to come to dinner. (blow blows blown blowing)
blind *blind* bl**i**nd	The man ⬚ is <u>blind.</u> cannot see. ⬚
block *block* blo**ck**	These are A B C <u>blocks.</u> (blocks)

40

Mother cut her finger. Red <u>blood</u> came from the cut.	blood *blood* bl<u>oo</u>d	B
Flowers ⎧ bloom ⎩ come out of buds ⎫ in the spring. <small>(blooms bloomed blooming)</small>	bloom *bloom* bl<u>oo</u>m	C D E F G H
This is a ⎧ blossom. ⎩ flower. ⎫ Fruit trees have <u>blossoms.</u> Flowers ⎧ blossom ⎩ come out of buds ⎫ in the spring. <small>(blossoms blossomed blossoming)</small>	blossom <small>blos-som</small> *blossom* blossom	I J K L M N O P
See Bob <u>blow</u> the whistle. The wind <u>blows</u> the leaves from the trees. <small>(blows blew blowing blown)</small>	blow *blow* bl<u>o</u>w	Q R S T U
The colors of the American flag are red, white and <u>blue</u>.	blue *blue* bl<u>ue</u>	V W X Y Z

B
C
D
E
F
G
H
I
J
K
L
M
N
O
P
Q
R
S
T
U
V
W
X
Y
Z

bluebird blue-bird *bluebird* bl u̲e̲b i̲rd	This bird is a bluebird. A bluebird has an orange colored breast. (bluebirds)
blue jay blue jay *blue jay* bl u̲e̲ j a̲y	This bird is a blue jay. The blue jay's back is blue. He has a knot of feathers on the top of his head. (blue jays)
board *board* b o̲a̲rd	The man made a box of wide boards. Boards are made of wood. (boards)
boast *boast* b o̲a̲st	Some people like to boast. talk about themselves too much. (boasts boasted boasting)
boat *boat* b o̲a̲t	This boat is large. Many people can ride on this boat. (boats)

This is a doll's <u>body</u>.
Boys and girls
  have <u>bodies,</u> too.
You should keep your <u>body</u> clean.

(bodies)

body
bod-y

body
body

Mary has a | boil / sore | on her arm.

Mother put the water on the fire.
When it gets so hot,

it will | boil. / steam and bubble.

(boils   boiled   boiling)

boil

boil
boil

The dog likes
  to eat a <u>bone.</u>

We have <u>bones</u> in our bodies.

(bones)

bone

bone
bone

Mother put
  the <u>bonnet</u>
  on the baby's head.

(bonnets)

bonnet
bon-net

bonnet
bonnet

B
C
D
E
F
G
H
I
J
K
L
M
N
O
P
Q
R
S
T
U
V
W
X
Y
Z

B
C
D
E
F
G
H
I
J
K
L
M
N
O
P
Q
R
S
T
U
V
W
X
Y
Z

book *book* bo͝ok	This is a <u>book</u>. I have a good <u>book</u> to read. (books)
bookcase book-case *bookcase* bo͝okcas̲e̲	The books are in the <u>bookcase</u>. (bookcases)
bookkeeper book-keep-er *bookkeeper* bo͝okkeeper	We played store. I was the <u>bookkeeper</u>. I wrote in the books how much money we spent and how much we took in. (bookkeepers)
bookstore book-store *bookstore* bo͝oksto̲re̲	We buy books at the <u>bookstore</u>. store where books are sold. (bookstores)
boot *boot* bo͝ot	See this leather <u>boot</u>? <u>Boots</u> are made of rubber, too. A <u>boot</u> is higher than a shoe. (boots)

Mary's handkerchief is white. It has a green │ border. edge. │ (borders)	border bor-der *border* b<u>or</u>d<u>er</u>	B
We have a new baby at our house. She was │ born brought into the world │ yesterday.	born *born* b<u>or</u>n	C D E F G
The baby broke │ both her her two │ dolls.	both *both* b<u>oth</u>	H I J K L M
Bob lost his hat. He did not │ bother take the trouble │ to look for it. (bothers bothered bothering)	bother both-er *bother* bo<u>th</u><u>er</u>	N O P Q R S T
This is a <u>bottle.</u> Milk is put into <u>bottles.</u> <u>Bottles</u> are made of glass. (bottles)	bottle bot-tle *bottle* b<u>o</u>ttl<u>e</u>	U V W X Y Z

B
C
D
E
F
G
H
I
J
K
L
M
N
O
P
Q
R
S
T
U
V
W
X
Y
Z

bottom bot-tom *bottom* bottom		The picture is at the top of the page. The story is at the <u>bottom</u> of the page. (bottoms)
bough *bough* bou̇g̈h		The bird is sitting on a ⎡bough⎤ ⎣branch⎦ of the tree. (boughs)
bought *bought* bou̇g̈ht	Father gave Tom a penny. Tom <u>bought</u> some candy with it. (buy buys buying)	
bound *bound* bou̲n̲d		Mary likes to ⎡bound⎤ the ball. ⎣bounce⎦ (bounds bounded bounding)
bow *bow* bo̲w̲	 	Jack has a <u>bow</u> and arrow. The <u>bow</u> is made with a stick and a string. Mary has a <u>bow</u> of ribbon on her hair. (bows)

46

Mary sang a song.
When the children
    clapped their hands
    she made a <u>bow</u>.
 	
(bows   bowed   bowing)
		bow
		bow
		b<u>o</u>w

This is a <u>bowl</u>. Baby eats from a <u>bowl</u>. (bowls)		bowl *bowl* b<u>o</u>wl
The dog said "<u>Bow-wow</u>."		bow-wow *bow-wow* b<u>ow</u>-w<u>ow</u>
This is a <u>box</u>. It had a lid on it. (boxes)		box *box* box
Tom is a small <u>boy</u>. (boys)		boy *boy* b<u>oy</u>

B
C
D
E
F
G
H
I
J
K
L
M
N
O
P
Q
R
S
T
U
V
W
X
Y
Z

47

B
C
D
E
F
G
H
I
J
K
L
M
N
O
P
Q
R
S
T
U
V
W
X
Y
Z

bran *bran* bran	Children eat bran. It is a good breakfast food. It is made from wheat and rye.
branch *branch* bran<u>ch</u>	The bird is sitting on a branch / bough of the tree. (branches)
brass *brass* brass	<u>Brass</u> is hard like gold. It is yellow, too. Bowls are sometimes made of <u>brass</u>.
brave *brave* br<u>a</u><u>v</u><u>e</u>	The soldier was brave. / not afraid. (braver bravest)
bread *bread* bre<u>a</u>d	This is a loaf of <u>bread</u>. One slice of <u>bread</u> has been cut.
break *break* bre<u>a</u>k	Did you <u>break</u> a bowl? (breaks broke breaking broken)

When I get up in the morning, I eat my <u>breakfast</u>. (breakfasts)	**breakfast** break-fast *breakfast* bre͜a kfast
The robin has a red <u>breast.</u> (breasts)	breast *breast* bre͜a st
To blow out a candle, blow your <u>breath</u> against it.	breath *breath* bre͜a th
You should <u>breathe</u> take in air through your nose. When you run, you <u>breathe</u> fast. (breathes breathed breathing)	breathe *breathe* bre͜a th̲e̲ₛ
A little <u>breeze</u> wind is blowing in the window. (breezes)	breeze *breeze* bre̲e̲z e̲ₛ
This house is made of <u>bricks.</u> (bricks)	brick *brick* br i c̲k̲

B
C
D
E
F
G
H
I
J
K
L
M
N
O
P
Q
R
S
T
U
V
W
X
Y
Z

B
C
D
E
F
G
H
I
J
K
L
M
N
O
P
Q
R
S
T
U
V
W
X
Y
Z

bridge *bridge* bri**dge**	 The <u>bridge</u> is over the river. We ride across the <u>bridge</u>. <div align="center">(bridges)</div>
bright *bright* br**igh**t	The sun is |bright.| |shiny.| (brighter brightest brightly)
bring *bring* bri**ng**	Mother went to the store. She said, "I will <u>bring</u> you an apple." <div align="center">(brings brought bringing)</div>
broad *broad* br**oa**d	One book is narrow. One is |broad.| |wide.|
broadcast broad-cast *broadcast* br**oa**dcast	The announcer will |<u>broadcast</u>| the news |send out | by radio. (broadcasts broadcasting)

50

Bob is ┌─────────┐ the meat │ broiling │ │ cooking │ └─────────┘ over the fire. (broil broils broiled)	broiling broil-ing *broiling* br<u>oi</u>li<u>ng</u>
Jack and Jill went up the hill To get a pail of water. Jack fell down and <u>broke</u> his crown, And Jill came tumbling after. (break breaks breaking broken)	broke *broke* br<u>o</u>k<u>e</u>
Father went fishing in the ┌──────────────┐ │ brook. │ small stream. └──────────────┘ (brooks)	brook *brook* br<u>oo</u>k
We sweep with a <u>broom</u>. (brooms)	broom *broom* br<u>oo</u>m
The man is Jack's father. The woman is Jack's mother. The girl is Jack's sister. The boy is Jack's <u>brother</u>. (brothers)	brother broth-er *brother* bro<u>th</u>er

B
C
D
E
F
G
H
I
J
K
L
M
N
O
P
Q
R
S
T
U
V
W
X
Y
Z

B
C
D
E
F
G
H
I
J
K
L
M
N
O
P
Q
R
S
T
U
V
W
X
Y
Z

brought *brought* br**ough**t	Mother asked Bob to bring her a book. Bob <u>brought</u> her a new book. (bring brings bringing)
brown *brown* br**ow**n	Leaves turn <u>brown</u> in autumn. Bob has blue eyes. Mary has <u>brown</u> eyes.
brownie brown-ie *brownie* br**ow**n**ie**	This is a <u>brownie</u>. <u>Brownies</u> are funny little fellows. (brownies)
brush *brush* bru**sh**	A toothbrush A scrub <u>brush</u> A paint <u>brush</u> I <u>brush</u> my teeth every day. Do you? (brushes brushed brushing)
bucket buck-et *bucket* bu**ck**et	This is a |bucket / pail| of water. (buckets)

	bud
  A <u>bud</u> A flower When the <u>bud</u> opens, it will be a flower (buds)	*bud* bud
  These are <u>bugs</u>. (bugs)	bug *bug* bug
This is a doll <u>buggy</u>. (buggies)	buggy bug-gy *buggy* buggy
Men $\boxed{\dfrac{\text{build}}{\text{make}}}$ houses. Birds <u>build</u> nests. Ants <u>build</u> ant hills. (builds built building)	build *build* b<u>u</u>ild

B
C
D
E
F
G
H
I
J
K
L
M
N
O
P
Q
R
S
T
U
V
W
X
Y
Z

bulb

bulb
bulb

The children
are planting
a lily <u>bulb</u>.

Some plants grow
from seeds.

Some grow
from <u>bulbs</u>.

This is
an electric light <u>bulb</u>.

(bulbs)

bulletin
bul-le-tin

bulletin
bŭlletin

It is raining today.
It will snow tomorrow.
It will be colder tomorrow.

This is a | bulletin / message | telling

about the weather.

(bulletins)

bumped

bumped
bumpĕd

Baby fell down.

She | bumped / hit | her head.

It made a big <u>bump</u> on her head.

(bump   bumps   bumping)

Mother made some

buns
rolls

for dinner.

Some <u>buns</u> are like cake
and some are like bread.

(buns)

bun

bun
bun

One flower   A <u>bunch</u> of flowers

One grape   A <u>bunch</u> of grapes.

(bunches)

bunch

bunch
bun<u>ch</u>

This is Bob's

bunny.
pet rabbit.

(bunnies)

bunny
bun-ny

bunny
bunny

The house is on fire.
It may <u>burn</u> down.

(burns   burned   burning)

burn

burn
b<u>ur</u>n

B
C
D
E
F
G
H
I
J
K
L
M
N
O
P
Q
R
S
T
U
V
W
X
Y
Z

bury bur-y *bury* b<u>ur</u>y	Dogs [bury / place] bones in the ground. When they get hungry, they dig them up and eat them. (buries buried burying)
bus *bus* bus	This is a big <u>bus</u>. Many people ride in a <u>bus</u>. (busses)
bush *bush* b<u>u</u>³<u>sh</u>	Apples grow on a tree. Roses grow on a <u>bush</u>. A tree is bigger than a <u>bush</u>. (bushes)
busy bus-y *busy* b<u>u</u>²sy	Tom worked all day. Father said, "What a <u>busy</u> boy you are." (busier busiest business)
but *but* b<u>ut</u>	The fox wanted the grapes, <u>but</u> he could not get them.
butcher butch-er *butcher* b<u>u</u>³t<u>ch</u>er	This man is a <u>butcher</u>. He has a meat market. He cuts and sells meat. (butchers)

Bread and <u>butter</u>
are good to eat.

<u>Butter</u> is made
from cream.

butter
but-ter

butter
but<u>te</u>r

This flower is a <u>buttercup.</u>

<u>Buttercups</u> are yellow.

(buttercups)

buttercup
but-ter-cup

buttercup
but<u>te</u>rcup

<u>Butterflies</u> have
bright colors.

They grow from
caterpillars

(butterflies)

A <u>butterfly.</u>

butterfly
but-ter-fly

butterfly
but<u>te</u>rfl<u>y</u>

Butter is made from cream.

The milk that is left from the cream
is called <u>buttermilk.</u>

<u>Buttermilk</u> is good to drink.

buttermilk
but-ter-milk

buttermilk
but<u>te</u>rmilk

B
C
D
E
F
G
H
I
J
K
L
M
N
O
P
Q
R
S
T
U
V
W
X
Y
Z

button
but-ton

button
button

I can <u>button</u> my dress.

These are <u>buttons</u>.

Some <u>buttons</u> are
flat and round.

<u>Buttons</u> are pretty
on dresses.

(buttons   buttoned   buttoning)

buy

buy
buy

Father gave Bob
a nickel to <u>buy</u> candy.

See him <u>buying</u> candy
with the money.

(buys   bought   buying)

buzz

buzz
buzz

Dogs say, "Bow-wow."

Robins say, "Cheer-up, cheer-up."

Bees say, "<u>Buzz</u> <u>buzz</u>."

(buzzes   buzzed   buzzing)

by

by
by

The man is standing

by
near

the tree.

This is a head of cabbage.

Some cabbages are white and some are red.

Cabbage is good to eat.

(cabbages)

cabbage

cab-bage

cabbage

cabb**a**g**e**

A bird is in this cage.

We saw a lion in a cage at the circus.

(cages)

cage

cage

c**a**g**e**

A round cake   A square cake

(cakes)

cake

cake

c**a**k**e**

This is a calendar.

It helps to tell which month and day it is.

(calendars)

calendar

cal-en-dar

calendar

calend**ar**

This is a cow and her baby calf.

(calves)

calf

calf

ca**l**f

C
D
E
F
G
H
I
J
K
L
M
N
O
P
Q
R
S
T
U
V
W
X
Y
Z

call *call* cȧll	Jack did not hear his mother's <u>call</u>. She <u>called</u> him again and again. (calls called calling)
came *came* <u>ca</u><u>me</u>	John called his dog. The dog <u>came</u> to him. (come comes coming)
camel cam-el *camel* camel	This is a <u>camel</u>. <u>Camels</u> can go a long time without drinking water. (camels)
camera cam-er-a *camera* cam<u>e</u>rȧ	This is a <u>camera</u>. We take pictures with a <u>camera</u>. (cameras)
camp *camp* camp	Father and I like to ⎡camp⎤ ⎣live⎦ by the roadside in a tent. Boy Scouts like to ⎡camp out⎤ ⎣live outdoors⎦ in the summer. These people are <u>camping</u>. (camps camped camping)

can

can
can

An oil <u>can</u>   A garbage   A coffee
                      <u>can</u>   <u>can</u>

I | <u>can</u>
know how to | make a kite.

Mother | <u>cans</u>
puts | fruit in jars.

(cans   canned   canning)

This is a <u>candle</u>.

Mother put six <u>candles</u>
on my birthday cake.

(candles)

candle
can-dle

candle
candl<u>e</u> ₄

This is a

<u>candlestick</u>.
<u>holder for a candle</u>.

(candlesticks)

candlestick
can-dle-stick

candlestick
candl<u>e</u>stick

Sticks of <u>candy</u>   A box of
                          <u>candy</u>

(candies)

candy
can-dy

candy
candy

C
D
E
F
G
H
I
J
K
L
M
N
O
P
Q
R
S
T
U
V
W
X
Y
Z

61

cane *cane* c̲a̲n̲e̲	The man walks with a cane. (canes)
cannot can-not *cannot* cannot	Birds can fly. Dogs cannot fly.
canoe ca-noe *canoe* cánȯe̲s	This boat is called a canoe. Indians used canoes. (canoes)
can't *can't* can't	Dogs $\dfrac{\text{can't}}{\text{cannot}}$ fly.
cap *cap* cap	Bob wears a cap on his head. (caps)
cape *cape* c̲a̲p̲e̲	Mary made a cape for her doll. (capes)
captain cap-tain *captain* captain	We call the leader in the game our captain. (captains)

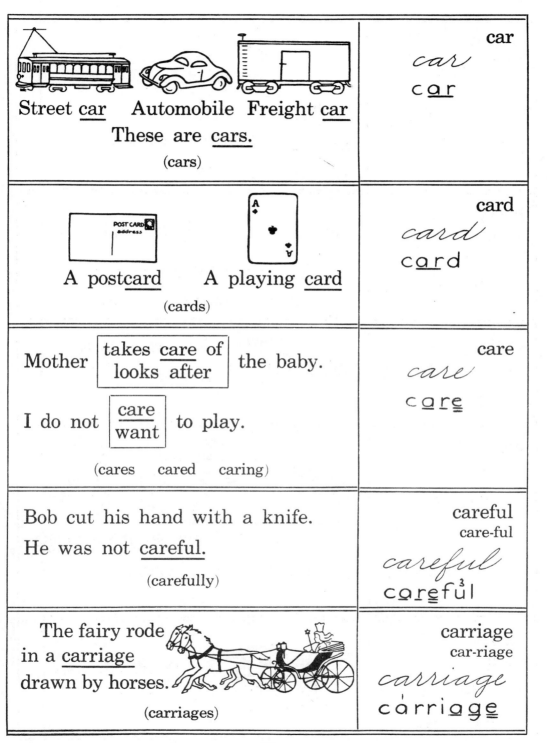

Street car   Automobile   Freight car
These are cars.
(cars)

car
car
c<u>a</u>r

A post<u>card</u>   A playing <u>card</u>
(cards)

card
card
c<u>a</u>rd

Mother | takes <u>care</u> of / looks after | the baby.

I do not | care / want | to play.

(cares   cared   caring)

care
care
c<u>a</u>r<u>e</u>

Bob cut his hand with a knife.
He was not <u>careful</u>.
(carefully)

careful
care-ful
careful
c<u>a</u>r<u>e</u>fŭl

The fairy rode in a <u>carriage</u> drawn by horses.
(carriages)

carriage
car-riage
carriage
cárri<u>age</u>

C
D
E
F
G
H
I
J
K
L
M
N
O
P
Q
R
S
T
U
V
W
X
Y
Z

63

carrot
car-rot

carrot
carrot

A <u>carrot</u>

<u>Carrots</u> are good to eat.

<u>Carrots</u> are orange in color.

(carrots)

carry
car-ry

carry
cárry

Father will $\boxed{\begin{array}{c} \text{carry} \\ \hline \text{take} \end{array}}$ the baby

in his arms to the church.

(carries   carried   carrying)

cart

cart
cart

This is a <u>cart.</u>

It has two wheels.

(carts)

case

case
case

A suit<u>case</u> A show<u>case</u> A book<u>case</u>

We put things in a case.

(cases)

castle
cas-tle

castle
castle

A <u>castle</u>

(castles)

I call my <u>cat</u> "Fluffy." (cats)	cat *cat* c a t
Bob is throwing the ball. Tom will <u>catch</u> it. (catches caught catching catcher)	catch *catch* c a <u>tc</u> h
Did you ever see a <u>caterpillar</u>? <u>Caterpillars</u> turn into butterflies. (caterpillars)	caterpillar cat-er-pil-lar *caterpillar* c a t <u>e</u> r p i l l <u>a</u> r

This plant is a <u>cattail</u>.
The leaves are green.
  The tail is brown.
<u>Cattails</u> grow
  in a wet place.
(cattails)
	cattail
	cat-tail
	cattail
	c a t t <u>a</u> i l

These are some
  of the animals
  that live on a farm.
They are called <u>cattle</u>.
	cattle
	cat-tle
	cattle
	c a t t l <u>e</u> 4

C
D
E
F
G
H
I
J
K
L
M
N
O
P
Q
R
S
T
U
V
W
X
Y
Z

C
D
E
F
G
H
I
J
K
L
M
N
O
P
Q
R
S
T
U
V
W
X
Y
Z

| caused | A broken wheel $\boxed{\frac{caused}{made}}$ the car to run into the post. |
| | (cause causes causing) |

caused
caused

| cave | The boys dug a big hole in the ground. They left a little door to get in. They called it their cave. |
| | (caves) |

cave
cave

| caw | The robin says, "Cheer-up, cheer-up." The crow says, "Caw-caw-caw." |
| | (caws cawed cawing) |

caw
caw

| celery | Celery is good to eat. Celery is covered up while it is growing. This makes it white. |

cel-er-y
celery
celery

| cent | Grandmother gave me one to buy candy. $\boxed{\frac{cent}{penny}}$ |
| | (cents) |

cent
cent

ONE CENT

UNITED STATES OF AMERICA

The cross is in the <u>center</u>
of the ring.

(centers)

center
cen-ter

center

cent<u>er</u>

We should eat <u>cereal</u> for breakfast.
<u>Cereal</u> is made from grain.

(cereals)

cereal
ce-re-al

cereal

c<u>e</u>r<u>e</u>ål

Bob was not | certain / sure | that
he could go.

(certainly)

certain
cer-tain

certain

c<u>e</u>r<u>tai</u>n

A <u>chain</u>

(chains)

chain

chain

<u>ch</u><u>ai</u>n

A kitchen <u>chair</u>   An arm<u>chair</u>

(chairs)

chair

chair

<u>ch</u><u>ai</u>r

C
D
E
F
G
H
I
J
K
L
M
N
O
P
Q
R
S
T
U
V
W
X
Y
Z

chalk *chalk* ch<u>ă</u><u>l</u>k	The teacher wrote on the blackboard with <u>chalk</u>.
champion cham-pi-on *champion* <u>ch</u>amp<u>i</u>on	Tom won all the games. He was the <u>champion</u>. (champions)
chance *chance* <u>ch</u>an<u>ce</u>,	Mary wanted to play but she did not have a <u>chance</u> to do so. (chances)
change *change* <u>ch</u>an<u>ge</u>	Bob got his shoes wet. He had to <u>change</u> his wet shoes for dry ones. (changes changed changing)
character char-ac-ter *character* <u>ch</u>áract<u>er</u>	Bob is a <u>character</u> an actor in the play. (characters)
chart *chart* <u>ch</u>art	Father is pasting a picture on the <u>chart</u>. (charts)

The dog likes to $\boxed{\frac{\text{chase}}{\text{run after}}}$ the cat. (chases chased chasing)	chase *chase* ch<u>a</u>s<u>e</u>
Mother bought a new dress for me. It $\boxed{\begin{array}{l}\text{was } \underline{\text{cheap.}} \\ \text{did not cost much money.}\end{array}}$ (cheaper cheapest)	cheap *cheap* ch<u>ea</u>p
This cloth has $\boxed{\frac{\text{checks}}{\text{squares}}}$ in it (checks)	check *check* ch<u>e</u>ck
Baby put her hand on her <u>cheek.</u> (cheeks)	cheek *cheek* ch<u>ee</u>k
Our team won the game. We all gave a loud $\boxed{\frac{\text{cheer.}}{\text{shout.}}}$ (cheers cheered cheering cheerfully)	cheer *cheer* ch<u>ee</u>r

C
D
E
F
G
H
I
J
K
L
M
N
O
P
Q
R
S
T
U
V
W
X
Y
Z

C
D
E
F
G
H
I
J
K
L
M
N
O
P
Q
R
S
T
U
V
W
X
Y
Z

cheerful cheer-ful *cheerful* cheerful	The children were cheerful. happy. (cheerfully)
cheese *cheese* cheese	Mice like to eat cheese. I like cheese, too. It is made from milk.
cherry cher-ry *cherry* cherry	A cherry (cherries)
chest *chest* chest	The boy put his hand on his chest. This is a chest for clothes. (chests)
chestnut chest-nut *chestnut* chestnut	Did you ever eat a toasted chestnut? Chestnuts grow on chestnut trees. They are big brown nuts. (chestnuts)

Baby put the candy
  into her mouth.
Father told her to <u>chew</u> it well
  with her new teeth.
(chews   chewed   chewing)

chew

chew
<u>ch</u>ew

A baby <u>chick</u>
(chicks)

chick

chick
<u>ch</u>i<u>ck</u>

A <u>chickadee</u> is
a small bird.

chickadee
chick-a-dee

chickadee
<u>ch</u>ick<u>a</u>d<u>ee</u>

A <u>chicken</u>
(chickens)

chicken
chick-en

chicken
<u>ch</u>i<u>ck</u>en

This is an Indian

<u>chief.</u>
<u>leader.</u>

(chiefs)

chief

chief
<u>ch</u>i<u>e</u>f

C
D
E
F
G
H
I
J
K
L
M
N
O
P
Q
R
S
T
U
V
W
X
Y
Z

child	
child c͟hild	This girl is a little c͟hild. (children)

children chil-dren	
children c͟hildren	These are c͟hildren. (child)

chimney chim-ney	
chimney c͟himney	A c͟himney Smoke goes out the c͟himney. (chimneys)

chin	
chin c͟hin	The boy is resting his c͟hin on his hand. (chins)

china chi-na	
china c͟hinå	This is a c͟hina cup.

China Chi-na	
China C͟hinå	This man came from C͟hina. C͟hina is a far-away country.

This is a chipmunk. He is a kind of squirrel. (chipmunks)		chipmunk chip-munk *chipmunk* chipmunk
The man is picking up [chips / small pieces of wood] to make a fire. (chip)		chips *chips* chips
A bar of chocolate A chocolate cake A cup of hot chocolate		chocolate choc-o-late *chocolate* chocolate
The children want to play a game. The leaders will [choose / pick out] the children to play. (chooses chose choosing choice)		choose *choose* choose
The woodcutter will [chop / cut] down the tree with an axe. (chops chopped chopping) A pork chop (chops)		chop *chop* chop

C
D
E
F
G
H
I
J
K
L
M
N
O
P
Q
R
S
T
U
V
W
X
Y
Z

C
D
E
F
G
H
I
J
K
L
M
N
O
P
Q
R
S
T
U
V
W
X
Y
Z

| chose | The leader chose / picked out me to play in the game. |
| | (choose   chooses   choosing   choice) |

chose
chose
cho̭s̭ḙ

Christmas	This is a <u>Christmas</u> tree.
Christ-mas	December 25th is
Christmas	<u>Christmas</u> day.
Christmas	

church	I go to <u>church</u>.
church	(churches)
church	

churn	Bob helped his grandmother
churn	churn / beat the butter
churn	from the cream.
	The machine for making butter is called a <u>churn</u>.
	(churns churned churning)

cigar	The man is smoking a <u>cigar</u>.
ci-gar	(cigars)
cigar	
cigar	

A circle / ring (circles)		**circle** cir-cle *circle* ci̲r̲cle̲ 4

The children went to the **circle.**

They saw the elephants and the clowns at the **circus.**

(circuses)

circus cir-cus *circus* ci̲rcus

Many people want to live in the United States.

These people are called **citizens.**

The laws make the country a safe place for **citizens** to live.

I am a **citizen** of the United States.

(citizens   citizenship)

citizen cit-i-zen *citizen* citizen

The farmer lives in the country.

I live in a   city. / large town.

(cities)

city cit-y *city* city

I liked the music.

See me **clap** my hands.

(claps   clapped   clapping)

clap *clap* clap

C D E F G H I J K L M N O P Q R S T U V W X Y Z

D
E
F
G
H
I
J
K
L
M
N
O
P
Q
R
S
T
U
V
W
X
Y
Z

class *class* class	Bob and Mary go to school. Bob is in a higher $\boxed{\begin{array}{c}\text{class}\\\hline\text{grade}\end{array}}$ than Mary. (classes)
claw *claw* cl<u>aw</u>	A <u>claw</u> is like a fingernail. The cat has sharp <u>claws</u>. She scratches with her <u>claws</u>. (claws)
clay *clay* cl<u>ay</u>	Mary made a bowl from $\boxed{\begin{array}{c}\text{clay.}\\\hline\text{mud.}\end{array}}$
clean *clean* cl<u>ea</u>n	Mother will $\boxed{\begin{array}{c}\text{clean}\\\hline\text{get the dirt}\\\text{out of}\end{array}}$ the house. Mother said, "Wash your hands <u>clean</u> with soap and warm water." (cleans cleaned cleaning) (cleaner cleanest)
cleaner clean-er *cleaner* cl<u>ea</u>n<u>er</u>	This man is a street <u>cleaner</u>. He makes the streets clean. (cleaners)

The water has dirt in it. It is not <u>clear</u>. (clearer clearest clearly)	clear *clear* cl<u>ea</u>r
Mary is a <u>clerk</u> in a store. She sells books and paper. (clerks)	clerk *clerk* cl<u>er</u>k
Bob can <u>climb / go up</u> the tree. (climbs climbed climbing) (climbers)	climb *climb* cl<u>i</u>m<u>b</u>
This is a paper <u>clip</u>. It is used to hold papers together. (clips)	clip *clip* clip
A <u>clock</u> (clocks)	clock *clock* clo<u>c</u>k
Mary said, "Do not get too <u>close to / near</u> me." (closer closest)	close *close* cl<u>o</u>s<u>e</u>

C
D
E
F
G
H
I
J
K
L
M
N
O
P
Q
R
S
T
U
V
W
X
Y
Z

C
D
E
F
G
H
I
J
K
L
M
N
O
P
Q
R
S
T
U
V
W
X
Y
Z

close *close* close	It is cold. Bob will close/shut the door. (closes closed closing)
cloth *cloth* cloth	Mother made a dress of pretty cloth.
clothes *clothes* clothes	Mother hung the clothes on the clothesline.

clothesline
clothes-line
clothesline
clothesline
	See the dress
	    on the clothesline.
	
	The clothesline
	    is a strong rope.
	
	(clotheslines)

cloud *cloud* cloud	I see a big cloud in the sky. (clouds)

	clover
A <u>clover</u> leaf A <u>clover</u> blossom	clo-ver
Bob fed his rabbits some <u>clover</u>.	*clover*
(clovers)	cl<u>o</u>v<u>e</u>r
I saw a <u>clown</u> at the circus.	clown
(clowns)	*clown*
	cl<u>ow</u>n
This is a <u>club.</u> / <u>heavy stick.</u>	club
(clubs)	*club*
Father belongs to a golf <u>club</u>.	club
(clubs)	
The hen said, "<u>Cluck! Cluck!</u> <u>Cluck!</u>"	cluck
	cluck
	cl<u>u</u><u>ck</u>
The king rode in a <u>coach</u> / carriage drawn by horses.	coach
(coaches)	*coach*
	c<u>oa</u><u>ch</u>

C
D
E
F
G
H
I
J
K
L
M
N
O
P
Q
R
S
T
U
V
W
X
Y
Z

coal		We burn <u>coal</u> in our furnace and stove.
coal		
c<u>oa</u>l		(coals)

coast		The children like to $\boxed{\begin{array}{c}\text{coast}\\\text{slide}\end{array}}$ down hill on their sleds. Some people like to live on the $\boxed{\begin{array}{c}\text{coast.}\\\text{seashore.}\end{array}}$
coast		
c<u>oa</u>st		(coasts coasted coasting)

coat		
coat		
c<u>oa</u>t		A <u>coat</u>
		(coats)

cock		This $\boxed{\begin{array}{c}\text{cock}\\\text{rooster}\end{array}}$ crows in the morning.
cock		
co<u>ck</u>		(cocks)

80

	cock-a-doodle-doo
The rooster says, "Cock-a-doodle-doo."	cock-a-doo-dle-doo *cock-a-doodle-doo* co<u>ck</u>-a-d<u>oo</u>dl<u>e</u>-d<u>oo</u>

	cocoa
Children drink <u>cocoa</u>. It makes them big and strong.	co-coa *cocoa* c<u>o</u>c<u>oa</u>

	cocoon
A butterfly will come out of this <u>cocoon</u>. (cocoons)	co-coon *cocoon* coc<u>oo</u>n

	coffee
Some children drink milk. It helps them grow. Some children drink <u>coffee</u>. It does not help them grow.	cof-fee *coffee* coff<u>ee</u>

	cold
The sun makes us warm. The snow makes us <u>cold</u>. (colder coldest)	*cold* c<u>o</u>ld

	collar
Father put a <u>collar</u> around the dog's neck. This is the <u>collar</u> to a man's shirt. (collars)	col-lar *collar* coll<u>ar</u>

C
D
E
F
G
H
I
J
K
L
M
N
O
P
Q
R
S
T
U
V
W
X
Y
Z

college
col-lege

college
college,

My brother goes to | college.
school.

(colleges)

---

color
col-or

color
color

We | color
paint | Easter eggs.

Red, yellow, and blue are colors.

(colors   colored   coloring)

---

colt

colt
colt

A mother horse and her baby colt.

(colts)

---

comb

comb
comb

A comb

(combs   combed   combing)

---

come

come
come,

Tom called his dog, but the dog did not come.

(comes   came   coming)

Some children came to our house. They were our <u>company</u>.	company com-pa-ny *company* company
Bob did not $\boxed{\begin{array}{c}\text{complete}\\\hline\text{finish}\end{array}}$ his picture. (completes completed completing)	complete com-plete *complete* compl<u>e</u>t<u>e</u>
This man is a streetcar <u>conductor</u>. He takes up the tickets. (conductors)	conductor con-duc-tor *conductor* conduct<u>o</u>r
An ice cream <u>cone</u> A pine <u>cone</u> (cones)	cone *cone* c<u>o</u>n<u>e</u>
This man is a <u>cook</u>. He will <u>cook</u> dinner for you. (cooks cooked cooking)	cook *cook* c<u>o</u>o k

C
D
E
F
G
H
I
J
K
L
M
N
O
P
Q
R
S
T
U
V
W
X
Y
Z

cooky
cook-y

cooky
cŏŏky

Jack ate a <u>cooky</u>.

It had a raisin on it.

(cookies)

---

cool

cool
cŏŏl

It is | cool / not warm | today.

(cooler   coolest)

(cools   cooled   cooling)

---

copy
cop-y

copy
copy

Bob tried to | <u>copy</u> Mary's picture. / make a picture just like Mary's.

(copies   copied   copying)

---

corn

corn
cŏrn

An ear of <u>corn</u>

---

corncob
corn-cob

corncob
cŏrncob

The corn has been eaten.

This is the <u>corncob</u>.

Little Jack Horner Sat in a <u>corner</u>. (corners)		corner cor-ner *corner* c<u>or</u>n<u>e</u>r
Mother bought a new dress. It <u>cost</u> four dollars. (costs costing)		cost *cost* cost
This small house is a <u>cottage</u>. We live in a <u>cottage</u> by the sea. (cottages)		cottage cot-tage *cottage* cott<u>a</u>g<u>e</u>
These men are picking <u>cotton</u>. Cloth is made from <u>cotton</u>.		cotton cot-ton *cotton* cotton
Mary is sick with a cold. She has a bad <u>cough</u>. (coughs coughed coughing)		cough *cough* c<u>ou</u>gh
Mother ┌ could ┐ get the apples. 　　　 └ was able to ┘		could *could* c<u>ou</u>ld

C
D
E
F
G
H
I
J
K
L
M
N
O
P
Q
R
S
T
U
V
W
X
Y
Z

couldn't could-n't *couldn't* c<u>ou</u>ldn't	I couldn't / could not / was not able to read the story.
count *count* c<u>ou</u>nt	1, 2, 3, 4, 5, 6, 7, 8, 9, 10. Can you <u>count</u> up to 10? (counts counted counting)
country coun-try *country* c<u>ou</u>ntry	Bob lives in the city, but Tom lives on a farm in the <u>country</u>. Mary lives in Canada, but Helen lives in another <u>country</u>. (countries)
course *course* c<u>ou</u>rse<u>s</u>	Of <u>course</u> / Surely I will go. This course / road goes to the country. (courses)
court *court* c<u>ou</u>rt	The boy would not go to school. The policeman took him to <u>court</u>. (courts)

Bob and Mary are
my aunt's children.

Bob is my <u>cousin</u>.

Mary is my <u>cousin</u>, too.

(cousins)

cousin
cous-in

cousin

cóusin

Mother will

| <u>cover</u> the baby with a blanket. |
| put the blanket over the baby. |

A can with a <u>cover</u>

A <u>cover</u> to
a can

(covers   covered   covering)

cover
cov-er

cover

cov<u>er</u>

A <u>cow</u>

(cows)

cow

cow

c<u>ow</u>

The cow sleeps
in the <u>cow barn</u>.

(cow barns)

cow barn

cow barn

c<u>ow</u> b<u>ar</u>n

C
D
E
F
G
H
I
J
K
L
M
N
O
P
Q
R
S
T
U
V
W
X
Y
Z

cowboy
cow-boy

cowboy
cow<u>bo</u>y

A <u>cowboy</u>

(cowboys)

---

crack

crack
cra<u>ck</u>

This bowl has a <u>crack</u> in it.

Bob will <u>crack</u> some nuts.

(cracks   cracked   cracking)

---

cracker
crack-er

cracker
cra<u>ck</u>er

Polly wants a <u>cracker</u>.

(crackers)

---

cradle
cra-dle

cradle
cr<u>a</u>dl<u>e</u>₄

This is a baby's

<u>cradle</u>.
bed with rockers.

(cradles)

---

cranberry
cran-ber-ry

cranberry
cranbérry

We ate <u>cranberry</u> sauce with our turkey.

<u>Cranberries</u> are red.

(cranberries)

The baby cannot walk
but she can <u>crawl.</u>

(crawls   crawled   crawling)

crawl

crawl

cr<u>aw</u>l

I like to color
pictures with
colored <u>crayons.</u>

One   A box
<u>crayon</u>   of <u>crayons</u>

(crayons)

crayon
cray-on

crayon

cr<u>ay</u>on

Mother has a bottle of milk.

<u>Cream</u> comes to the top of the milk.

cream

cream

cr<u>ea</u>m

Baby cannot walk

but she can | creep.
             crawl.

(creeps   crept   creeping)

creep

creep

cr<u>ee</u>p

Put a | cross
        + | after your name.

Bob will | cross
           go across | the street

at the corner.

(crosses   crossed   crossing)

cross

cross

cross

C
D
E
F
G
H
I
J
K
L
M
N
O
P
Q
R
S
T
U
V
W
X
Y
Z

C
D
E
F
G
H
I
J
K
L
M
N
O
P
Q
R
S
T
U
V
W
X
Y
Z

crow *crow* crow	This bird is a big black <u>crow</u>. Roosters <u>crow</u>. (crows crowed crowing)
crowd *crowd* crowd	One boy and one girl A <u>crowd</u> of children Bad boys try to $\boxed{\begin{array}{c}\text{crowd}\\\hline\text{push}\end{array}}$ in the line. The room is $\boxed{\begin{array}{c}\text{crowded.}\\\hline\text{filled very full.}\end{array}}$ (crowds crowded crowding)
crown *crown* crown	The king wore a <u>crown</u>. (crowns)
cruel cru-el *cruel* cruel	The man is very <u>cruel</u>. He likes to see others in pain.
crumbs *crumbs* crumbs	Birds eat $\boxed{\begin{array}{c}\text{crumbs}\\\hline\text{small pieces}\end{array}}$ of bread. (crumb)

The rabbit could not get the goats
   out of the turnip patch.

The bee said, "Do not <u>cry</u>.
   I will get them out for you."

(cries   cried   crying)

cry

cry

cr<s>y</s>

A <u>cup</u>

(cups)

cup

cup

cup

Old Mother Hubbard
Went to the <u>cupboard</u>.

(cupboards)

cupboard
cup-board

cupboard

cup<u>bo</u>ard

If you are sick, the doctor

will | <u>cure</u> you.
     | make you well.

(cures   cured   curing)

cure

cure

c<u>ure</u>

Mother curls Mary's hair
with a <u>curling iron</u>.

A <u>curling iron</u>

(curling irons)

curling iron
curl-ing i-ron

curling iron

c<u>url</u>i<u>ng</u> <u>i</u>ron

curls	Mary has her hair in <u>curls</u>.
curls	Her mother <u>curls</u> it
c<u>ur</u>l̇s	for her on a curling iron.
	(curl curled curling)
curtain	Mother is putting up
cur-tain	the <u>curtain</u>
curtain	at the window
c<u>ur</u>t<u>ai</u>n	(curtains)
curved	A straight line A <u>curved</u> line
curved	
c<u>ur</u>v<u>e</u>d	(curves curving)
cushion	This is a cushion. / pillow.
cush-ion	
cushion	I like to sit on a soft <u>cushion</u>.
c<u>u</u>sh<u>io</u>n	(cushions)
cut	Tom <u>cut</u> his hand with a knife.
cut	
cut	(cuts cutting)
cute	The baby is cute. / little and pretty.
cute	
c<u>u</u>t<u>e</u>	(cuter cutest)

Some children call their father <u>dad</u>. (dads daddy)	dad *dad* dad
We went to the <u>dairy</u>. They sell milk and butter at the <u>dairy</u>. (dairies)	dairy dair-y *dairy* d<u>ai</u>ry
This flower is a <u>daisy</u>. It is white with a yellow center. (daisies)	daisy dai-sy *daisy* d<u>ai</u>sy
See the children <u>dance</u>. (dances danced) dancing)	dance *dance* danc<u>e</u>₃
This flower is a <u>dandelion</u>. <u>Dandelions</u> are yellow. (dandelions)	dandelion dan-de-li-on *dandelion* dand<u>e</u>l<u>i</u>on

Do not cross the street
   when the light is red.
 	
It means danger.
            you may get hurt.
 	
(dangers   dangerous)
	danger
	dan-ger
	danger
	d<u>a</u>ng<u>er</u>

93

dare *dare* d<u>a</u>r<u>e</u>	Tom was afraid of the water. Bob said, "I will <u>dare</u> you to jump into the lake." (dares dared daring)
dark *dark* d<u>a</u>rk	At night the sky is <u>dark.</u> (darker darkest darkness)
dash *dash* d<u>a</u><u>sh</u>	We watched the men ___ past the fire. **dash / hurry** (dashes dashed dashing)
date *date* d<u>a</u>t<u>e</u>	Have you eaten a <u>date</u>? The <u>date</u> of my birthday is May 5, 1931. What is the <u>date</u> of your birthday? (dates)
daughter daugh-ter *daughter* d<u>au</u><u>gh</u>t<u>e</u>r	A boy is a son of his father and mother. A girl is a <u>daughter</u> of her mother and father. (daughters)

Do you know the name of the first <u>day</u> of the week? Monday, Tuesday, and Wednesday are some of the <u>days</u>. (days)	day *day* d<u>ay</u>	
I have a very $\boxed{\begin{array}{c}\text{dear}\\\hline\text{nice}\end{array}}$ mother. (dears dearie dearly)	dear *dear* d<u>ea</u>r	
<u>December</u> is the twelfth month of the year. Christmas comes in <u>December.</u>	December De-cem-ber *December* D<u>e</u>cemb<u>e</u>r	
Father will $\boxed{\begin{array}{c}\text{decide}\\\hline\text{make up his mind}\end{array}}$ whether we'll have a picnic. (decides decided deciding)	decide de-cide *decide* d<u>e</u>c<u>i</u>d<u>e</u>	
Bob can dig a <u>deep</u> hole in the ground. (deeper deepest)	deep *deep* d<u>ee</u>p	
This is a <u>deer.</u>	deer *deer* d<u>ee</u>r	

D
E
F
G
H
I
J
K
L
M
N
O
P
Q
R
S
T
U
V
W
X
Y
Z

delight de-light *delight* d<u>e</u>l<u>igh</u>t	Father takes ⎡ **delight** / great joy ⎤ in surprising the children. (delights delighted delighting)
deliver de-liv-er *deliver* d<u>e</u>liv<u>e</u>r	The postman will ⎡ **deliver** / bring ⎤ the letters. (delivers delivered delivering)
demand de-mand *demand* d<u>e</u>mand	Father will ⎡ **demand** / ask ⎤ that you bring back our books. (demands demanded demanding)
den *den* den	The fox went into his ⎡ **den.** / home. ⎤ (dens)
dentist den-tist *dentist* dentist	This man is a <u>dentist.</u> He fixes teeth. (dentists)

Bob wanted to ⎡describe / tell about⎤ his visit to the farm. (describes described describing)	describe de-scribe *describe* d<u>e</u>scr<u>i</u>b<u>e</u>
The camel travels through the ⎡desert. / land without water and trees.⎤ (deserts)	desert des-ert *desert* des<u>e</u>rt
Helen does good work in school. She ⎡deserves / should have⎤ a good mark. (deserve deserved deserving)	deserves de-serves *deserves* d<u>e</u>s<u>e</u>rv<u>e</u>s
These are <u>desks</u>. Which kind of <u>desk</u> do you have? (desks)	desk *desk* desk
Fire will ⎡destroy / put an end to⎤ the house. (destroys destroyed destroying)	destroy de-stroy *destroy* d<u>e</u>str<u>oy</u>

D
E
F
G
H
I
J
K
L
M
N
O
P
Q
R
S
T
U
V
W
X
Y
Z

dew *dew* de̬w	In the morning we found $\boxed{\dfrac{\text{dew}}{\text{drops of water}}}$ on the grass. (dewy)
diamond di-a-mond *diamond* di̯åmond	Mother has a <u>diamond</u> ring. The <u>diamond</u> sparkles. (diamonds)
did *did* did	The girl <u>did</u> her work well. (do does done doing)
didn't did-n't *didn't* didn't	The girl $\boxed{\dfrac{\text{didn't}}{\text{did not}}}$ do her work well.
die *die* di̬e	The mouse will $\boxed{\dfrac{\text{die}}{\text{stop living}}}$ if the cat catches him. (dies died dying dead death)
different dif-fer-ent *different* diffe̬rent	Bob has a new book. It is $\boxed{\dfrac{\text{different from}}{\text{not like}}}$ ours. (difference)

D
E
F
G
H
I
J
K
L
M
N
O
P
Q
R
S
T
U
V
W
X
Y
Z

	Bob can <u>dig</u> in the sand with his shovel. (digs dug digging)	dig *dig* dig

Ten pennies make a <u>dime.</u>

Two nickels make a <u>dime.</u>

(dimes)

dime
dime
d<u>im</u>e

<u>Ding</u>, dong bell,
Pussy's in the well.

ding
ding
di<u>ng</u>

These children are eating

in the [dining / eating] room.

(dine   dines   dined)

dining
din-ing
dining
d<u>i</u>ni<u>ng</u>

The family is eating <u>dinner.</u>

We have <u>dinner</u> at six o'clock.

(dinners)

dinner
din-ner
dinner
dinn<u>er</u>

D
E
F
G
H
I
J
K
L
M
N
O
P
Q
R
S
T
U
V
W
X
Y
Z

99

direction	The children were going north.
di-rec-tion	That was the wrong <u>direction.</u>
direction	Bob did not make his picture right.
d<u>i</u>rec<u>ti</u>on	He did not listen to the teacher's <u>directions.</u>
	(directions)

dirt	Mary fell down.
dirt	She got $\boxed{\dfrac{\text{dirt}}{\text{mud}}}$ on her dress.
d<u>ir</u>t	

dirty	The children played in the sand.
dirt-y	Their hands were $\boxed{\dfrac{\text{dirty.}}{\text{not clean.}}}$
dirty	
d<u>ir</u>ty	

disappeared	
dis-ap-peared	The cat $\boxed{\dfrac{\text{disappeared}}{\text{ran from sight}}}$ up a tree.
disappeared	
disapp<u>ea</u>red	(disappear disappears disappearing)

disease	
dis-ease	A <u>disease</u> is a kind of sickness.
disease	(diseases)
dis<u>ea</u>se<u></u>s	

dish	
dish	A <u>dish</u> Dishes
di<u>sh</u>	(dishes)

I wash dishes in a <u>dishpan.</u> (dishpans)		dishpan dish-pan *dishpan* di<u>sh</u>pan
It is a long $\boxed{\dfrac{\text{distance}}{\text{way}}}$ from here to our school. (distances distant)		distance dis-tance *distance* distanc<u>e</u>₃
Bob cut the apple in two. He said, "I will $\boxed{\begin{array}{l}\underline{\text{divide}}\text{ my apple with you."}\\ \text{share my apple with you."}\\ \text{give you a part}\\ \text{of my apple."}\end{array}}$ (divides divided dividing)		divide di-vide *divide* div<u>id</u><u>e</u>
I <u>do</u> my work well. (did doing does done)		do *do* dŏ³
Father is sick. The <u>doctor</u> came to make him well. (doctors)		doctor doc-tor *doctor* doct<u>or</u>
Bob <u>does</u> his work well. (do did doing done)		does *does* dŏ³<u>e</u>s¹

D
E
F
G
H
I
J
K
L
M
N
O
P
Q
R
S
T
U
V
W
X
Y
Z

D
E
F
G
H
I
J
K
L
M
N
O
P
Q
R
S
T
U
V
W
X
Y
Z

dog *dog* dog	A <u>dog</u> (dogs)
doll *doll* doll	This is a baby <u>doll</u>. (dolls dolly)
dollar dol-lar *dollar* doll<u>ar</u>	$ This is a <u>dollar</u> sign. A <u>dollar</u> is 100 cents. (dollars)
dollhouse doll-house *dollhouse* dollh<u>ou</u>s<u>e</u>₅	The doll lives in a | dollhouse. / house made for dolls. (dollhouses)
done *done* don<u>e</u>₅	You may go home when your work is | done. / finished.
donkey don-key *donkey* donk<u>e</u>y	A <u>donkey</u> (donkeys)

I $\boxed{\dfrac{\text{don't}}{\text{do not}}}$ sing well.	don't *don't* don't
A <u>door</u> (doors)	door *door* d<u>oo</u>r
A man is ringing the <u>doorbell</u>. Mother will go to the door. (doorbells)	doorbell door-bell *doorbell* d<u>oo</u>rbell
Bob is sitting on the <u>doorstep</u>. (doorsteps)	doorstep door-step *doorstep* d<u>oo</u>rstep
Mary is standing in the <u>doorway</u>. (doorways)	doorway door-way *doorway* d<u>oo</u>rway

D
E
F
G
H
I
J
K
L
M
N
O
P
Q
R
S
T
U
V
W
X
Y
Z

dot *dot* dot	This cloth has <u>dots</u> in it. (dots)
double dou-ble *double* d<u>ou</u>ble	We spell book with | **double** / two | o's. (doubles doubled doubling)
dove *dove* dov<u>e</u>	This bird is a <u>dove.</u> A <u>dove</u> is sometimes called a pigeon. (doves)
down *down* d<u>ow</u>n	The squirrel ran <u>down</u> the tree.
downstairs down-stairs *downstairs* d<u>ow</u>nst<u>ai</u>rs	The boy is coming | <u>downstairs.</u> / down the stairs. |
downtown down-town *downtown* d<u>ow</u>nt<u>ow</u>n	Mother went | **downtown** / to town | to buy a dress.

Helen went to the store to buy a dozen / twelve eggs.	**dozen** doz-en *dozen* dozen
The baby drank the milk. (drink drinks drinking)	**drank** *drank* drank
Tom can draw pictures. (draws drew drawing drawn)	**draw** *draw* draw
"Something dreadful / terrible has happened," said the boy. "The goats are in the turnip patch and I can't get them out."	**dreadful** dread-ful *dreadful* dreadful
Bob had a dream when he was asleep. He dreamed he was riding on an elephant. (dreams dreamed dreaming)	**dream** *dream* dream
A dress (dresses)	**dress** *dress* dress

D
E
F
G
H
I
J
K
L
M
N
O
P
Q
R
S
T
U
V
W
X
Y
Z

D
E
F
G
H
I
J
K
L
M
N
O
P
Q
R
S
T
U
V
W
X
Y
Z

dresser dress-er *dresser* dress**er**	This is a <u>dresser</u>. We keep clothes in a <u>dresser</u>. (dressers)
drill *drill* drill	We are giving a play. We will │ <u>drill</u> / practice │ on our parts today. (drills drilled drilling)
drink *drink* drink	See baby <u>drink</u> her milk. (drinks drank drinking)
drinking fountain drink-ing foun-tain *drinking fountain* drinki<u>ng</u> fo<u>un</u>t<u>ai</u>n	Mary is getting a drink from the <u>drinking</u> fountain. (drinking fountains)
drive *drive* dr<u>i</u>v<u>e</u>	This man can <u>drive</u> the auto. He is the <u>driver</u>. He makes the car go. (drives drove driving driver)

The car is standing in the <u>driveway</u>. (driveways)		**driveway** drive-way *driveway* dr<u>i</u>v<u>ewa</u>y
A <u>drop</u> of rain fell on Mary's dress. Did you see Mary <u>drop</u> a package? (drops dropped dropping)		**drop** *drop* drop
The cat fell into the water. She could not swim. I pulled her out so she would not drown. die under the water. (drowns drowned drowning)		**drown** *drown* dr<u>ow</u>n
Father was sick. Bob ran to the <u>drug</u> store to get some drugs medicine for him. (drugs)		**drug** *drug* drug
A <u>drum</u> (drums)		**drum** *drum* drum

D
E
F
G
H
I
J
K
L
M
N
O
P
Q
R
S
T
U
V
W
X
Y
Z

dry	The rain makes the ground wet.
dry	The sun makes the ground <u>dry</u>.
dry	The sun <u>dries</u> the ground.
	(dries dried drying)

duck	
duck	A <u>duck</u>
duck	(ducks)

duckling	
duck-ling	A <u>duckling</u>
duckling	(ducklings)
duckling	

during	We ate apples
dur-ing	during / while we / were having our play class.
during	
d<u>uring</u>	

dust	The wind blew dust / fine dirt into my eyes.
dust	
dust	Mother <u>dusts</u> the furniture.
	(dusts dusted dusting)

	Dutch
This is a little <u>Dutch</u> girl. She lives in Holland.	*Dutch* Du<u>tch</u>
This man did not grow big. We call him a <u>dwarf</u>. <center>(dwarfs)</center>	dwarf *dwarf* dw<u>ar</u>f
We $\boxed{\dfrac{\text{dwell}}{\text{live}}}$ in a brick house. <center>(dwells dwelled dwelling)</center>	dwell *dwell* dwell
The $\boxed{\dfrac{\text{dwellers}}{\text{people who live}}}$ in this town are Americans. <center>(dweller)</center>	dwellers dwell-ers *dwellers* dwell<u>er</u>s

D
E
F
G
H
I
J
K
L
M
N
O
P
Q
R
S
T
U
V
W
X
Y
Z

E e $\mathcal{E}$ e E e

each *each* <u>each</u>	I gave <u>each</u> boy one apple.
eager ea-ger *eager* <u>eager</u>	Bob ⎡ is <u>eager</u> / wants ⎤ to see my kite. (eagerly)
eagle ea-gle *eagle* <u>eagle</u>₄	This bird is an <u>eagle</u>. He is very large. His picture is on money. (eagles)
ear *ear* <u>ea</u>r	We hear with our <u>ears</u>. An <u>ear</u>. (ears)
early ear-ly *early* <u>ear</u>ly	I started to school <u>early</u> so that I would not be late. (earlier earliest)
earned *earned* <u>ea</u>rn<u>e</u>d	I have a dime. I <u>earned</u> it by working for father. (earn earns earning)
earth *earth* <u>ea</u>rth	The farmer put the seeds into the ⎡ <u>earth</u>. / ground. ⎤

The sun comes up in the <u>east</u>.	east *east* <u>e</u><u>a</u>st
We color eggs for <u>Easter</u>.	Easter East-er *Easter* E<u>a</u>st<u>e</u>r
This flower is an <u>Easter</u> <u>lily</u>. (Easter lilies)	Easter lily East-er lil-y *Easter lily* E<u>a</u>st<u>e</u>r lily
Your book is hard to read. My book is <u>easy</u> to read. (easier easiest easily)	easy eas-y *easy* e<u>a</u>sy
The boy will <u>eat</u> the apple. (eats ate eating eaten)	eat *eat* <u>e</u><u>a</u>t
Bob put a line near the <u>edge</u> of the paper. (edges)	edge *edge* e<u>d</u><u>g</u>e
Hens lay <u>eggs</u>. The <u>eggs</u> are in the nest. <u>Eggs</u> are good to eat. (eggs)	egg *egg* egg

E
F
G
H
I
J
K
L
M
N
O
P
Q
R
S
T
U
V
W
X
Y
Z

E
F
G
H
I
J
K
L
M
N
O
P
Q
R
S
T
U
V
W
X
Y
Z

eight *eight* <u>eigh</u>t	Here are $\frac{\text{eight}}{8}$ apples. Count them. (eighth)
either ei-ther *either* <u>ei</u>t<u>her</u>	You may have either dog. this dog or that one.
electric e-lec-tric *electric* <u>e</u>lectric	This is an <u>electric</u> light. This is an <u>electric</u> iron.
electricity e-lec-tric-i-ty *electricity* <u>e</u>lectricity	The electric iron is kept warm by <u>electricity</u>.
elephant el-e-phant *elephant* el<u>e</u><u>ph</u>ant	I saw an <u>elephant</u> at the zoo. <u>Elephants</u> are very big. (elephants)
elevator el-e-va-tor *elevator* el<u>e</u>v<u>a</u>t<u>or</u>	The children went up in the <u>elevator</u>. (elevators)

The boy saw <u>eleven</u> stars. · Count them. (eleventh)	eleven e-lev-en *eleven* <u>e</u>leven
This is an <u>elf</u>. · An <u>elf</u> is like a fairy. (elves)	elf *elf* elf

Who <u>else</u>
 What <u>other persons</u> will come
 to my party?
	else
	 else
	 els<u>e</u>,

The box is <u>empty</u>. has nothing in it. Bob <u>emptied</u> the apples took out all from the basket. (empties emptied emptying)	empty emp-ty *empty* empty
Mary is holding one <u>end</u> of the rope. Bob is holding the other <u>end</u>. The children were fighting. Mother came and the fighting <u>ended</u>. stopped. (ends ended ending)	end *end* end

E F G H I J K L M N O P Q R S T U V W X Y Z

enemy en-e-my *enemy* enemy	A soldier does not fight friends. He fights the enemy. people who are against him. (enemies)
engine en-gine *engine* engine	This is an engine. It pulls the railroad cars. (engines engineer engineers)
enjoy en-joy *enjoy* enjoy	Did you enjoy the story? Did the story make you happy? (enjoys enjoyed enjoying)
enough e-nough *enough* enough	Mother did not have enough apples. as many apples as we needed.
envelope en-ve-lope *envelope* envelope	This is an envelope. We put letters in envelopes. (envelopes)
errand er-rand *errand* errand	Bob went to the store for Mother. Mary went on an errand for Mother, too. (errands)

The lion is trying to | escape from / get out of | the cage.

(escapes   escaped   escaping)

escape
es-cape
escape
esc<u>a</u>p<u>e</u>

This is an <u>Eskimo</u> mother.

<u>Eskimos</u> live in the North.

(Eskimos)

Eskimo
Es-ki-mo
Eskimo
Eskim<u>o</u>

Can you fold the paper so that the edges will be <u>even?</u>

Bob's and Mary's pencils are | even. / the same size. |

The boys divided the sand into | <u>even</u> / equal | piles.

Mother | <u>evened</u> / smoothed | the frosting on the cake.

(evens   evened   evening)

even
e-ven
even
<u>e</u>ven

When the sun goes down, it is <u>evening.</u>

After the <u>evening,</u> it is night.

(evenings)

evening
eve-ning
evening
<u>e</u>veni<u>ng</u>

E
F
G
H
I
J
K
L
M
N
O
P
Q
R
S
T
U
V
W
X
Y
Z

ever ev-er *ever* ev<u>er</u>	Did you $\boxed{\dfrac{\text{ever}}{\text{at any time}}}$ see a cow?
every ev-er-y *every* ev<u>er</u>y	I drink milk $\boxed{\dfrac{\text{every}}{\text{each}}}$ day.
everybody ev-er-y-bod-y *everybody* ev<u>er</u>ybody	She gave $\boxed{\dfrac{\text{everybody}}{\text{each person}}}$ an apple.
everyone ev-er-y-one *everyone* ev<u>er</u>yone	She gave $\boxed{\dfrac{\text{everyone}}{\text{everybody}}}$ an apple.
everything ev-er-y-thing *everything* ev<u>er</u><u>thing</u>	They put $\boxed{\dfrac{\text{everything}}{\text{all the things}}}$ into the box.
everywhere ev-er-y-where *everywhere* ev<u>er</u>y<u>where</u>	Mary looked $\boxed{\dfrac{\text{everywhere}}{\text{every place}}}$ for her doll.
evil e-vil *evil* <u>e</u>vil	Some people do $\boxed{\dfrac{\text{evil}}{\text{bad}}}$ things. (evils)

I go to school every day $\boxed{\dfrac{\text{except}}{\text{but}}}$ Saturday and Sunday.	**except** ex-cept *except* except
My new shoes are too small. Mother will <u>exchange</u> them for a larger pair. Tom and Betty will <u>exchange</u> books. (exchanges exchanged exchanging)	**exchange** ex-change *exchange* ex<u>ch</u>a<u>ng</u><u>e</u>₃
The fire bell rang. The children were <u>excited</u>. (excite excites exciting)	**excited** ex-cit-ed *excited* exc<u>it</u><u>ed</u>

Mary is polite.
She says, "<u>Excuse</u> me,"
   when she walks in front of you.
 	
The teacher will $\boxed{\dfrac{\text{excuse you}}{\text{let you go}}}$
   if you are sick.
 	
Bob's father wrote an <u>excuse</u>
   to the teacher.
 	
(excuses   excused   excusing)
	excuse
	ex-cuse
	
	excuse
	exc<u>us</u><u>e</u>

E
F
G
H
I
J
K
L
M
N
O
P
Q
R
S
T
U
V
W
X
Y
Z

exercise ex-er-cise *exercise* exerc<u>i</u>s<u>e</u>	Playing ball is good <u>exercise</u>. Running is good <u>exercise</u>. (exercises exercised exercising)
expect ex-pect *expect* expect	Mother will $\boxed{\begin{array}{c}\text{expect}\\\hline\text{look for}\end{array}}$ you to come to our house. (expects expected expecting)
express ex-press *express* express	Mary can $\boxed{\begin{array}{c}\text{express herself}\\\hline\text{say what she}\\\text{wants to say}\end{array}}$ well. (expresses expressed expressing) This is $\boxed{\begin{array}{c}\text{an express}\\\hline\text{a fast}\end{array}}$ train.
eye *eye* <u>eye</u>	We see with our <u>eyes</u>. An <u>eye</u> (eyes)

E
F
G
H
I
J
K
L
M
N
O
P
Q
R
S
T
U
V
W
X
Y
Z

F f F f **F f**

I wash my hands and <u>face</u>. We ⎡ face / look toward ⎤ the window. (faces faced facing)	face *face* f<u>a</u><u>c</u><u>e</u>
Bob told one ⎡ fact / truth ⎤ about the accident. (facts)	fact *fact* fact
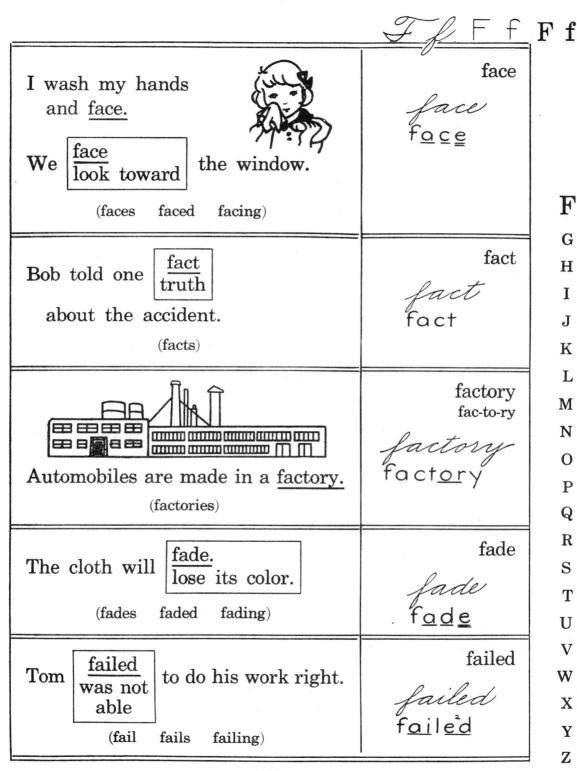 Automobiles are made in a <u>factory</u>. (factories)	factory fac-to-ry *factory* fact<u>or</u>y
The cloth will ⎡ <u>fade</u>. / lose its color. ⎤ (fades faded fading)	fade *fade* f<u>a</u><u>d</u><u>e</u>
Tom ⎡ <u>failed</u> / was not able ⎤ to do his work right. (fail fails failing)	failed *failed* f<u>ai</u>le͞d

F
G
H
I
J
K
L
M
N
O
P
Q
R
S
T
U
V
W
X
Y
Z

F
G
H
I
J
K
L
M
N
O
P
Q
R
S
T
U
V
W
X
Y
Z

fair	Bob is ┌fair / honest┐ about his work.
	This is a ┌fair / clear┐ day.
fair	We are going to the fair.
f<u>ai</u>r	People show and sell all kinds of things at the fair.
	(fairs fairer fairest fairly)

fairy	See this fairy!
fair-y	Fairies are make-believe people.
fairy	
f<u>ai</u>ry	(fairies fairyland)

fall	Humpty Dumpty sat on a wall.
	Humpty Dumpty had a great fall.
fall	Leaves ┌fall / come down┐ from the trees
fȧll	in autumn.
	(falls fell falling)

false	The story is ┌false. / not true.┐
false	
fȧlse₅	

false face	On Halloween we wear false faces.
false face	
fȧlse₅ face	A false face (false faces)

120

This is a <u>family</u>.

In this <u>family</u> there is the father, mother and two children.

(families)

family
fam-i-ly

family
family

This is a <u>fan</u>.

It helps keep you cool.

Do you have a <u>fan?</u>

(fans   fanned   fanning)

fan

fan
fan

Mary cannot throw the ball as <u>far</u> as Bob can.

Grandmother lives | <u>far</u> away. |
| a long way off. |

(farther   farthest)

far

far
far

The Eskimos live

in a | <u>faraway</u> | land.
| far off |

faraway
far-a-way

faraway
faraway

The conductor took

the streetcar | <u>fare</u>. |
| money or tickets. |

(fares)

fare

fare
fare

F
G
H
I
J
K
L
M
N
O
P
Q
R
S
T
U
V
W
X
Y
Z

farm

farm

f<u>a</u>rm

We went to a <u>farm</u> in the country.

We saw horses and cows
on the <u>farm</u>.

(farms)

farmer

farm-er

farmer

f<u>ar</u>m<u>e</u>r

This man is a <u>farmer</u>.

He lives on a farm.

He grows things to eat.

(farmers)

farmhouse

farm-house

farmhouse

f<u>a</u>rmh<u>ou</u>s<u>e</u>.

The farmer lives in the

| farmhouse. |
| house on |
| the farm. |

fast

fast

f<u>a</u>st

Mary runs slowly.

I can run <u>fast</u>.

(faster   fastest)

fasten

fas-ten

fasten

f<u>a</u>s<u>t</u>en

Tom tried to | fasten |
| lock | the door.

Mother | fastened |
| buttoned | Mary's dress.

(fastens   fastened   fastening)

This man is **fat.** / **not thin.** (fatter fattest)		fat *fat* fat
That woman is Jack's mother. That man is Jack's <u>father.</u> <u>Father</u> earns money to care for his children. (fathers)		father fa-ther *father* fáther
Our teacher found <u>fault</u> with / mistakes in our work. (faults)		fault *fault* fault
Mother has no fear of the dog. Mother is not afraid of the dog. (fears feared fearing)		fear *fear* fear
The Pilgrims had a <u>feast</u> / many things to eat on Thanksgiving. (feasts feasted feasting)		feast *feast* feast
This is a <u>feather.</u> Chickens and ducks have <u>feathers.</u> (feathers feathery)		feather feath-er *feather* feáther

F
G
H
I
J
K
L
M
N
O
P
Q
R
S
T
U
V
W
X
Y
Z

F
G
H
I
J
K
L
M
N
O
P
Q
R
S
T
U
V
W
X
Y
Z

February Feb-ru-ar-y *February* February	The second month of the year is <u>February</u>. February has 28 days. Every four years February has 29 days.
feed *feed* f<u>ee</u>d	See the girl <u>feed</u> the chickens. (feeds fed feeding)
feel *feel* f<u>ee</u>l	See Bob | <u>feel</u> / touch | the elephant's trunk. (feels felt feeling feelings)
feelers feel-ers *feelers* f<u>ee</u>lers	Many bugs have <u>feelers</u>. Bugs feel their way on the ground with their <u>feelers</u>. The rabbit's <u>feelers</u> are his whiskers. (feeler)
feet *feet* f<u>ee</u>t	We have two <u>feet</u>. Horses have four <u>feet</u>. A <u>foot</u> is twelve inches long. I am three <u>feet</u> tall. (foot)

The baby **fell** down. It did not hurt her. (fall falls falling)	fell *fell* fell
This is a little \boxed{fellow. / boy.} (fellows)	fellow fel-low *fellow* fell<u>ow</u>
Bob \boxed{felt / touched} the elephant's trunk. (feel feels feeling)	felt *felt* felt
The **fence** is around the field. The calf cannot get over the **fence**. (fences)	fence *fence* fenc<u>e</u>$_3$
This car has a bumped **fender**. **Fenders** keep dirt off the car. (fenders)	fender fend-er *fender* fend<u>er</u>
This is a **fern** leaf. **Ferns** have leaves but no flowers. (ferns)	fern *fern* f<u>er</u>n

F
G
H
I
J
K
L
M
N
O
P
Q
R
S
T
U
V
W
X
Y
Z

few	
few fe̲w̲	Here are many flowers. Here are only a few not many flowers.

fiddle fid-dle	
fiddle fiddle̲=₄	This is a fiddle. / violin. Do you like the music of a fiddle? (fiddles)

field	
field fi̲e̲ld	The children play in the field. Cows eat grass in the field. (fields)

fierce	
fierce fi̲e̲rc̲e̲₃	The lion is a fierce / wild animal. (fiercer fiercest)

fifteen fif-teen	
fifteen fift̲e̲e̲n	five ten fifteen 5 10 15 Can you count to fifteen? Can you write the numbers from 1 to 15?

This is a whole pie
   cut into five
   pieces.

This is one <u>fifth</u> or one
   of the five pieces.

(fifths)

fifth

fifth
fif<u>th</u>

---

thirty   forty   <u>fifty</u>
30   40   50

<u>Fifty</u> cents make one-half dollar.

fifty
fif-ty

fifty
fifty

The tin soldiers
   went to <u>fight</u>
   for the king.

Some bad boys | <u>fight.</u>
| hit each other.

(fights   fought   fighting   fighter)

fight

fight
fi<u>gh</u>t

---

1 2 3 4 5 6 7 8 9 10

Each number is a <u>figure.</u>

Some cloth is plain.

Some cloth has | <u>figures</u>
| flowers or
| shapes | in it.

(figures)

figure
fig-ure

figure
fig<u>ure</u>

F
G
H
I
J
K
L
M
N
O
P
Q
R
S
T
U
V
W
X
Y
Z

file

file
file

This is a nail <u>file</u>.

This <u>file</u> makes the fingernails smooth.

The children walked

in | a single <u>file</u>.
one line behind each other.

(files   filed   filing)

fill

fill
fill

Bob can | <u>fill</u> his pail with
make his pail full of | sand.

(fills   filled   filling)

finally
fi-nal-ly

finally
finally

Finally
At last | the three bears

came home.

find

find
find

Little Bo-Peep has lost her sheep

And can't tell where to | find
go get | them.

(finds   found   finding)

Peter Rabbit said, "How _fine_ I look." The man drove too fast. He had to pay a _fine_. Flour is _fine_ but oatmeal is coarse. (finer finest) (fines fined fining)		fine *fine* fi̲n̲e̲
I have five _fingers_ on each hand. Which _finger_ is longest? (fingers)		finger fin-ger *finger* fi̲n̲g̲e̲r̲
Jack is reading a book. He will [_finish_ it / come to the end] soon. (finishes finished finishing)		finish fin-ish *finish* fini̲s̲h̲
The house is on _fire_. It may burn down. (fires)		fire *fire* fi̲r̲e̲
This is a _fire alarm_. We use it to call the firemen.		fire alarm fire a-larm *fire alarm* fi̲r̲e̲ a̲l̲a̲r̲m̲

F
G
H
I
J
K
L
M
N
O
P
Q
R
S
T
U
V
W
X
Y
Z

firecracker fire-crack-er *firecracker* f<u>i</u>r<u>e</u>cr<u>a</u>ck<u>e</u>r	We had <u>firecrackers</u> on the Fourth of July. Did you ever shoot a <u>firecracker</u>? (firecrackers)
fire engine fire en-gine *fire engine* f<u>i</u>r<u>e</u> <u>e</u>ng<u>i</u>ne<u>e</u>s	A <u>fire</u> <u>engine</u> is used to throw water on a fire. (fire engines)
firelight fire-light *firelight* f<u>i</u>r<u>e</u>l<u>ig</u>ht	The Indian sat by the <u>firelight.</u> light of the fire. (firelights)
fireman fire-man *fireman* f<u>i</u>r<u>e</u>man	The <u>fireman</u> helped put out the fire. (firemen)
fireplace fire-place *fireplace* f<u>i</u>r<u>e</u>pl<u>a</u>c<u>e</u>	They made a fire in the <u>fireplace.</u> (fireplaces)

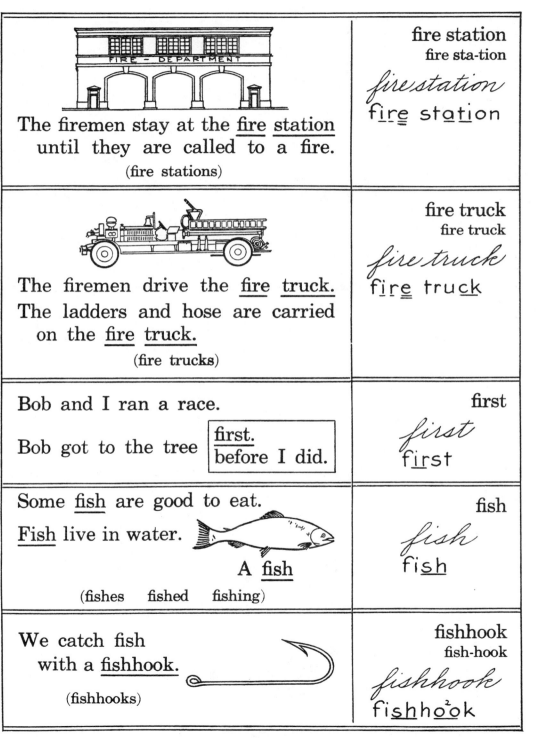

The firemen stay at the <u>fire</u> station until they are called to a fire. (fire stations)	fire station fire sta-tion *fire station* f<u>i</u>r<u>e</u> st<u>a</u>t<u>i</u>on
The firemen drive the <u>fire</u> truck. The ladders and hose are carried on the <u>fire</u> truck. (fire trucks)	fire truck fire truck *fire truck* f<u>i</u>r<u>e</u> tru<u>ck</u>
Bob and I ran a race. Bob got to the tree <u>first.</u> / before I did.	first *first* f<u>ir</u>st
Some <u>fish</u> are good to eat. <u>Fish</u> live in water. A <u>fish</u> (fishes fished fishing)	fish *fish* fi<u>sh</u>
We catch fish with a <u>fishhook.</u> (fishhooks)	fishhook fish-hook *fishhook* fi<u>sh</u>ho͞ok

F
G
H
I
J
K
L
M
N
O
P
Q
R
S
T
U
V
W
X
Y
Z

G
H
I
J
K
L
M
N
O
P
Q
R
S
T
U
V
W
X
Y
Z

fishline
fish-line

fishline
fishline

The <u>fishline</u> is tied
to the pole.

The <u>fishline</u>
is a strong string.

(fishlines)

fit

fit
fit

My shoes are not too big.

They just <u>fit</u> my feet.

(fits   fitted   fitting)

five

five
five

Here are $\dfrac{\text{five}}{5}$ stars.

Count them.

fix

fix
fix

See father
$\dfrac{\text{fix}}{\text{mend}}$ the tire.

(fixes   fixed   fixing)

flag

flag
flag

This is an American <u>flag</u>.

(flags)

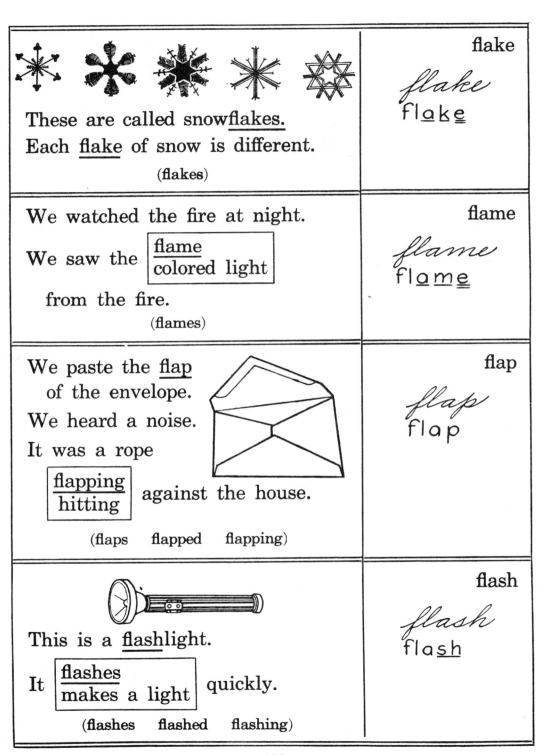

These are called snow<u>flakes</u>.
Each <u>flake</u> of snow is different.

(flakes)

flake

flake
f<u>la</u>k<u>e</u>

We watched the fire at night.

We saw the | flame |
| colored light |

from the fire.

(flames)

flame

flame
fl<u>a</u>m<u>e</u>

We paste the <u>flap</u>
of the envelope.

We heard a noise.

It was a rope

| flapping |
| hitting | against the house.

(flaps   flapped   flapping)

flap

flap
flap

This is a <u>flashlight</u>.

It | flashes |
| makes a light | quickly.

(flashes   flashed   flashing)

flash

flash
fl<u>a sh</u>

flat

flat
flat

See the flat tire.

The table has a | flat / even | top.

flea

flea
flea

The dog scratched his head.

| A flea / An insect | was biting him.

Fleas bite the dog to get his blood.
A flea does not have wings.

(fleas)

flew

flew
flew

The bird flew away.

(fly   flies   flying)

flicker
flick-er

flicker
flicker

This bird is a flicker.
He is a kind of woodpecker.
He has yellowish wings.

(flickers)

float

float
float

The boat can | float on / stay on / top of | the water.

(floats   floated   floating)

The children are sitting on the <u>floor</u> by the fireplace. (floors)	floor *floor* fl<u>oo</u>r
Bread is made of <u>flour.</u> <u>Flour</u> is made of wheat.	flour *flour* fl<u>ou</u>r
See the water ⏐flow⏐ ⏐run⏐ out of the pipe. (flows flowed flowing)	flow *flow* fl<u>ow</u>
Here are many <u>flowers.</u> Here is one <u>flower.</u> (flowers)	flower flow-er *flower* fl<u>ow</u><u>er</u>
The bird can <u>fly</u> high into the sky. This is a <u>fly.</u> (flies flew flying)	fly *fly* fl<u>y</u>
We <u>fold</u> the paper to make a box. (folds folded folding)	fold *fold* f<u>o</u>ld

F
G
H
I
J
K
L
M
N
O
P
Q
R
S
T
U
V
W
X
Y
Z

G
H
I
J
K
L
M
N
O
P
Q
R
S
T
U
V
W
X
Y
Z

follow fol-low *follow* foll**o͞w**	My dog likes to [follow / come after] me. (follows followed following)
fond *fond* fond	Mother [is fond of / likes] the baby. (fonder fondest)
food *food* f**o͞o**d	The things we eat are foods. We should eat good food. Bread and milk are good foods. (foods)
foot *foot* f**o͞o**t	The man stands on one foot. Twelve inches make a foot. We measure things with a foot ruler. (feet)
footprints foot-prints *footprints* f**o͞o**tprints	We could see [footprints / marks of feet] in the sand. (footprint)
for *for* f**o**r	I have a gift for Mother. I know Bob is here [for / because] I saw him.
forehead fore-head *forehead* f**o**reh**e**ad	Baby put her hand on her forehead. (foreheads)

The land is covered with trees. We call it a [forest. / thick woods.] (forests)	forest for-est *forest* f<u>o</u>re st
I cannot buy an apple if I [forget / do not remember] to bring my money. (forgets forgetting forgot forgotten)	forget for-get *forget* f<u>o</u>rget
Bob was a bad boy. Mother said she would [forgive / not feel angry at] him if he would promise to be good. (forgives forgiven forgiving forgave)	forgive for-give *forgive* f<u>o</u>rg<u>i</u>v<u>e</u>
This is a <u>fork</u>. We eat with a <u>fork</u>. The farmer uses a hay <u>fork</u> to pick up hay. (forks)	fork *fork* f<u>o</u>rk
The soldiers built a <u>fort</u>. The <u>fort</u> will protect them from their enemies. (forts)	fort *fort* f<u>o</u>rt

F
G
H
I
J
K
L
M
N
O
P
Q
R
S
T
U
V
W
X
Y
Z

forward for-ward *forward* f**or**w**a**rd	The soldier stepped ┌ forward. out in front. forth. ┐
fought *fought* f**ou**ght	The soldier ┌ fought went to war against ┐ the enemy. Tom ┌ fought hit ┐ Bob. (fight fights fighting)
found *found* f**ou**nd	Mary lost her book. Bob <u>found</u> it and gave it to her. (find finds finding)
fountain foun-tain *fountain* f**ou**nt**ai**n	There is a <u>fountain</u> in the park. We drink from a drinking <u>fountain</u>. (fountains)
four *four* f**ou**r	Here are ┌ four 4 ┐ balls. Count them. (fourth)
fox *fox* fox	A <u>fox</u> looks something like a dog. We put the fur of a <u>fox</u> on coats. (foxes)

	frame
This is a frame for a picture. This is a picture in a frame. (frames)	*frame* fr**a**m**e**
The man was | frank / not afraid to talk | about the fight.	frank *frank* fr**a**nk
Bob set the dog | free. / loose. | (freedom)	free *free* fr**ee**
Water | freezes / turns to ice | when it gets cold enough. The rain froze on our window. (froze frozen freezing freezer)	freeze *freeze* fr**ee**z**e** s
The cake is | fresh. / newly made. | The teacher opened the window. The | fresh / cool | air blew in. (fresher freshest freshly)	fresh *fresh* fr**e**s**h**

F
G
H
I
J
K
L
M
N
O
P
Q
R
S
T
U
V
W
X
Y
Z

F
G
H
I
J
K
L
M
N
O
P
Q
R
S
T
U
V
W
X
Y
Z

Friday Fri-day *Friday* Friday	Monday, Tuesday, Wednesday, Thursday, and <u>Friday</u> are five days of the week. What are the other days?
friend *friend* friend	Bob and Jack like each other. They are <u>friends</u>. Bob is Jack's <u>friend</u>. Jack is Bob's <u>friend</u>. (friends friendly)
frighten fright-en *frighten* frighten	The dog ran toward the baby. It did not <u>frighten</u> her. / make her afraid. (frightens frightened frightening)
fro *fro* fro	The swing went to and fro. / from me.
frog *frog* frog	The <u>frog</u> lives near the water. (frogs)
from *from* from	The gingerbread boy ran away <u>from</u> the cow. I have a letter <u>from</u> Mother. The school is not far <u>from</u> here.

140

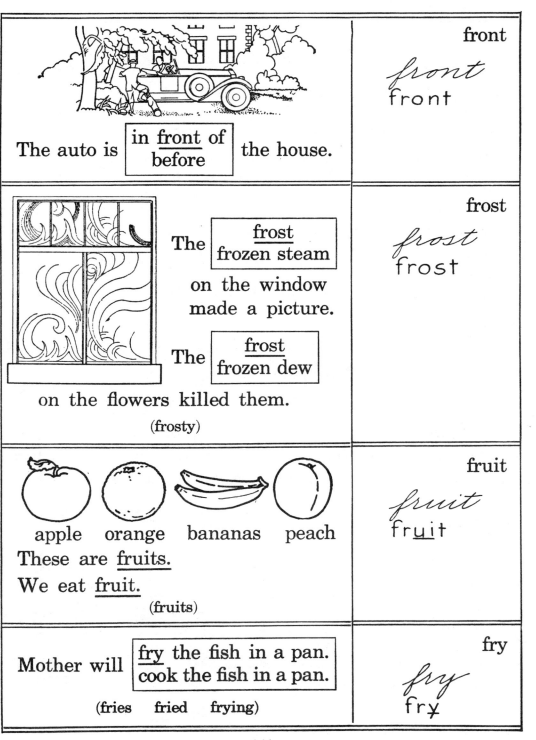

front

front
front

The auto is | in front of / before | the house.

---

frost

frost
frost

The | frost / frozen steam | on the window made a picture.

The | frost / frozen dew | on the flowers killed them.

(frosty)

---

fruit

fruit
fruit

apple   orange   bananas   peach

These are <u>fruits</u>.

We eat <u>fruit</u>.

(fruits)

---

fry

fry
fry

Mother will | <u>fry</u> the fish in a pan. / cook the fish in a pan. |

(fries   fried   frying)

full *full* full	One box is empty. The other is <u>full</u>.
fun *fun* fun	We had <u>fun</u> / a nice time playing in the water.
funny fun-ny *funny* funny	Father told a <u>funny</u> story. We laughed at the <u>funny</u> story. (funnier funniest)
fur *fur* f<u>ur</u>	Mother has a <u>fur</u> coat. The cat has a coat of <u>fur</u>. (furs)
furnace fur-nace *furnace* f<u>ur</u>n<u>a</u>c<u>e</u>₃	We have a fire in the <u>furnace</u>. The fire in the <u>furnace</u> keeps the house warm. (furnaces)
furniture fur-ni-ture *furniture* f<u>ur</u>nit<u>ur</u><u>e</u>	This is <u>furniture</u>.

The boy did not **gain** / **get** anything by telling what was not true.

(gains   gained   gaining)

ɡain

gain

gain

See this horse gallop.

Gallop is one way a horse goes.

Galloping is something like jumping or leaping.

(gallops   galloped   galloping)

gallop
gal-lop

gallop

gallop ·

These boys are playing a game.

It is a ball game.

(games)

game

game

game

Father put the car into the garage.

(garages)

garage
ga-rage

garage

garage

garden gar-den *garden* g<u>a</u>rden	The children are planting a garden. They are planting flowers and carrots in their garden. (gardens)
gas *gas* g<u>a</u>s	Mother lights the gas in the stove. The gas makes the fire.
gasoline gas-o-line *gasoline* g<u>a</u>s<u>o</u>l<u>i</u>n<u>e</u>ₛ	This is a gasoline station. Gasoline makes the auto go.
gate *gate* g<u>a</u>t<u>e</u>	The dog cannot get through the gate. (gates)
gather gath-er *gather* g<u>a</u>th<u>er</u>	Flowers grow in the garden. I will ⎡gather / pick⎤ some for Mother. (gathers gathered gathering)
gave *gave* g<u>a</u>v<u>e</u>	I had seven apples but I gave two to Mary. (give gives giving given)

144

The children were [gay. / happy.] (gayly)	gay *gay* g<u>a</u>y
When the farmer wants his horse to turn to the right, he says, "<u>Gee</u>."	gee *gee* g<u>ee</u>
Here are two <u>geese</u>. <u>Geese</u> can swim. (goose)	geese *geese* g<u>ee</u>s<u>e</u>₅

Bob's father is a captain
   in the army.
Mary's father is a <u>general</u>
   in the army.
Both men are officers in the army.
They lead the other men.
 	
      (generals)
	general
	gen-er-al
	general
	gen<u>e</u>ral

Our teacher has a [gentle / soft / kind] voice. (gently)	gentle gen-tle *gentle* gentl<u>e</u>₄

A <u>gentleman</u> is a man who
   is kind and polite.
 	
      (gentlemen)
	gentleman
	gen-tle-man
	gentleman
	gentl<u>e</u>₄man

G
H
I
J
K
L
M
N
O
P
Q
R
S
T
U
V
W
X
Y
Z

145

get *get* get	Jack and Jill went up the hill, to <u>get</u> a pail of water. (gets got getting gotten)
giant gi-ant *giant* g<u>i</u>ant	This man is a <u>giant.</u> A <u>giant</u> is large and strong. (giants)
gift *gift* gift	Today is my birthday. Mother gave me a nice <u>gift.</u> present. (gifts)
gingerbread gin-ger-bread *gingerbread* ging<u>er</u>bre<u>a</u>d	I like <u>gingerbread.</u> cake with ginger in it. This is a <u>gingerbread</u> boy mother made for me.
giraffe gi-raffe *giraffe* g<u>i</u>raff<u>e</u>s	See how long this <u>giraffe's</u> neck and legs are. He has spots on his body. He can eat from tall trees. (giraffes)

This <u>girl</u> is Mary. (girls)	girl *girl* g<u>ir</u>l
I have two apples. I will │ give you make you a gift of │ one. (gives gave giving given)	give *give* g<u>i</u><u>v</u><u>e</u>
Mary went to the party. Bob said, "I am │ glad happy │ that you came." (gladly)	glad *glad* glad
Every time the fire engine goes by, I │ glance look quickly │ out the window. (glances glanced glancing)	glance *glance* glan<u>ce</u>₃
Windows are made of <u>glass</u>. Some dishes are made of <u>glass</u>. This is a <u>glass</u> with milk in it. (glasses)	glass *glass* glass

G
H
I
J
K
L
M
N
O
P
Q
R
S
T
U
V
W
X
Y
Z

glossy gloss-y *glossy* glossy	Bob rubbed his shoes until they were	glossy. smooth and shiny.	 (gloss)
glove *glove* glov<u>e</u>₂	 This is a woolen <u>glove</u>. Two <u>gloves</u> make a pair of <u>gloves</u>. (gloves)
glue *glue* glu<u>e</u>₂	Mary broke her doll. Father said, "I will	glue stick	it together for you." <u>Glue</u> is sticky. It holds things together. (glues glued gluing)
go *go* g<u>o</u>	Father has an auto. We will <u>go</u> for a ride. (goes gone going)

Some people drink goat's milk.

(goats)

goat

goat

g<u>oa</u>t

The duck says, "Quack, quack."
The turkey says, "Gobble, gobble."

Some children | gobble their food.
                eat their food fast.

(gobbles   gobbled   gobbling)

gobble
gob-ble

gobble

g o b b l<u>e</u>₊

This is a gocart.

Mother took baby
for a ride
in the gocart.

gocart
go-cart

gocart

g<u>o</u>c<u>a</u>rt

God made the world.

God is ruler of the world.

God

God

God

These things are made of gold.
Gold is yellow.

(golden)

gold

gold

g<u>o</u>ld

G
H
I
J
K
L
M
N
O
P
Q
R
S
T
U
V
W
X
Y
Z

goldenrod gold-en-rod *goldenrod* g<u>o</u>ldenrod	 This yellow flower is the <u>goldenrod</u>. It blossoms in autumn. It grows in fields and by the roadside.
goldfish gold-fish *goldfish* g<u>o</u>ldfi<u>sh</u>	 There are two <u>goldfish</u> in the bowl.
golf *golf* golf	 A <u>golf</u> stick A <u>golf</u> bag A <u>golf</u> ball Father plays <u>golf</u>.
gone *gone* gon<u>e</u> s	Father has <u>gone</u> to work. (go goes going)
good *good* g<u>oo</u>d	Tom is a <u>good</u> / not a bad boy.
good-by *good-by* g<u>oo</u>d-by	 The children said <u>good-by</u> to their mother.

Mary says <u>good</u> <u>morning</u> to her mother when she gets up in the morning.	**good morning** good morn-ing *good morning* g o͞o d m o r n i n g
Mary says <u>good</u> <u>night</u> to her mother when she goes to bed at night.	**good night** *good night* g o͞o d n i g h t
Cake and candy are called <u>goodies</u>. A <u>goody</u> is sweet and good to eat. (goodies)	**goody** good-y *goody* g o͞o d y
This is a <u>goose</u>. A <u>goose</u> is good to eat. A <u>goose</u> can swim. (geese)	**goose** *goose* g o͞o s e s
We <u>got</u> good marks at school. Father <u>got</u> a new hat. (get getting gotten)	**got** *got* g o t
A <u>gown</u> is a dress. This is mother's evening <u>gown</u>. (gowns)	**gown** *gown* g o w n

G
H
I
J
K
L
M
N
O
P
Q
R
S
T
U
V
W
X
Y
Z

graceful grace-ful *graceful* gr**a**c**e**fûl³	Mary is a \[graceful / beautiful \] dancer. (gracefully)
grade *grade* gr**a**d**e**	I go to school. I am in the first \[grade. / class. \] (grades)
grain *grain* gr**ai**n	A potato is a vegetable. Wheat is a \[grain. / seed of a plant. \] Corn is a grain, too. (grains)
grand *grand* gr**a**nd	The children live in a \[grand / very fine \] house. (grander grandest)
grandfather grand-fa-ther *grandfather* grandfá³th²**e**r	Your father's father is your grandfather. Your mother's father is your grandfather, too. (grandfathers)

I call my grandmother, "Grandma." (grandmas)	grandma grand-ma *grandma* grandmă
Your father's mother is your grandmother. Your mother's mother is your grandmother, too. (grandmothers)	grandmother grand-moth-er *grandmother* grandmŏther
I call my grandfather, "Grandpa." (grandpas)	grandpa grand-pa *grandpa* grandpă
The fairy would not <u>grant / give</u> the woodcutter his wish. (grants granted granting)	grant *grant* grant
These are grapes. Grapes are red, purple, and green. Did you ever eat a grape? (grapes)	grape *grape* grape

G
H
I
J
K
L
M
N
O
P
Q
R
S
T
U
V
W
X
Y
Z

grapevine
grape-vine

grapevine

grap̲e̲vin̲e̲

Berries grow on a bush.
Cherries grow on a tree.
Grapes grow on a vine.
We call it a grapevine.

(grapevines)

grass

grass

grass

Green grass grows
in the yard.

Cows eat grass.

(grasses)

grasshopper
grass-hop-per

grasshopper

grasshopp̲e̲r

The grasshopper hops.

See how long
his legs are.

Grasshoppers eat the
things farmers grow.

Farmers do not like grasshoppers.

(grasshoppers)

gravel
grav-el

gravel

gravel

Gravel is small stones.

Some roads are made of gravel.

gray

gray

gra̲y̲

Some mice are white
and some are gray.

Mother gave a party for me.
 	
It was a <u>great</u> | big surprise.
 	
George Washington was
  a <u>great</u> man.
He did many good things
  for his country.
 	
(greater greatest)
	great
	
	great
	gr**ea**t

Two dogs were eating.
 	
The bigger dog was <u>greedy</u>.
  wanted more
  than his share.
	greedy
	greed-y
	greedy
	gr**ee**dy

Grass is <u>green.</u> When the traffic light is <u>green,</u> the children cross the street.	green *green* gr**ee**n
The flower <u>grew</u> in the garden. (grow grows growing grown)	grew *grew* gr**ew**

The man who sells
  things to eat is called
  a <u>grocer.</u>
(grocers)
	grocer
	gro-cer
	grocer
	gr**o**c**e**r

We buy crackers, sugar,
  and other things to eat
  at a <u>grocery</u> store.
(groceries)
	grocery
	gro-cer-y
	grocery
	gr**o**c**e**ry

G
H
I
J
K
L
M
N
O
P
Q
R
S
T
U
V
W
X
Y
Z

groceryman	Sometimes the man
gro-cer-y-man	who runs the grocery store
groceryman	is called the groceryman.
groceryman	(grocerymen)

ground

ground

ground

We put the seeds into the ground.

The groceryman ground the coffee.

(grind   grinds   grinding)

group

group

group

This is one boy.

This is

a | group / number | of boys.

(groups)

grow

grow

grow

Rain makes the flowers | grow. / become / larger.

(grows   grew   growing   grown)

The dog is cross. I heard him <u>growl</u> at us. (growls growled growling)	growl *growl* g r<u>o</u>wl
Jack is a <u>grown-up</u> boy now. He will get no larger.	grown-up *grown-up* gr<u>o</u>wn-up
The Billy Goat has a <u>gruff</u> / deep voice.	gruff *gruff* gruff
The dog will <u>guard</u> / watch over the baby. (guards guarded guarding)	guard *guard* g<u>ua</u>rd
Bob had some apples in a box. I tried to <u>guess</u> how many there were. (guesses guessed guessing)	guess *guess* g<u>u</u>ess

G
H
I
J
K
L
M
N
O
P
Q
R
S
T
U
V
W
X
Y
Z

guest *guest* g‿u‿est	We had a guest / company for dinner. (guests)
guide *guide* g‿u‿i‿d‿e	Bob will guide you / show you the way to the zoo. (guides guided guiding)
gum *gum* gum	The children do not chew <u>gum</u> in school. It is not polite.
gun *gun* gun	This is a <u>gun.</u> Men shoot with a <u>gun.</u> (guns)

H h H h H h

Bob asked Mother for some milk. She gave him all she <u>had</u>. (have has)	had *had* had
Mary is combing her <u>hair</u>. (hairs hairy)	hair *hair* h<u>ai</u>r
The apple is cut into two pieces. Each piece is a <u>half</u>. (halves)	half *half* ha<u>l</u>f
John put his coat in the <u>hall</u>. There is a <u>hall</u> between the bedroom and the bathroom. (halls)	hall *hall* håll
The children are having a <u>Halloween</u> party. See their Jack-o'-lantern.	Halloween Hal-low-een *Halloween* Hall<u>o</u>w<u>ee</u>n

H
I
J
K
L
M
N
O
P
Q
R
S
T
U
V
W
X
Y
Z

159

ham *ham* ham	This meat is <u>ham</u>. We get <u>ham</u> from pigs. (hams)
hammer ham-mer *hammer* hamm<u>er</u>	This is a <u>hammer</u>. We pound with a <u>hammer</u>. (hammers hammered hammering)
hand *hand* hand	This is a <u>hand</u>. We have two <u>hands</u>. (hands)
handkerchief hand-ker-chief *handkerchief* handk<u>er</u><u>chie</u>f	Mary wiped her nose with a clean <u>handkerchief</u>. (handkerchiefs)
handle han-dle *handle* handl<u>e</u>₄	The cup has a broken <u>handle</u>. (handles handled handling)
handsome hand-some *handsome* handsom<u>e</u>₅	The baby is very <u>handsome</u>. good looking.
hang *hang* ha<u>ng</u>	I like to <u>hang</u> clothes on the clothesline. (hangs hanging hung)

160

They put the airplane in the <u>hangar</u>. (hangars)	hangar hang-ar *hangar* h a n g <u>a r</u>
Cross the street with the green light, or something may happen. take place. (happens happened happening)	happen hap-pen *happen* h a p p e n
John is a good boy. This makes mother feel happy. joyful. (happiness happily happier happiest)	happy hap-py *happy* h a p p y
Fur is soft. Stones are <u>hard.</u> (harder hardest)	hard *hard* h <u>a r</u> d

This is a <u>hare</u>.
 	
He looks like a
   rabbit but
   he is larger.
 	
(hares)
	hare
	
	hare
	h <u>a r e</u>

H
I
J
K
L
M
N
O
P
Q
R
S
T
U
V
W
X
Y
Z

I
J
K
L
M
N
O
P
Q
R
S
T
U
V
W
X
Y
Z

harm *harm* h<u>a</u>rm	This dog will not ┌─────┐ you. │ harm │ │ hurt │ └─────┘ (harms　　harmed　　harming)　　(harmful)
has *has* ha<u>s</u>	I have a big doll and 　Betty <u>has</u> a small one. (have　　had)
hat *hat* hat	 This is a boy's <u>hat</u>.　　　This is 　　　　a girl's <u>hat</u>. I wear a <u>hat</u> on my head. (hats)
hatch *hatch* ha<u>tch</u>	The hen is sitting 　on the eggs. In three weeks chicks will ┌──────────┐ │ hatch from │ │ come out of │ └──────────┘ the eggs. (hatches　　hatched　　hatching)
hate *hate* h<u>ate</u>	The rats ┌──────────┐ the cat. │ hate │ │ do not like │ └──────────┘ (hates　　hated　　hating)

Give me all the money

that you | have. / own. | (having)

have

have

h a v e₂

Bob and **Mary** have some apples

but we | haven't / do not have | any.

haven't

haven't

haven't

This bird
is a <u>hawk</u>.

He eats chickens.

(hawks)

hawk

hawk

h a w k

Cows eat <u>hay</u>.

<u>Hay</u> is grass
that is dried.

hay

hay

h a y

Little Boy Blue was
sleeping under

the | <u>haycock</u>. / stack of hay. |

(haycocks)

haycock

hay-cock

haycock

haycock

See the boy run.

<u>He</u> runs fast.

| <u>He</u> / Father | is home.

he

he

h e

head *head* head		Father has his hat on his <u>head</u>. (heads)
hear *hear* hear		Mother called to Bob but he did not <u>hear</u> her. We <u>hear</u> with our ears. (hears heard hearing)
heard *heard* heard		Mother called Bob again. He <u>heard</u> her that time. (hear hears hearing)
heart *heart* heart		This valentine is shaped like a <u>heart</u>. The doctor listened to the beating of my <u>heart</u>. (hearts)
heat *heat* heat		The fire will <u>heat</u> / warm the soup. (heats heated heating)
heavy heav-y *heavy* heavy		Mary could not carry the big chair. It was too <u>heavy</u>. (heavier heaviest)

 A heel on a shoe A person's heel. (heels)		heel *heel* h ee l
The baby cried so Mother held her in her arms. (hold holds holding)		held *held* held
When I meet the children I say hello to them.		hello hel-lo *hello* hell o
I could not read my story. Bob said, "I will help you." (helpers helper helps helped helping)		help *help* help
Can you read the story about the Little Red Hen?/hen? (hens)		hen *hen* hen
The hen lives in a henhouse. (henhouses)		henhouse hen-house *henhouse* henhouse,
The girl has the doll in her arms.		her *her* h er

H
I
J
K
L
M
N
O
P
Q
R
S
T
U
V
W
X
Y
Z

here *here* h<u>e</u>r<u>e</u>	Jack was a bad boy. Mother said, "Come $\boxed{\text{here."} \atop \text{to this place."}}$
herself her-self *herself* h<u>er</u>self	The little girl can dress all by <u>herself</u>.
hid *hid* hid	Jack <u>hid</u> his ball in the box so that the baby would not find it. (hide hiding hidden)
hide *hide* h<u>id</u>e	The boy said, "Shut your eyes while I <u>hide</u> the ball." (hides hiding hidden hid)
hide-and-seek *hide-and-seek* h<u>id</u>e-and-s<u>ee</u>k	The children play <u>hide-and-seek.</u>
high *high* h<u>igh</u>	The bird flew <u>high</u> up in the sky. (higher highest)
hill *hill* hill	Jack and Jill Went up the <u>hill.</u> (hills)

Bob asked me for some pennies. I gave <u>him</u> all I had.	him *him* him
The little boy can dress <u>himself</u>.	himself him-self *himself* himself
The boy plays with │ <u>his</u> dog. │ the dog he owns.	his *his* hi̇́s
The boy will <u>hit</u> the ball with the bat. (hits hitting)	hit *hit* hit
This is a bee's │ <u>hive</u>. │ house. Bees live in the <u>hive</u>. (hives)	hive *hive* h<u>i</u><u>v</u><u>e</u>
Mother likes to <u>hold</u> the baby in her arms. (holds held holding)	hold *hold* h<u>o</u>ld
Mother carries hot pans with a <u>holder</u>. (holders)	holder hold-er *holder* h<u>o</u>ld<u>e</u>r

H
 I
 J
 K
 L
 M
 N
 O
 P
 Q
 R
 S
 T
 U
 V
 W
 X
 Y
 Z

I
J
K
L
M
N
O
P
Q
R
S
T
U
V
W
X
Y
Z

hole *hole* h o l e	There is a <u>hole</u> in the window. (holes)
hollow hol-low *hollow* h o l l o w	The rabbit lives in a <u>hollow</u> tree. / empty tree.
home *home* h o m e	Father goes to work in the morning. He comes <u>home</u> / to the house / where we live at night. (homes)
honest hon-est *honest* <u>h</u>onest	An <u>honest</u> man tells the truth. He does not steal or cheat.
honey hon-ey *honey* h o n e y	Bees make <u>honey</u> from the juice they get from flowers. It is sweet and good to eat.
honk *honk* h o n k	Hear the <u>honk</u> / noise of the auto horn! (honks honked honking)
hood *hood* h o o d	Little Red Riding <u>Hood</u> wore a <u>hood</u> on her head. (hoods)

		hook
The man hung his coat on the <u>hook</u>. (hooks)		*hook* ho͝ok
Bob is rolling a <u>hoop</u>. (hoops)		hoop *hoop* ho͞op
See these boys <u>hop</u> on one foot. Can you <u>hop</u>? (hops hopped hopping hopper)		hop *hop* hop
These children are playing <u>hoppity</u> skip.	hoppity skip hoppity skip	hoppity skip hop-pit-y skip
This is a <u>horn</u> to blow. A goat has <u>horns</u> on his head. (**horns**)		horn *horn* ho͝rn

H
I
J
K
L
M
N
O
P
Q
R
S
T
U
V
W
X
Y
Z

horse *horse* h<u>or</u>s<u>e</u>,	Grandfather rides a <u>horse</u>. He let Bob ride on the <u>horse's</u> back. (horses)
horse chestnut horse chest-nut *horse chestnut* h<u>or</u>s<u>e</u>,chestnut	This tree is a <u>horse</u> <u>chestnut</u>. It has very big leaves. The seed is a big brown nut. (horse chestnuts) <u>Horse</u> <u>chestnut</u> tree Leaves Seeds
hose *hose* h<u>o</u>s<u>e</u>	These are hose. stockings. We use a garden <u>hose</u> to water the garden.
hospital hos-pi-tal *hospital* hospital	When father was sick, we sent him to the <u>hospital</u>. The nurse was good to father while he was in the <u>hospital</u>. (hospitals)

In summer the sun makes us [hot. / very warm.] (hotter hottest)	hot *hot* hot
When Mary went to the city, she stayed in a <u>hotel</u>. The <u>hotel</u> has many rooms. She ate and slept in the <u>hotel</u>. (hotels)	hotel ho-tel *hotel* hotel
From 8 o'clock until 9 o'clock is one <u>hour</u>. One <u>hour</u> is 60 minutes. There are 24 <u>hours</u> in a day. (hours)	hour *hour* <u>h</u>our
People live in <u>houses</u>. This <u>house</u> is made of wood. (houses)	house *house* house_s
The girl has two books. <u>How</u> many have you?	how *how* how
<u>However</u>, if you are a good girl you may go to the party.	however how-ever *however* however

H
I
J
K
L
M
N
O
P
Q
R
S
T
U
V
W
X
Y
Z

huff

huff

huff

The wolf said, "I'll | huff / get angry |

and I'll puff and I'll blow

your house in."

(huffs   huffed   huffing)

hug

hug

hug

See Mary hug the baby.

See Mary put her arms

around the baby.

(hugs   hugged   hugging)

huge

huge

huge

A | huge / very large | tree grew

by the door.

hump

hump

hump

This camel has
one hump
on his back.

This camel has
two humps
on his back.

(humps)

172

Can you count to [one hundred? / 100?] (hundreds)	hundred hun-dred *hundred* hundred
   Mother <u>hung</u> clothes on the line. (hang hangs hanging)	hung *hung* hu<u>ng</u>
Please give me something to eat. I am so <u>hungry</u>. (hungrier hungriest)	hungry hun-gry *hungry* hu<u>ng</u>ry
Father went into the woods to [hunt for / look for] rabbits. I lost my hat. Will you help me [hunt / look for] it? (hunts hunted hunting hunter hunters)	hunt *hunt* hunt
The children cheered the flag. They said "Hurrah! Hurrah!"	hurrah hur-rah *hurrah* h<u>u</u>rr<u>a</u>h

hurry hur-ry *hurry* hu<u>rr</u>y	The fire bell is ringing. We must ⟦ hurry. move fast. ⟧ (hurries hurried hurrying)
hurt *hurt* h<u>ur</u>t	I cut my hands. They ⟦ hurt pain ⟧ me. (hurts hurting)
husband hus-band *husband* hu<u>s</u>band	Father is my mother's <u>husband</u>. Mother is the wife. (husbands)
hush *hush* hu<u>sh</u>	The baby is asleep. ⟦ Hush! Be still ⟧ you may wake her. (hushes hushed hushing)
husk *husk* husk	This ear of corn has the <u>husk</u> on it. This is the ⟦ husk cover ⟧ without the corn. (husks husked husking)

The hunter lives in a little old | hut. / house.

(huts)

hut

hut

hut

Do not park near the fire hydrant.

The firemen could not get to the hydrant for water if there were a fire.

(hydrants)

hydrant

hy-drant

hydrant

hydrant

H
I
J
K
L
M
N
O
P
Q
R
S
T
U
V
W
X
Y
Z

I i *I i* I i

I *I* l	Jack has a cat but <u>I</u> have a dog.

ice *ice* i<u>ce</u>	The iceman brings the <u>ice</u>.
	We put it in the icebox.
	I like to skate on <u>ice</u>
	    in the winter.
	        (icy)

icebox *icebox* i<u>ce</u>box	This is an <u>icebox.</u> It keeps food cool. (iceboxes)
ice cream *ice cream* i<u>ce</u> cr<u>ea</u>m	Do you like <u>ice</u> <u>cream</u> in a cone?
idea i-de-a *idea* i d<u>e</u>a	I have an <u>idea</u> / think that my rabbit is lost.
if *if* if	Father went to see if / whether the postman had gone.

I
J
K
L
M
N
O
P
Q
R
S
T
U
V
W
X
Y
Z

176

The Eskimos live in an <u>igloo</u>. It is made of hard snow.	igloo ig-loo *igloo* igl<u>oo</u>
I am $\boxed{\dfrac{\text{ill}}{\text{sick}}}$ today.	ill *ill* ill
$\boxed{\dfrac{\text{``I'll}}{\text{``I will}}}$ get the goats out of the turnip patch," said the bee.	I'll *I'll* <u>I</u>'ll
$\boxed{\dfrac{\text{I'm}}{\text{I am}}}$ a big boy.	I'm *I'm* <u>I</u>'m
Bob was $\boxed{\dfrac{\text{impolite}}{\text{not polite}}}$ to his sister. He used very bad manners.	impolite im-po-lite *impolite* imp<u>o</u><u>lite</u>
Where is the cat? She is <u>in</u> the box.	in *in* in
This line is one <u>inch</u> long. ——— Twelve <u>inches</u> make a foot. (inches)	inch *inch* in<u>ch</u>

I
J
K
L
M
N
O
P
Q
R
S
T
U
V
W
X
Y
Z

increase in-crease *increase* incr<u>ea</u>s<u>e</u>₅	If you blow air into the balloon it will ⟦ <u>increase</u> in size. / become larger. ⟧ (increases increased increasing)
indeed in-deed *indeed* ind<u>ee</u>d	Simple Simon met a pieman Going to the fair. Said Simple Simon to the pieman, "Let me taste your ware." Said the pieman to Simple Simon, "Show me first your penny." Said Simple Simon to the pieman, ⟦ "<u>Indeed</u> / "Truthfully ⟧ I haven't any."

Indian
In-di-an
Indian
Indian
	See this <u>Indian.</u>
	His hat is made
	   of feathers.
	<u>Indians</u> lived
	   in America when the
	   white people came.
	(Indians)

ink
ink
ink
	In the first grade the children
	   write with a pencil.
	In the third grade they write
	   with pen and <u>ink.</u>

The bee is an <u>insect</u>. Flies are <u>insects</u>, too. <p align="center">(insects)</p>		insect in-sect *insect* insect
Where is the hen? The hen is │ <u>inside</u> / not outside │ the barn.		inside in-side *inside* insid̲e̲
Mary will go │ <u>instead</u> of / in the place of │ Bob.		instead in-stead *instead* inste̲a̲d
The children were <u>interested</u> in the story. They wanted to hear all of it. <p align="center">(interest interests interesting)</p>		interested in-ter-est-ed *interested* inte̲re̲ste̲d̲
Where did the Pied Piper take the children? <u>Into</u> the side of the hill.		into in-to *into* into̊
We are having a party. We will │ <u>invite</u> / ask │ teacher to come. <p align="center">(invites invited inviting invitation)</p>		invite in-vite *invite* invi̲t̲e̲

I
J
K
L
M
N
O
P
Q
R
S
T
U
V
W
X
Y
Z

I
J
K
L
M
N
O
P
Q
R
S
T
U
V
W
X
Y
Z

iris i-ris *iris* i̱ris	This flower is an <u>iris.</u> The <u>irises</u> are of many colors. (irises)
iron i-ron *iron* i̱ron	This is an electric <u>iron.</u> Mother will <u>iron</u> the clothes. Many tools are made of <u>iron.</u> (irons ironed ironing)
ironing board i-ron-ing board *ironing board* i̱roni̱ng bo̱o̱rd	This is an <u>ironing board.</u> Mother irons the clothes on an <u>ironing</u> board. (ironing boards)
is *is* i̱s	Bob <u>is</u> playing. This <u>is</u> a nice day.
island is-land *island* i̱sland	This land is an <u>island.</u> It has water all around it. (islands)

180

This \[isn't / is not\] my birthday.	isn't *isn't* isn't
Mary has a doll. Father gave <u>it</u> to her.	it *it* it
\[It's / It is\] raining today.	it's *it's* it's
The barn stood in the field all by <u>itself</u>.	itself it-self *itself* itself
\[I've / I have\] a box of toys.	I've *I've* <u>I've</u>

I
J
K
L
M
N
O
P
Q
R
S
T
U
V
W
X
Y
Z

J j _J_ _j_ J J

jacket jack-et _jacket_ jac<u>k</u>et	This is a $\boxed{\begin{array}{l}\text{jacket.}\\ \text{short coat.}\end{array}}$ (jackets)
jack-in-the-pulpit jack-in-the-pul-pit _jacksinthepulpit_ ja<u>ck</u>-in-<u>th</u>e-pulpit	This flower is called a <u>jack-in-the-pulpit.</u>
jack-o'-lantern jack-o'-lan-tern _jack-o'-lantern_ ja<u>ck</u>-<u>o</u>'-lant<u>er</u>n	These children made this <u>jack-o'-lantern.</u> (jack-o'-lanterns)
jail _jail_ j<u>ai</u>l	Bad people often are put in <u>jail.</u> (jails)
jam _jam_ jam	Most boys and girls like to eat raspberry <u>jam</u> on their bread. It is made of berries and sugar.
janitor jan-i-tor _janitor_ janit<u>or</u>	The man who keeps the school clean is the <u>janitor.</u> (janitors)

J
K
L
M
N
O
P
Q
R
S
T
U
V
W
X
Y
Z

The first month of the year is <u>January</u>. New Year's Day is in <u>January</u>.	January Jan-u-ar-y *January* January
Mother cans fruit in a glass <u>jar</u>. (jars)	jar *jar* j<u>a</u>r
I like <u>jelly</u> on my bread. Grape <u>jelly</u> is made from sugar and grape juice.	jelly jel-ly *jelly* jelly
Jack had fun. He told Jane a <u>joke.</u> / funny story. (jokes joked joking joker)	joke *joke* j<u>o</u>k<u>e</u>
Bob is very <u>jolly.</u> / full of fun.	jolly jol-ly *jolly* jolly
This flower is a <u>jonquil</u>. It is yellow. It blossoms in spring. (jonquils)	jonquil jon-quil *jonquil* jon<u>qu</u>il

J
K
L
M
N
O
P
Q
R
S
T
U
V
W
X
Y
Z

journey	Mary and her father are going
jour-ney	on a long ⎢journey / trip⎢
journey	
journey	to the country.
	(journeys)

joy	The gifts brought ⎢joy / happiness⎢
joy	
joy	to the sick children.
	(joyful joyfully joyous)

judge	The teacher will
judge	⎢judge our work. / see if our work is good.⎢
judge	
	(judges judged judging)

juice	Mother is squeezing the juice out of the orange.
juice	We like orange juice.
juice,	(juices juicy juicier juiciest)

July	July is the seventh month of the year.
Ju-ly	We have firecrackers on the Fourth of July.
July	
July	

	jump
The boy can <u>jump</u> the rope. (jumps jumped jumping)	*jump* jump
<u>June</u> is the sixth month of the year. School is out in May or <u>June.</u>	June *June* J<u>un</u><u>e</u>
Lions live in the <u>jungle.</u> The trees and bushes in a <u>jungle</u> are all tangled together. (jungles)	jungle jun-gle *jungle* jungl<u>e</u>₄
Father just came. came a short time ago. The party was just very fine.	just *just* just

J
K
L
M
N
O
P
Q
R
S
T
U
V
W
X
Y
Z

K k *K k* K k

keep *keep* k**ee**p	Father gave me a rabbit to keep. / to have always. I keep / have it in a box. (keeps kept keeping keeper)
kept *kept* kept	Father gave me a rabbit. When it was sick, I kept it / took care of it in the house. (keep keeps keeping keeper keepers)
kernel ker-nel *kernel* k**er**nel	This is an ear of corn. This is a kernel / seed of corn. This is a walnut. This is the kernel of the walnut. (kernels)

K
L
M
N
O
P
Q
R
S
T
U
V
W
X
Y
Z

	kettle
	ket-tle

A <u>kettle</u> to cook in   A tea <u>kettle</u>

We cook in this <u>kettle</u>.

We boil water in a tea <u>kettle.</u>

(kettles)

kettle

kettl<u>e</u>⁺

This is a <u>key.</u>

We lock our door.
with a <u>key.</u>

(keys)

key

key

k<u>ey</u>

The soldier's **clothes** are
made of <u>khaki</u> cloth.

khaki

kha-ki

khaki

kh<u>a</u>ki

⊙ See Tom <u>kick</u> the ball
with his foot.

(kicks   kicked   kicking)

kick

kick

ki<u>ck</u>

Mother wears <u>kid</u> gloves.

They are made of leather like
fine shoes.

<u>Kid</u> is a young goat's skin.

kid

kid

kid

K
L
M
N
O
P
Q
R
S
T
U
V
W
X
Y
Z

L
M
N
O
P
Q
R
S
T
U
V
W
X
Y
Z

kill *kill* kill	I saw a cat $\boxed{\begin{array}{c}\text{kill}\\ \hline \text{put to death}\end{array}}$ a bird. (kills killed killing)

kimono
ki-mo-no
kimono
kimono
	This is a kimono.
	It is a loose dress.
	Some women wear
	    kimonos in the house
	    in the morning.
	
	(kimonos)

kind *kind* kind	Mother $\boxed{\begin{array}{c}\text{is kind to}\\ \text{does nice things for}\end{array}}$ her children. (kinds kinder kindest kindly)

kindergarten
kin-der-gar-ten
kindergarten
kindergarten
	I go to school.
	I am in the first grade.
	Last year I was
	    in the kindergarten.
	We learn to work together
	    in the kindergarten.
	
	(kindergartens)

king *king* king	This man is a king. He is something like our president. He is a ruler. (kings)

The land which a king rules is a <u>kingdom</u>. (kingdoms)	kingdom king-dom *kingdom* kin**g**dom
See Tom <u>kiss</u> the baby's cheek. (kisses kissed kissing)	kiss *kiss* kiss
This is a <u>kitchen</u>. Mother cooks in the <u>kitchen</u>. (kitchens)	kitchen kitch-en *kitchen* ki<u>tch</u>en
This <u>kite</u> has a tail and a string. (kites)	kite *kite* k<u>i</u>t<u>e</u>

K
L
M
N
O
P
Q
R
S
T
U
V
W
X
Y
Z

kitten	
kit-ten *kitten* kitten	The baby cat is called a <u>kitten</u>. (kittens)
kitty	
kit-ty *kitty* kitty	Jane calls her pet kitten "<u>Kitty</u>." (kitties)
knee	
knee <u>knee</u>	Bob fell and hurt his <u>knee</u>. (knees)
kneeling	
kneel-ing *kneeling* <u>kneeling</u>	This boy is kneeling. / <u>kneeling.</u> standing on his knees. (kneel kneels knelt)
knew	
knew <u>knew</u>	Mary read her story. She <u>knew</u> all the words. (know knows knowing)

190

This is a table <u>knife</u>.

This is Bob's jackknife.

(knives)

knife

knife

<u>kn<u>i</u>f<u>e</u></u>

I saw a small girl

knock
rap

on the door.

(knocks   knocked   knocking)

knock

knock

<u>kn</u>o<u>ck</u>

There was an old woman
Who lived in a shoe.

She had so many children
She didn't <u>know</u> what to do.

(knows   knew   knowing   known)

know

know

<u>kn</u>o<u>w</u>

K
L
M
N
O
P
Q
R
S
T
U
V
W
X
Y
Z

lace *lace* l<u>ace</u>	This is <u>lace</u> for a dress. This is a shoe ⎹ <u>lace.</u> ⎹ string. The boy <u>laces</u> his shoes with a shoe <u>lace.</u> (laces laced lacing)
lad *lad* l a d	This is a small ⎹ lad. ⎹ boy. (lads laddie)
ladder lad-der *ladder* l a d d <u>e</u> r	Father uses a <u>ladder</u> when he paints the house. (ladders)
lady la-dy *lady* l<u>a</u>dy	A <u>lady</u> is a woman who is kind and polite. (ladies)
lake *lake* l<u>a</u>k<u>e</u>	This water is a <u>lake.</u> There is land all around it. (lakes)

A baby sheep
is called a <u>lamb</u>.

(lambs)

lamb

lamb

lam<u>b</u>

A little lamb is sometimes
called a <u>lambkin</u>.

(lambkins)

lambkin

lamb-kin

lambkin

lam<u>b</u>kin

These are <u>lamps</u>.
They make light for us at night.

(lamps)

lamp

lamp

lamp

Boats sail on the water.

Autos run on the | <u>land</u>.
ground.

(lands   landed   landing)

land

land

land

L
M
N
O
P
Q
R
S
T
U
V
W
X
Y
Z

language lan-guage *language* language	I speak the English <u>language</u>. What <u>language</u> do you speak? <center>(languages)</center>
lantern lan-tern *lantern* lantern	This is a <u>lantern</u>. Some <u>lanterns</u> use oil to make the light. Some <u>lanterns</u> use a flashlight for the light. <center>(lanterns)</center>
lap *lap* lap	Mother held the baby in her <u>lap</u>. <center>(laps)</center>
lard *lard* lard	<u>Lard</u> is a fat. It comes from pigs. We use <u>lard</u> for cooking.
large *large* large	The elephant is not small. He is <u>large.</u> / big. <center>(larger largest)</center>

194

This bird is a
meadow <u>lark</u>.

He makes his nest
on the ground.

He sings a pretty song.

(larks)

lark

lark

l<u>a</u>rk

<u>Larva</u> is another name
for caterpillar.

(larvae)

larva

lar-va

larva

l<u>a</u>rvå

Jane is first in the line.

Bob is <u>last</u> in the line.

How long did the show | <u>last?</u> / go on?

It <u>lasted</u> one hour.

(lasts   lasted   lasting)

last

last

l<u>a</u>st

Tom came to school early, but

Mary came | late. / after time.

(later   latest)

late

late

l<u>a</u>t<u>e</u>

L
M
N
O
P
Q
R
S
T
U
V
W
X
Y
Z

L
M
N
O
P
Q
R
S
T
U
V
W
X
Y
Z

laugh *laugh* laugh	Tom told a funny story. See Bob <u>laugh</u> at it. (laughs laughed laughing)
law *law* law	The man was bad. He did not live up to the \[<u>laws</u> / rules \] made for this country. (laws)
lawn *lawn* lawn	Father is mowing the <u>lawn</u>. (lawns)
lay *lay* lay	Mother will \[<u>lay</u> / place \] the baby on the bed. (lays laid laying)
lazy la-zy *lazy* lazy	Some people \[are <u>lazy</u>. / will <u>not</u> work. \] (lazier laziest)

196

The children are playing a game.

Bob wanted to lead.
show them how.

He wanted to be the leader.

(leads   led   leading   leader)

lead

lead
l**ea**d

This is a lead pencil.

We write with
a lead pencil.

lead

lead
l**ea**d

A maple leaf   An oak leaf

These are leaves from trees.

(leaves)

leaf

leaf
l**ea**f

Jack Spratt would eat no fat.
His wife would eat no lean.
And so between them both, you see,
They kept the platter clean.

The ladder leans
rests

against the house.

(leans   leaned   leaning)

lean

lean
l**ea**n

L
M
N
O
P
Q
R
S
T
U
V
W
X
Y
Z

leap *leap* leap	A frog can $\boxed{\dfrac{\text{leap}}{\text{jump}}}$ high. (leaps leaped leaping)
learn *learn* learn	We go to school to $\boxed{\dfrac{\text{learn}}{\text{find out how}}}$ to read. (learns learned learning)
leather leath-er *leather* leather	Shoes are made of <u>leather</u>. Belts are made of <u>leather</u>. Pocketbooks are made of <u>leather</u>.
leave *leave* leave	Mary had to $\boxed{\dfrac{\text{leave}}{\text{go away from}}}$ the party before we did. (leaves leaving left)
led *led* led	The boy <u>led</u> the pony to the barn. (lead leads leading)

Tom writes with his right hand, but Bob writes with his <u>left</u> hand. We $\boxed{\begin{array}{c}\underline{\text{left}}\\ \text{went away from}\end{array}}$ the party early. Mary has one apple <u>left</u>.	left *left* left
We stand on our <u>legs</u>. We have two <u>legs</u>. Dogs and horses have four <u>legs</u>. My dog broke one <u>leg</u>. <div align="center">(legs)</div>	leg *leg* leg
This is a <u>lemon</u>. Lemons are yellow and sour. <div align="center">(lemons)</div>	lemon lem-on *lemon* lemon
<u>Lemonade</u> is made of lemon juice, sugar and water. <u>Lemonade</u> is good to drink.	lemonade lem-on-ade *lemonade* lemon<u>ade</u>
My ruler is twelve inches $\boxed{\begin{array}{l}\text{in }\underline{\text{length.}}\\ \text{long.}\end{array}}$	length *length* le<u>ng</u>th

L
M
N
O
P
Q
R
S
T
U
V
W
X
Y
Z

less *less* less	I have $\boxed{\begin{array}{l}\underline{less}\text{ money than}\\\text{not as much money as}\end{array}}$ you. (little least)
let *let* let	Be good and mother will $\boxed{\begin{array}{l}\underline{let}\text{ you}\\\text{allow you to}\end{array}}$ play. (lets letting)
let's *let's* let's	$\boxed{\begin{array}{l}\underline{Let's}\\\text{Let us}\end{array}}$ sing a song.
letter let-ter *letter* letter	A. B. C. These are <u>letters.</u> Do you know all the A B C's? I will send this <u>letter</u> through the mail. (letters)
lettuce let-tuce *lettuce* lettuce₃	This is a head of <u>lettuce.</u> It looks like cabbage.
library li-brar-y *library* library	This is a <u>library.</u> We get books to read from the <u>library.</u> (libraries)

L
M
N
O
P
Q
R
S
T
U
V
W
X
Y
Z

I saw a bad boy ⎡lick / whip⎤ his dog. (licks licked licking)	lick *lick* li<u>ck</u>
Mother puts a ⎡lid / cover⎤ on top of the kettle when she cooks. (lids)	lid *lid* lid
I am sleepy. I will <u>lie</u> on the bed and sleep. (lay lain lying)	lie *lie* l<u>ie</u>
Tom read a story about the ⎡<u>life</u> of George Washington. / way George Washington lived.⎤ (lives)	life *life* l<u>ife</u>
The box was heavy. Bob could not ⎡lift / raise⎤ it very high. (lifts lifted lifting)	lift *lift* lift

L
M
N
O
P
Q
R
S
T
U
V
W
X
Y
Z

light	One box was heavy but the other was <u>light</u>.
light	It is dark at night but it is <u>light</u> in the day time.
l<u>igh</u>t	This is an electric <u>light</u>.
	(lights lighted lighting)
	(lighter lightest lightly)

like	Your dress is $\boxed{\dfrac{\text{like}}{\text{the same as}}}$ mine.
like	I $\boxed{\dfrac{\text{like}}{\text{enjoy}}}$ milk.
l<u>ike</u>	(likes liked liking)

lily	
lil-y	
lily	
lily	This flower is a <u>lily</u>.
	It grows from a bulb, not a seed.
	(lilies)

limb	The boy climbed out
limb	on the $\boxed{\dfrac{\text{limb}}{\text{branch}}}$ of the tree.
lim<u>b</u>	Legs and arms are called <u>limbs</u>.
	(limbs)

This man is
Abraham <u>Lincoln.</u>

He was president of the
United States once.

Lincoln
Lin-coln
Lincoln
Linco<u>l</u>n

A straight
<u>line</u>

A fish
<u>line</u>

A clothes
<u>line</u>

There are many kinds of <u>lines.</u>

Here are three kinds.

(lines)

line
line
li<u>ne</u>

This is a <u>lion.</u>
He is wild.
He lives in a jungle.

(lions)

lion
li-on
lion
l<u>i</u>on

These are <u>lips.</u>

We speak with our <u>lips.</u>

John had a cold sore on his <u>lip.</u>

(lips)

lip
lip
lip

Mary wrote a <u>list</u> of many names

on her paper.

(lists   listed   listing)

list
list
list

L
M
N
O
P
Q
R
S
T
U
V
W
X
Y
Z

L
M
N
O
P
Q
R
S
T
U
V
W
X
Y
Z

listen lis-ten *listen* lis<u>t</u>en	Mother wanted to hear the music. She sat down to <u>listen</u> to the music on the radio. (listens iistened listening)
little lit-tle *little* littl<u>e</u>₄	One doll is big but the other is ⸢little.⸥ ⸤small.⸥ (littler littlest)
live *live* liv<u>e</u>₂	The old woman <u>lived</u> in a shoe. I <u>live</u> in a house. (lives lived living)

load
load
l<u>oa</u>d
	This is
	a ⸢load of hay.⸥
	    ⸤wagon filled with hay.⸥
	The men ⸢load⸥ the wagon
	          ⸤fill⸥
	with hay.
	(loads loaded loading)

loaf
loaf
l<u>oa</u>f
	This is a <u>loaf</u> of bread.
	Mother makes
	          meat <u>loaf</u> sometimes.
	We slice off pieces
	          of a <u>loaf.</u>
	(loaves)

This is a lock.

Father will | lock / fasten | the auto door with a key.

(locks   locked   locking)

lock

lock

lo**ck**

The frog is sitting on a | log. / part of the tree trunk.

(logs)

log

log

log

My pencil is short but
Bob's pencil is <u>long.</u>

(longer   longest)

long

long

lo**ng**

Father lost his hat.

I will | <u>look</u> for / try to find | it.

| <u>Look</u> at / See | my new shoes.

(looks   looked   looking)

look

look

lo͞ok

Jack can see
himself in the | <u>looking glass.</u> / mirror.

(looking glasses)

looking glass

look-ing glass

looking glass

lo͞oking glass

loose *loose* lo͟o͟se͟,	Tom's hat is loose. / not tight. The dog is loose. / not tied up. (looser loosest loosen loosely)
lost *lost* lost	Little Bo Peep has <u>lost</u> her sheep, And can't tell where to find them. Leave them alone, and they'll come home, And bring their tails behind them. (lose loses losing)
lot *lot* lot	Bob had a lot of / great many marbles. Father built a house on his lot. / piece of land. (lots)
loud *loud* lo͟u͟d	Mother dropped a pan. It made a <u>loud</u> noise. (louder loudest loudly)

Mother	loves her baby. likes her baby very much. (love loved loving) (lovely lovelier loveliest) (lovers)	loves *loves* lo<u>ve</u>s
One airplane is high in the sky. The other one is <u>low</u>. (lower lowest)		low *low* l o w
Mother sang a	lullaby soft song to the baby.	lullaby lull-a-by *lullaby* lullaby
Tom fell down and hit his head. It made a big <u>lump</u>. Father put a big	lump piece of coal on the fire. (lumps)	lump *lump* lump

I eat my <u>lunch</u> when
  I go home at noon.
We do not eat as much for <u>lunch</u>
  as we do for dinner.
 	
(lunches)
		lunch
		lunch
		lun<u>ch</u>

L
M
N
O
P
Q
R
S
T
U
V
W
X
Y
Z

M
N
O
P
Q
R
S
T
U
V
W
X
Y
Z

machine

ma-chine

machine

máchine

A sewing machine A washing machine A machine in an auto factory

These are machines.
Machines make work easy.

(machines)

---

mad

mad

mad

The man was | mad. / crazy. |

The dog is | mad. / sick and may bite. |

(madder   maddest)

---

made

made

made

Tom wanted a kite.
Grandfather made a kite for him.

(make   makes   making)

---

magic

mag-ic

magic

magic

The fairy waved her magic wand,
    and three rabbits hopped
out of the basket.

(magical)

---

maid

maid

maid

A girl is sometimes called a maid.

Grandmother has a | maid / girl |
    to do her work.

(maids)

208

A girl is called a maid or
a <u>maiden</u>.

(maidens)

maiden

maid-en

maiden

m<u>ai</u>den

This is a <u>mail</u> box.
Mary put

the | <u>mail</u>
letters and packages |

in the <u>mail</u> box.

mail

mail

m<u>ai</u>l

The postman carries

a | <u>mailbag</u>
bag for letters |

on his back.

(mailbags)

mailbag

mailbag

m<u>ai</u>lbag

The | <u>main</u>
largest | street in our town

is Second Street.
The <u>main</u> thing to do is to listen
when someone else is talking.

main

main

m<u>ai</u>n

maize *maize* m<u>ai</u>z<u>e</u>₅	This corn is sometimes called <u>maize</u>.
make *make* m<u>a</u>k<u>e</u>	Mother wants a bird house. I will <u>make</u> it for her. (makes made making)
mamma mam-ma *mamma* mămmă	Did you see my <table><tr><td><u>mamma?</u></td></tr><tr><td>mother?</td></tr></table> (mammas)
man *man* man	This is a <u>man</u>. (men)
manners man-ners *manners* mann<u>er</u>s	Some children have nice <table><tr><td><u>manners.</u></td></tr><tr><td>ways of saying and doing things.</td></tr></table> (manner)
many man-y *many* many	Grandfather has <table><tr><td><u>many</u></td></tr><tr><td>a large number of</td></tr></table> chickens.

M
N
O
P
Q
R
S
T
U
V
W
X
Y
Z

This is a │ **map** │
─────────
flat picture
of the United States.

(maps)

map
map
map

A <u>maple</u> tree   A <u>maple</u> leaf

The <u>maple</u> tree makes shade.

<u>Maple</u> syrup is made from the sap
of a <u>maple</u> tree.

maple
ma-ple
maple
m<u>a</u>pl<u>e</u>₄

These boys are playing a game
with <u>marbles</u>.

(marbles)

marble
mar-ble
marble
m<u>a</u>rbl<u>e</u>₄

<u>March</u> is the third month
of the year.

March
March
M<u>a</u>r<u>ch</u>

M
N
O
P
Q
R
S
T
U
V
W
X
Y
Z

M
N
O
P
Q
R
S
T
U
V
W
X
Y
Z

march *march* m<u>a</u>r<u>ch</u>	The play soldiers like to <u>march</u>. They keep time with the drum. (marches marched marching)
marigold mar-i-gold *marigold* már<u>i</u>g<u>o</u>ld	This flower is a <u>marigold</u>. <u>Marigolds</u> are yellow or orange color. (marigolds)

mark
mark
m<u>a</u>rk
	The girl made a <u>mark</u>
	  on the blackboard.
	Tom had good <u>marks</u>
	  on his report card.
	(mar<u>k</u>s marked marking)

market mar-ket *market* m<u>a</u>rket	We go to the <u>market</u> to buy food. Father buys cattle at the <u>market</u>. A <u>market</u> is a place where things are bought and sold. (markets)

Father and mother	marry
	mar-ry
were <u>married.</u> became husband and wife long ago.	*marry* márry
When I grow up, I will <u>marry</u> someone.	
(marries married marrying)	

The dog	master
	mas-ter
likes | his <u>master.</u> the <u>man who owns him.</u>	*master* mast<u>er</u>
(masters)	

This is a table <u>mat.</u>	mat
	mat mat
This is a door <u>mat.</u> We wipe our shoes on a door <u>mat.</u>	
(mats)	

	match
	match ma<u>tch</u>
One <u>match</u> A box of <u>matches</u>	
We use <u>matches</u> to start a fire.	
(matches)	

M
N
O
P
Q
R
S
T
U
V
W
X
Y
Z

material
ma-te-ri-al
material
material
	Paper, pencil, and paints
	   are drawing <u>materials.</u>
	Silk and cotton cloth
	   are <u>dress materials.</u> / things dresses are made of.
	Father is going to make a table.
	He will get the <u>material</u> tonight.
	<div align="center">(materials)</div>

matted mat-ted *matted* matt<u>ed</u>	The baby's hair was <u>matted.</u> / tangled. <div align="center">(mat mats matting)</div>
matter mat-ter *matter* matt<u>er</u>	My dog is sick. We do not know what the <u>matter</u> is / is wrong with with him.
may *may* m<u>ay</u>	Bob said, "May I / "Will you let me have an apple?" Mother said, "You <u>may</u>." <div align="center">(might)</div>
May *May* M<u>ay</u>	The girl's name is <u>May.</u> The fifth month of the year is <u>May.</u>

Maybe It may be that │ I can go with you.	maybe may-be *maybe* m<u>ay</u>be
You have a doll. Will you give the doll to <u>me</u>?	me *me* m<u>e</u>
 The cows are in a │ meadow. field of grass. (meadows)	meadow mead-ow *meadow* me²ad<u>ow</u>
We eat three times a day. The first <u>meal</u> is breakfast. The second <u>meal</u> is lunch. What is the third <u>meal</u>? (meals)	meal *meal* m<u>ea</u>l
I do not know what you │ mean. have in your mind. are thinking about. The boy is │ mean. not good. (means meant meaning)	mean *mean* m<u>ea</u>n

measure meas-ure *measure* me͝ȧs̄u͟re	How long is this rope? The boys will measure it. see how long it is. (measures measured measuring)
meat *meat* m e͟a͟t	This is meat. We eat meat. Dogs like meat, too.
medicine med-i-cine *medicine* medicine͟s	When the baby is sick, the doctor gives her medicine. Medicine will make her well. (medicines)
meet *meet* m e͟e͟t	When Tom heard his father coming, he went to meet him. (meets met meeting)
melon mel-on *melon* melon	A watermelon A muskmelon or cantaloupe These melons are good to eat. (melons)

M
N
O
P
Q
R
S
T
U
V
W
X
Y
Z

When the sun shines on the ice, it [melts it. / turns it back to water.] (melts melted melting)	melt *melt* melt
These <u>men</u> can walk fast. (man)	men *men* men
The dog said, "Bow, wow." The cat said, "<u>Meow</u>, <u>meow</u>."	meow *meow* meow
The man is a [merchant. / storekeeper.] (merchants)	merchant mer-chant *merchant* merchant
The children were [merry. / joyful.] I wish you a <u>Merry</u> Christmas.	merry *merry* merry
Bob <u>met</u> his father at the gate to help carry the packages. (meet meets meeting)	met *met* met

mew	The dog says, "Bow, wow."
mew	The kitten says, "Mew, mew."
m<u>ew</u>	

mice	These are <u>mice</u>.
mice	Mice are gray.
m<u>ice</u>	(mouse)

microphone	The man is talking
mi-cro-phone	into a <u>microphone</u>.
microphone	You can hear him
m<u>icr</u>o<u>ph</u>o<u>ne</u>	if you will listen
	to the radio.
	(microphones)

middle	
mid-dle	
middle	The big The <u>middle</u> The baby
middl<u>e</u>	bear sized bear bear
	The girl stood	in the <u>middle</u> of
	half way across
	the road.

Mother said that I <u>might</u> go. It <u>might</u> rain tomorrow. (may)	might *might* m<u>igh</u>t
Grandfather lives in the country many <u>miles</u> away. A <u>mile</u> is a long way to go. We drive our car 30 <u>miles</u> an hour. (miles)	mile *mile* m<u>ile</u>
The <u>milk</u> is in the bottle. <u>Milk</u> is good to drink. Cows give <u>milk</u>.	- milk *milk* milk
A farmer boy is <u>milking</u> the cow. (milk milks)	milking milk-ing *milking* milki<u>ng</u>
The <u>milkman</u> brings the milk to our house. (milkmen)	milkman milk-man *milkman* milkman

M
N
O
P
Q
R
S
T
U
V
W
X
Y
Z

milk wagon milk wag-on *milk wagon* milk wagon	This is a <u>milk</u> <u>wagon</u>. The milkman carries milk in this wagon. (milk wagons)
milkweed milk-weed *milkweed* milkw<u>ee</u>d	This plant is a <u>milkweed</u>. There is a kind of milk in the stems. The feathery seeds fly and plant themselves. (milkweeds)
mill *mill* mill	This is a Dutch wind<u>mill</u>. This is a wind<u>mill</u> to pump water. The farmer takes wheat to the <u>mill</u> to be ground into flour. (mills)
miller mill-er *miller* mill<u>er</u>	The man at the mill who grinds wheat for the farmer is a <u>miller</u>. (millers)

Some people have a <u>million</u> dollars.
A <u>million</u> is a very big number.
This is the way to write
   one <u>million</u>. 1,000,000.
 	
       (millions)
	million
	mil-lion
	million
	million

Mary is a good girl.
She <u>minds</u> her mother.
      does what mother asks her
        to do.
Do you <u>mind</u> your mother?
I do not know
what you have in <u>mind</u>.
         are thinking about.
 	
  (minds   minded   minding)
	mind
	mind
	mind

This pencil is not yours.
It is <u>mine</u>.
   belongs to me.
 	
       (my)
	mine
	mine
	mine

What time is it?
It is ten <u>minutes</u> past 9.
There are 60 <u>minutes</u>
   in an hour.
Wait a <u>minute</u> for me.
    (minutes)
	minute
	min-ute
	minute
	minutes

M
N
O
P
Q
R
S
T
U
V
W
X
Y
Z

| miss **miss** miss | Mother went away. I <u>miss</u> her so much. (misses   missed   missing) |

| Miss **Miss** Miss | This is "Little <u>Miss</u> Muffet." My sister is not married. She is <u>Miss</u> Smith. (Misses) |

| mistake mis-take **mistake** mist<u>a</u><u>ke</u> | I did not get a good mark on my paper. I made a \| mistake / wrong answer \| on two questions. (mistakes   mistook   mistaking   mistaken) |

| mistress mis-tress **mistress** mistress | The cat likes \| her <u>mistress</u>. / the woman who owns her. \| (mistresses) |

| mitten mit-ten **mitten** mitten | A <u>mitten</u> does not have a place for each finger. It has a place for the thumb. (mittens) |

See mother mix / stir together the cake. (mixes mixed mixing)	mix *mix* mix
Father will be here in a moment. / very short time. (moments)	moment mo-ment *moment* moment
Monday is the second day of the week.	Monday Mon-day *Monday* Monday
This is money. We buy things with money.	money mon-ey *money* money
This is a monkey. Monkeys have long tails. (monkeys)	monkey mon-key *monkey* monkey

M
N
O
P
Q
R
S
T
U
V
W
X
Y
Z

month *month* month	When is your birthday? Mine is in the <u>month</u> of May. There are 12 <u>months</u> in a year. May is the fifth <u>month</u>. (months)
moo *moo* moo	The lamb says, "Ba, ba, ba." The cow says, "Moo, <u>moo</u>, <u>moo</u>."
moon *moon* moon	The <u>moon</u> is in the sky at night. (moons)
moonlight moon-light *moonlight* moonlight	The children sat in the moonlight. light made by the moon.
more *more* more	Jack liked the candy I gave him. He said, "Please give me some <u>more</u>." (most)
morning morn-ing *morning* morning	I go to bed at night. I get up in the <u>morning</u>. (mornings)

This flower is a <u>morning-glory</u>.

It blossoms early in the morning.

It then closes up for the rest of the day.

(morning-glories)

morning-glory

morn-ing-glo-ry

morning-glory

m<u>or</u>n<u>ing</u>-gl<u>o</u>ry

<u>Moss</u> is a green plant.

It grows close to the ground and sometimes on trees.

It is soft like velvet.

moss

moss

moss

I have some candy.

Mary has more candy than I have.

Jack has the <u>most</u> of all.

(more)

most

most

most

This is a <u>moth</u>.

It looks like a butterfly.

<u>Moths</u> fly at night.

(moths)

moth

moth

mo<u>th</u>

mother
moth-er
mother
mother
	I live at home
	   with my <u>mother</u> and father.
	<u>Mother</u> takes care of me.
	       (mothers)

motion
mo-tion
motion
motion
	Some people cannot see or hear.
	They talk by making <u>motions</u>
	   with their fingers.
	Tom will come here if I <u>motion</u> to
	   him.
	(motions motioned motioning)

mountain
moun-tain
mountain
mountain
	This is a <u>mountain</u>.
	A <u>mountain</u> is a
	   big hill.
	     (mountains)

mouse *mouse* mouse,	This is a <u>mouse</u>. A <u>mouse</u> is not as big as a rat. (mice)

mouth
mouth
mouth
	Baby put the spoon
	   in her <u>mouth</u>.
	She likes to feed herself.
	     (mouths)

The baby is trying to <u>move</u> the chair across the room. (moves moved moving)	move *move* mŏv͟e̱₂	
I went to the <u>moving picture</u> show. I saw a funny picture. (moving pictures)	moving picture mov-ing pic-ture *moving picture* mŏvin͟g pictu͟r͟e	
My father is <u>Mr.</u> Brown.	Mr. *Mr.* Mr.	M
My mother is <u>Mrs.</u> Brown.	Mrs. *Mrs.* Mrs.	N O P Q R
Bob is sick. He ate too <u>much</u> candy.	much *much* mu͟c͟h	S T U
The children like to play in the mud. / wet earth. They make <u>mud</u> pies. (muddy)	mud *mud* mud	V W X Y Z

music	
mu-sic *music* mu͜sic	This is <u>music</u>. We sing in <u>music</u> class. I listen to <u>music</u> over the radio.
must *must* must	Children must / have to go to school.
muzzle	
muz-zle *muzzle* muzzle	The dog has a <u>muzzle</u> over his mouth. He cannot bite you now. (muzzles)
my *my* my	This is not your book. It is <u>my</u> book.
myself	
my-self *myself* myself	I read all the stories <u>myself</u>.

Father made a box.

He pounded the <u>nails</u>
with a hammer.

A <u>nail</u>

(nails   nailed   nailing)

nail

𝓷𝓪𝓲𝓵

n<u>a</u>il

My <u>name</u> is Jack.

What is your <u>name</u>?

What is the <u>name</u> of the flower?

We <u>named</u> our baby Jane.

(names   named   naming)

name

𝓷𝓪𝓶𝓮

n<u>a</u><u>m</u><u>e</u>

Baby was sleepy.

She took a | <u>nap.</u>
short sleep.

(naps)

nap

𝓷𝓪𝓹

nap

Jane folded her <u>napkin</u>
after eating her dinner.

She put the <u>napkin</u>
by her plate.

(napkins)

napkin

nap-kin

𝓷𝓪𝓹𝓴𝓲𝓷

napkin

The road is not <u>narrow</u>. It is wide.

(narrower   narrowest)

narrow

nar-row

𝓷𝓪𝓻𝓻𝓸𝔀

na̍rro͝w

nasturtium nas-tur-tium *nasturtium* nasturtium	This flower is a <u>nasturtium</u>. <u>Nasturtiums</u> are yellow and red. (nasturtiums)
native na-tive *native* native,	Grandfather is a <u>native</u> of America because he was born in America. (natives)
naughty naugh-ty *naughty* naughty	Mary was a <u>naughty</u> / bad girl. (naughtier naughtiest)
near *near* near	The swing is <u>near</u> / close to the house. (nearer nearest)
neat *neat* neat	The cupboard is <u>neat.</u> / clean and in order. (neater neatest)

The dog has a collar around his <u>neck</u>. Girls wear beads around their <u>necks</u>. (necks)	neck *neck* ne<u>ck</u>
John wanted to write. He had no pencil. He said, "I $\boxed{\begin{array}{c}\underline{\text{need}}\\ \text{must have}\end{array}}$ a pencil." (needs needed needing)	need *need* n<u>ee</u>d
Mother can sew. This is her <u>needle</u> and thread. (needles)	needle nee-dle *needle* n<u>ee</u>dl<u>e</u>₄
Mary $\boxed{\begin{array}{c}\text{is a } \underline{\text{neighbor}}\\ \text{lives next door}\end{array}}$ to Betty. (neighbors)	neighbor neigh-bor *neighbor* n<u>eigh</u>b<u>or</u>
This is a bird's <u>nest</u>. It has eggs in it. (nests)	nest *nest* nest

N
O
P
Q
R
S
T
U
V
W
X
Y
Z

net *net* n e t	The men put **a** <u>net</u> over the lion. The <u>net</u> is made of heavy rope. (nets)
never nev-er *never* n e v <u>e r</u>	The dog ran away. He <u>never</u> came back again.
new *new* n e<u>w</u>	This shoe is old. This one is <u>new</u>. (newer newest newly)
news *news* n <u>e w</u> s	Father told us the $\begin{array}{l}\underline{\text{news.}}\\ \text{things that happened.}\end{array}$
newspaper news-pa-per *newspaper* n <u>e w</u> s p a p <u>e r</u>	We read the news in the <u>newspaper</u>. Do you like the funnies in the <u>newspapers</u>? (newspapers)

N
O
P
Q
R
S
T
U
V
W
X
Y
Z

The boy $\boxed{\frac{\text{next}}{\text{nearest}}}$ to me is Dan. The teacher said, "Dan, you may read <u>next</u>."	next *next* n e x t

The mouse $\boxed{\frac{\text{nibbled}}{\text{ate little bits of}}}$
   the cheese.
   (nibble   nibbles   nibbling)
	nibbled
	nib-bled
	nibbled
	ni bbl<u>ed</u>

Mother is a $\boxed{\frac{\text{nice}}{\text{very pleasant}}}$ woman. (nicer nicest nicely)	nice *nice* n<u>ice</u>

Mother gave me a <u>nickel</u>
   to buy candy.
A <u>nickel</u> is five cents.
      (nickels)
	nickel
	nick-el
	nickel
	ni<u>ck</u>el

It is light in the daytime. It is dark at <u>night</u>. We go to bed at <u>night</u>. (nights)	night *night* ni<u>gh</u>t

nightdress night-dress *nightdress* n<u>igh</u>tdress	I wear a <u>nightdress</u> when I go to bed at night. (nightdresses)
nightgown night-gown *nightgown* n<u>igh</u>tg<u>ow</u>n	Mother put the $\boxed{\begin{array}{c}\text{nightgown}\\ \hline \text{nightdress}\end{array}}$ on the baby. (nightgowns)
nine *nine* n<u>i</u>n<u>e</u>	How many stars are here? There are $\boxed{\dfrac{\text{nine}}{9}}$ stars.
no *no* n<u>o</u>	The teacher said, "<u>No,</u> I do not have a book for you." I said, "I have <u>no</u> book to read."
nobody no-bod-y *nobody* n<u>o</u>body	I thought I heard someone in the hall. I looked but I saw $\boxed{\begin{array}{c}\text{nobody.}\\ \hline \text{no one.}\end{array}}$

When baby is sleepy, her head begins to ⎡nod.⎤ ⎣bow.⎦ (nods nodding nodded)	nod *nod* n o d
The ball hit the window. I heard the ⎡noise.⎤ ⎣sound.⎦ (noises)	noise *noise* n o̲i̲s̲e̲ₛ
Mary said, "Give me an apple, Bob." Bob said, "I have ⎡none."⎤ ⎣not one."⎦	none *none* n o n e̲ₛ
At 12 o'clock in the daytime it is <u>noon</u>. We eat lunch at <u>noon</u>. (noons)	noon *noon* n o̲o̲ n
I have no pencil ⎡nor⎤ paper. ⎣and no⎦	nor *nor* n o̲r̲

N
O
P
Q
R
S
T
U
V
W
X
Y
Z

north *north* n o̲r̲t̲h̲	North West ← → East South "Which direction are you going from here?" said Tom. "I am going north," said Bob. Eskimos live in the North.
nose *nose* n o̲s̲e̲	I breathe through my nose. (noses) A nose
not *not* n o t	Mary can play with the ball. Baby cannot play with the ball. Not once did she catch it.
note *note* n o̲t̲e̲	Bob wrote mother a | note. / short letter. | (notes)
nothing noth-ing *nothing* no̲t̲h̲in̲g	Jack ate all of his lunch. He had | nothing / not anything | left to eat.

I did not \[notice / see\] the fire engine when it passed. We put up a <u>notice</u> in our yard. It said, "Please keep off the grass." (notices noticed noticing)	notice no-tice *notice* n<u>o</u>tic<u>e</u>₃
The eleventh month of the year is <u>November</u>. Thanksgiving comes in <u>November</u>.	November No-vem-ber *November* N<u>o</u>vemb<u>er</u>
When can you go home? I can go \[now. / at this time.\]	now *now* n<u>ow</u>
4 9 1 7 8 2 4 5 0 These are <u>numbers</u>. Do you know the name of each <u>number</u>? (numbers)	number num-ber *number* numb<u>er</u>
This is a <u>nurse</u>. She takes care of sick people. (nurses nursed nursing)	nurse *nurse* n<u>urse</u>₅

N
O
P
Q
R
S
T
U
V
W
X
Y
Z

nut

nut

n u t

These <u>nuts</u> are
good to eat.

Did you ever see a squirrel
eat a <u>nut</u>?

(nuts)

N
O
P
Q
R
S
T
U
V
W
X
Y
Z

O o O o O o

oak

oak
o a k

This tree is an oak. This is the leaf of an oak tree.

An acorn

This is the seed of an oak tree.

It is called an acorn.

(oaks)

I eat oatmeal for breakfast.

It is made from oats.

Oats are a kind of grain.

(oats)

oat

oat
o a t

Oatmeal is a breakfast food.

It is made of oats.

Oatmeal is good to eat.

oatmeal
oat-meal

oatmeal
o a t m e a l

Bob is a good boy.

He obeys his mother.
does what his mother tells him.

Do you obey your mother?

(obeys obeyed obeying)

obey
o-bey

obey
o b e y

O
P
Q
R
S
T
U
V
W
X
Y
Z

239

object ob-ject *object* object	An <u>object</u> is anything that you can see or touch. A table is an <u>object.</u> A box is an <u>object.</u> <div align="right">(objects)</div>
ocean o-cean *ocean* <u>oce</u>an	The Pilgrims crossed the <u>ocean</u> in a boat. The <u>ocean</u> is a very big sea. The water in the <u>ocean</u> is salty. <div align="right">(oceans)</div>
o'clock o'clock *o'clock* <u>o</u>'clo<u>ck</u>	What time is it? It is 10 o'clock. I go to school at 9 <u>o'clock.</u>
October -Oc-to-ber *October* Oct<u>ober</u>	<u>October</u> is the tenth month of the year. Halloween comes in <u>October.</u>
odd *odd* odd	There are 4 boys in row 1. There are 5 boys in row 2. If each boy in row 1 chooses a partner there will be one │ <u>odd</u> boy / boy left over │ in row 2. He is <u>odd</u> or queer looking. <div align="right">(odder oddest)</div>

Give me a box <u>of</u> candy. My dress is made <u>of</u> silk.	of *of* o<u>f</u>
My hat blew $\boxed{\begin{array}{c}\text{off.}\\\hline\text{away.}\end{array}}$	off *off* off

My sister is a bookkeeper
   in an <u>office.</u>
 	
When I was sick, mother took me
   to the doctor's <u>office.</u>
 	
The postman works
   in the post <u>office.</u>
 	
      (offices)
	office
	of-fice
	office
	offi<u>ce</u>,

We play games $\boxed{\begin{array}{c}\text{often.}\\\hline\text{many times.}\end{array}}$	often of-ten *often* of<u>t</u>en
Father puts <u>oil</u> into his auto. <u>Oil</u> makes the car run well. Castor <u>oil</u> is used for medicine. (oils oiled oiling)	oil *oil* <u>oi</u>l

O
P
Q
R
S
T
U
V
W
X
Y
Z

old *old* <u>o</u>ld	Grandmother is <u>old</u> but I am young. (older oldest)
on *on* o n	 Where did Mary put the dishes? She set them <u>on</u> the table.
once *once* on<u>c</u><u>e</u>,	<u>Once</u> upon a time there were three bears. I will call you just	once. one time. All the children ate ice cream at	once. the same time.
one *one* o n e	How many apples do you see? I see	one / 1	apple. (ones)
onion on-ion *onion* on<u>i</u>on	This is an <u>onion</u>. <u>Onions</u> are good to eat. Sometimes <u>onions</u> make tears come to the eyes. (onions)

I see $\boxed{\frac{\text{only}}{\text{just}}}$ one apple.	only
	on-ly
Grandfather has two cars.	*only*
We have $\boxed{\begin{array}{l}\text{only one.}\\\text{one and no more.}\end{array}}$	only

The door is $\boxed{\begin{array}{l}\text{open.}\\\text{not closed.}\end{array}}$	open
	o-pen
Bob opened it.	*open*
(opens opened opening)	open

Black is the opposite of white.	opposite
Large is the opposite of small.	op-po-site
Cold is the opposite of hot.	*opposite*
(opposites)	opposites

Did you choose the red dress or the green one?	or
Do you like apples or oranges best?	*or*
You must go now or you will be late.	or

This is an orange.	orange
I like oranges better than any other fruit.	or-ange
(oranges)	*orange*
	oranges

O
P
Q
R
S
T
U
V
W
X
Y
Z

orchard or-chard *orchard* o̲r̲ch̲a̲rd	Apples, pears, and peaches grow in our <u>orchard</u>. Fruits grow in <u>orchards</u>. (orchards)

order
or-der
order
o̲rd e̲r
	1 4 5 3 2
	These numbers are not in <u>order</u>.
	1 2 3 4 5
	These numbers are in <u>order</u>.
	They follow each other
	  as they should.
	Mother put the house in <u>order</u>.
	She placed things where
	  they belonged.
	(orders ordered ordering)

organ
or-gan
organ
o̲rg a̲n
	Tom's sister plays the piano
	  and the <u>organ</u>
	  at the church.
	(organs)

other oth-er *other* ot̲h̲e̲r	Rain, rain, go away. Come again some <u>other</u> / a different day. Little Johnny wants to play.

You $\boxed{\begin{array}{c}\underline{\text{ought}}\text{ to go}\\ \text{should go}\end{array}}$ to school.	ought *ought* o͝ught
Father brought us a cat. It $\boxed{\begin{array}{c}\text{is }\underline{\text{our}}\text{ cat}\\ \text{belongs to us}\end{array}}$ now. <div align="right">(ours)</div>	our *our* o͝ur
This is our kite. We made it all by <u>ourselves.</u>	ourselves our-selves *ourselves* o͝urselv̯e͟s
A gentleman came to see father. Father was $\boxed{\begin{array}{l}\text{out.}\\ \text{away.}\\ \text{not in.}\end{array}}$ The bird flew in the window. The bird flew <u>out</u> again.	out *out* o͝ut
We do not play ball in the house. We play ball <u>outdoors.</u>	outdoors out-doors *outdoors* o͝utdo͝ors

O
P
Q
R
S
T
U
V
W
X
Y
Z

outside out-side *outside* <u>ou</u>t<u>si</u>d<u>e</u>	 One apple is inside the basket. Two apples are <u>outside</u> the basket.
oven ov-en *oven* oven	Mother put the cake in the <u>oven</u> to bake. (ovens)
over o-ver *over* <u>o</u>v<u>er</u>	 The airplane flew <u>over</u> the house. The show is <u>over</u> / has ended and the children are going home.
owe *owe* <u>ow</u><u>e</u> ₅	Mary could not pay for the milk. She owes / has to pay the grocer ten cents. Do you <u>owe</u> the grocer any money? (owes owed owing)

This bird is an <u>owl</u>.

It says, "Whoo, whoo."

<u>Owls</u> look for their food
   at night.

(owls)

owl

owl
<u>ow</u>l

Jack gave me this ball.

It is my <u>own</u> now.

Bob $\boxed{\dfrac{\text{owns}}{\text{has}}}$ a bicycle.

Grandmother gave it to him.

(owns   owned   owning)

own

own
o<u>w</u>n

ox

ox
o x

An <u>ox</u> looks like a cow.

The farmer drives the <u>ox</u>.

It helps him with his work.

(oxen)

O
P
Q
R
S
T
U
V
W
X
Y
Z

P p *P p P p*

pa *pa* pà	<u>Pa</u> is another name for father.
pack *pack* pa<u>ck</u>	We are going away. Mother will ⎡pack / put together⎤ our clothes in the bag. (packs packed packing)

package pack-age *package* pa<u>ck</u>a<u>ge</u>	See the ⎡packages / things wrapped up⎤ under the Christmas tree. I put a <u>package</u> there for the baby. (packages)

pad *pad* pad	This is a ⎡pad / tablet⎤ of paper. This is a ⎡pad / cushion⎤ for the baby's carriage. (pads)

P
Q
R
S
T
U
V
W
X
Y
Z

248

The book is opened to <u>page</u> 10.

Read the story on <u>page</u> 10.

(pages)

page

page

p<u>a</u>g<u>e</u>

This is a | pail. / bucket. |

(pails)

pail

pail

p<u>a</u>il

Baby burned her hand.

It | <u>pained</u> / hurt | her very much.

Did you ever have a <u>pain</u>
from being burned?

(pains   pained   paining)

pain

pain

p<u>a</u>in

See the man
<u>painting</u> the house.

He is using
white <u>paint</u>.

What color <u>paint</u> do you like?

(paints   painted   painting)

paint

paint

p<u>a</u>int

pair	This is one shoe. This is a <u>pair</u> of shoes.
pair	He bought a <u>pair</u> of shoes for me.
pair	(pairs)

pajamas	This is a pair of <u>pajamas</u>.
pa-ja-mas	Some people wear nightdresses to sleep in
pajamas	and other people
pajamas	wear <u>pajamas</u>.

palace	This house is a <u>palace</u>.
pal-ace	A king lives in a <u>palace</u>.
palace	(palaces)
palace	

pale	When mother cut her finger,
pale	her face became	pale.
pale		white-like.
	(paler palest)

palm	This is a <u>palm</u> tree.
palm	The <u>palm</u> of the hand is the inside of the hand.
palm	(palms)

This is a <u>pan</u>. Mother cooks pudding in a <u>pan</u>. (pans)	pan *pan* pan
Mother fried these <u>pancakes</u> for my breakfast. Did you ever eat a <u>pancake</u> with butter and syrup on it? (pancakes)	pancake pan-cake *pancake* pancake

This flower is a <u>pansy</u>.
<u>Pansies</u> are of many
    colors.
Some <u>pansies</u> look like
    faces.
 	
(pansies)
	pansy
	pan-sy
	pansy
	pansy

The dog is warm and tired. See him <u>pant</u>. breathe fast and hard. (pants panted panting)	pant *pant* pant

This is
  a pair of boy's
 	
  <u>pants</u>.
  trousers.
	pants
	pants
	pants

P
Q
R
S
T
U
V
W
X
Y
Z

| papa
pa-pa
papa
på på |  That man is Bob's | papa.
father. |
| | (papas) | |

| paper
pa-per
paper
paper | We write on <u>paper</u>.
Books are made of <u>paper</u>.
We wrap things in <u>paper</u>.
We read the news<u>papers</u>.
(papers) |

| parachute
par-a-chute
parachute
pårå<u>chute</u> |  This is a <u>parachute</u>.
Sometimes men jump
from airplanes
in <u>parachutes</u>.
(parachutes) |

| parade
pa-rade
parade
pårad<u>e</u> |  |
| | This is a circus <u>parade</u>.
I saw the <u>parade</u> march by.
(parades   paraded   parading) |

When Mary ran into Bob she said, "I beg your pardon." / "Excuse me."	pardon par-don *pardon* p a r d o n
Everyone has two parents. Your father is one parent. Your mother is the other parent. (parents)	parent par-ent *parent* p a r e n t
 See father park the car. This is a park where children play. (parks parked parking)	park *park* p a r k
Bob had a whole apple. He gave Mary a part / piece of it. Mary took part in the show. (parts)	part *part* p a r t

P
Q
R
S
T
U
V
W
X
Y
Z

party par-ty *party* party	Tomorrow is Jane's birthday. She will have a birthday <u>party</u>. She has asked seven boys and girls to her <u>party</u>. <div align="right">(parties)</div>
pass *pass* pass	The brown car tried to pass go by the blue one. Jack will pass hand out the books. <div align="center">(passes passed passing)</div>
past *past* past	Mother went past by the window.
paste *paste* paste	This is a jar of <u>paste</u>. We use <u>paste</u> to stick things together. <div align="center">(pastes pasted pasting)</div>
pasture pas-ture *pasture* pasture	Cows eat grass in the pasture. grassy field. <div align="center">(pastures)</div>

See me ⎡pat / tap⎤ the horse with my hand. (pats patted patting)	pat *pat* pat
Father tore a hole in his coat. Mother sewed ⎡a patch / piece of cloth⎤ over the hole. (patches patched patching)	patch *patch* pa<u>tch</u>
The cows walked down the ⎡path. / narrow road.⎤ (paths)	path *path* pa<u>th</u>
Hear the ⎡patter, patter / tap, tap⎤ of the rain on the window pane. (patters pattered pattering)	patter pat-ter *patter* patt<u>er</u>
Grandmother will make a new dress for me. She will buy a paper <u>pattern</u> today. She will cut the dress just like the paper <u>pattern</u>. (patterns)	pattern pat-tern *pattern* patt<u>ern</u>

P
Q
R
S
T
U
V
W
X
Y
Z

paw *paw* p a w	The dog held up his	paw foot.	 (paws)
pay *pay* p a y	Tom bought some candy. He had to	pay give	a nickel for it. (pays paid paying)

pea
pea
p e a
	There are seven <u>peas</u>
	  in this pod.
	<u>Peas</u> are good
	  to eat.
	
	(peas)

peach *peach* p e a ch	A <u>peach</u> A <u>peach</u> pit or stone A <u>peach</u> is a fruit. <u>Peaches</u> are good to eat. (peaches)
peacock pea-cock *peacock* p e a co ck	This bird is a <u>peacock.</u> He has beautiful feathers. (peacocks)

I like to eat peanuts. Squirrels like peanuts, too. A peanut (peanuts)	peanut pea-nut *peanut* peanut
A pear is a fruit. Pears are sweet and juicy. (pears)	pear *pear* pear
Father bought a peck of potatoes. A peck is as much as eight quarts. A woodpecker │ pecks │ │ taps with his bill │ on the tree. (pecks)	peck *peck* peck
The little chicken says, "Peep, peep." Mother │ peeped │ through the door │ looked │ to see if the baby was asleep. (peeps peeped peeping)	peep *peep* peep

P
Q
R
S
T
U
V
W
X
Y
Z

pen *pen* pen	This is a <u>pen</u> to keep the pig in. This is a <u>pen</u> to write with.
pencil pen-cil *pencil* pencil	Sometimes we write with a pen and sometimes with a <u>pencil</u>. (pencils)
penny pen-ny *penny* penny	I can buy candy with this <u>penny</u>. A <u>penny</u> is one cent. (pennies)
people peo-ple *people* people	See these <u>people.</u> men and women, boys and girls.

Mary's paper **was perfect.** **had no mistakes.** (perfectly)	perfect per-fect *perfect* p<u>er</u>fect
If you are good **perhaps** **maybe** you may go.	perhaps per-haps *perhaps* p<u>er</u>haps
A <u>period</u> is the dot used at the end of a sentence. (periods)	period pe-ri-od *period* p<u>er</u>iod
There isn't a **person** **man, woman or child** in the room. (persons)	person per-son *person* p<u>er</u>son
 These animals are my <u>pets.</u> I love my <u>pets.</u> Do you have a <u>pet?</u> (pets petted petting)	pet *pet* pet

P
Q
R
S
T
U
V
W
X
Y
Z

petal pet-al *petal* petal	This is a rose. This is a <u>petal</u> from the rose. The <u>petals</u> are of many colors. (petals)
petunia pe-tu-ni-a *petunia* pétunia	This flower is a <u>petunia</u>. <u>Petunias</u> are bright colored. (petunias)
piano pi-an-o *piano* piano	This is a <u>piano</u>. I can play the <u>piano</u>. (pianos)
pick *pick* pick	See Bob [<u>pick</u> / gather] apples. (picks picked picking)
pickle pick-le *pickle* pickle	This is a jar of <u>pickles</u>. Some <u>pickles</u> are sweet and some are sour. (pickles)

P
Q
R
S
T
U
V
W
X
Y
Z

picnic

pic-nic

picnic

picnic

These children are having a picnic.

It is an outdoor party.

We eat outdoors at a picnic.

(picnics picnicked picnicking)

picture

pic-ture

picture

picture

This is a picture of trees.

Did you ever have
  your picture taken?

(pictures)

pie

pie

pie

This is a pie.

I like apple pie best.

What kind do you like best?

(pies)

P
Q
R
S
T
U
V
W
X
Y
Z

piece *piece* pi̲e̲c̲e̲₃	This is a whole pie. This is a piece. part. (pieces)
pierce *pierce* pi̲e̲rc̲e̲₃	Bob pierced punched a hole in the paper. (pierces pierced piercing)
pig *pig* pig	This is a pig. The meat of a pig is called pork. (pigs)
pigeon pi-geon *pigeon* pi̲g̲e̲o̲n	This bird is a pigeon. dove. Some people have pet pigeons. (pigeons)

This is a <u>pile</u> of sand.

This is a <u>pile</u> of wood.

Father | piled
put in order | the wood near the fence.

(piles   piled   piling)

pile

pile

p<u>i</u>l<u>e</u>

Tom was sick.

The doctor gave him

some | pills.
balls of medicine.

A <u>pill</u> is easy to take.

(pills)

pill

pill

pill

The baby's head is on the <u>pillow</u>.

(pillows)

pillow

pil-low

pillow

pill<u>o</u>w

This man drives an airplane.

He is a <u>pilot</u>.

(pilots)

pilot

pi-lot

pilot

p<u>i</u>lot

P
Q
R
S
T
U
V
W
X
Y
Z

pin *pin* pin	 These are <u>pins</u>. We use <u>pins</u> to fasten things together. (pins pinned pinning)
pine *pine* pine	This is a <u>pine</u> tree. We use <u>pine</u> trees for Christmas trees. Its leaves are called needles. Its seed is called a cone. The needles stay on all winter. (pines)
pineapple pine-ap-ple *pineapple* pineapple	This is a <u>pineapple.</u> derline>Pineapple</u> is a fruit. It is good to eat. (pineapples)
pink *pink* pink	The baby has | **pink** / light red | cheeks.
pint *pint* pint	The larger bottle is a quart. The smaller bottle is a <u>pint</u>. A <u>pint</u> is one half as much as a quart. (pints)

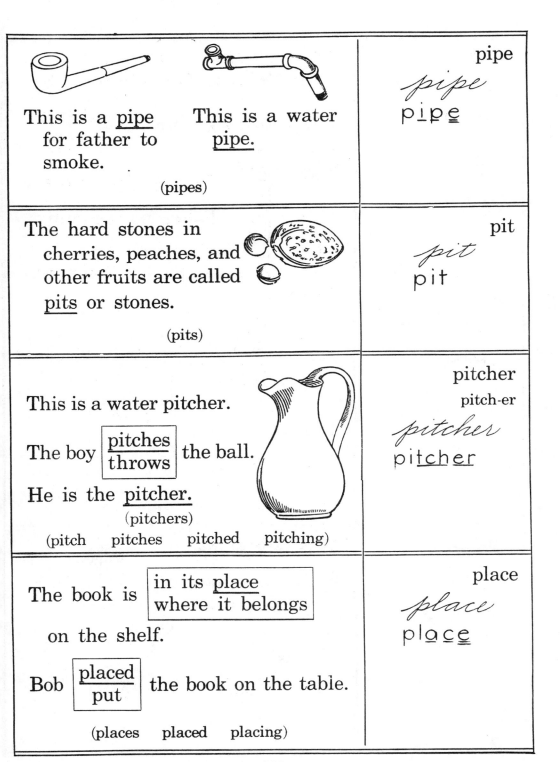

This is a <u>pipe</u>
for father to
smoke.

This is a water
<u>pipe.</u>

(pipes)

pipe

pipe

p<u>i</u>p<u>e</u>

The hard stones in
cherries, peaches, and
other fruits are called
<u>pits</u> or stones.

(pits)

pit

pit

pit

This is a water pitcher.

The boy | pitches / throws | the ball.

He is the <u>pitcher.</u>

(pitchers)

(pitch   pitches   pitched   pitching)

pitcher

pitch-er

pitcher

pi<u>tch</u><u>e</u>r

The book is | in its <u>place</u> / where it belongs |

on the shelf.

Bob | placed / put | the book on the table.

(places   placed   placing)

place

place

pl<u>a</u>c<u>e</u>

P
Q
R
S
T
U
V
W
X
Y
Z

265

plain	Bob could not understand

plain

plain

Bob could not understand
the directions for making the box.

The directions were not | plain. |
| clear. |

This is a plain dress.

It has no trimmings.

(plainer   plainest   plainly)

---

plan

plan

plan

The boys

will | plan |
| think out a way to do | their

work before they start to work.

The boys have a | plan |
| drawing |

that tells how to make a kite.

(plans   planned   planning)

---

plane

plane

plane

This is a plane.

Father uses it
to make the wood smooth.

This is
an airplane.

(planes   planed   planing)

This is a <u>plant</u> in a jar.

The farmer

> <u>plants</u> the corn.
> puts the corn in the ground.

(plants   planted   planting)

plant

plant

plant

The walls are covered with <u>plaster</u>.

Wallpaper is put on
  next to the <u>plaster</u>.

(plasters   plastered   plastering)

plaster

plas-ter

plaster

plast<u>er</u>

This is a <u>plate</u>.

A <u>plate</u> is a flat dish.

I eat from a <u>plate</u>.

(plates)

plate

plate

pl<u>a</u>t<u>e</u>

This is a <u>platform</u>.

It is like a little stage.

It is higher than
  the floor.

(platforms)

platform

plat-form

platform

platf<u>o</u>rm

P
Q
R
S
T
U
V
W
X
Y
Z

play *play* play	Father likes to work. I do not like to work but I like to ⎡play. / have fun.⎤ (plays played playing) (player playful)
player play-er *player* pl**ay**er	Bob plays baseball. He is a baseball player. (players)
playhouse play-house *playhouse* pl**ayhouse**₅	The children play in the ⎡playhouse. / small house.⎤ (playhouses)
playmate play-mate *playmate* pl**aymate**	Mary has two ⎡playmates. / children to play with.⎤ Do you have a playmate? (playmates)

P
Q
R
S
T
U
V
W
X
Y
Z

We went to a picnic. We had a \[pleasant / happy\] time.	pleasant pleas-ant *pleasant* pleăsănt
Mary is polite. She said, "Please give me an apple." Bob tries to \[please his mother. / make his mother glad.\] (pleases pleased pleasing)	please *please* pleăsĕs
It is a \[pleasure / joy\] to see you. (pleasures)	pleasure- pleas-ure *pleasure* pleăsŭre
We have \[plenty of books / all the books we need\] for the class.	plenty plen-ty *plenty* plenty
This is a plow. The farmer uses the plow for \[plowing. / turning over the ground.\] (plows plowed plowing)	plow *plow* plow

P
Q
R
S
T
U
V
W
X
Y
Z

plum *plum* plum	This is a <u>plum</u>. A <u>plum</u> is a fruit. <u>Plums</u> are red, green, yellow, and purple. They are good to eat. (plums)
plump *plump* plump	The baby is | plump. | fat.
pocket pock-et *pocket* po<u>ck</u>et	The boy put his hand in his <u>pocket</u>. (pockets)
pod *pod* pod	These are peas in a <u>pod</u>. The cover is called a <u>pod</u>. (pods)

This is a <u>poem</u>. Little boy, little boy, 　Down by the tree. I like the bird house 　You made for me. (poems)	poem po-em *poem* p<u>o</u>em
My pencil has a sharp <div style="border:1px solid"><u>point</u>. end.</div> Mother told me to <div style="border:1px solid"><u>point</u> to put my finger toward</div> the sun. (points　pointed　pointing)	point *point* p<u>o</u>int
This sign means <u>poison</u>. Some drugs are <u>poison</u>. Do not touch things 　with the <u>poison</u> sign 　on them. They may hurt you. (poisons　poisoned　poisoning)	poison poi-son *poison* p<u>oi</u>son
This is a <u>polar</u> <u>bear</u>. He is white. He came from 　a very cold land. (polar bears)	polar bear po-lar bear *polar bear* p<u>o</u>l<u>ar</u> be<u>a</u>r

pole *pole* p<u>o</u>l<u>e</u>	The flag is fastened to the flag <u>pole</u>. (poles)
policeman po-lice-man *policeman* p<u>o</u>l<u>i</u>c<u>e</u>man	This is a <u>policeman</u>. He is a helper. He sees that people obey the rules of the country. (policemen)
polite po-lite *polite* p<u>o</u>l<u>i</u>t<u>e</u>	Tom is <u>polite</u>. has good manners. (politeness politely)
pond *pond* pond	Father went fishing i̇n the <u>pond</u>. A <u>pond</u> is smaller than a lake. (ponds)
pony po-ny *pony* p<u>o</u>ny	See Tom's <u>pony</u>. He is not as big as a horse. (ponies)

P
Q
R
S
T
U
V
W
X
Y
Z

Father threw the firecrackers into the fire. We could hear them <u>pop</u>. Popcorn pops bursts open when it gets hot. (pops popped popping)	pop *pop* p o p
<u>Popcorn</u> is corn that pops open when it gets hot. It is good to eat. Crackerjack is made of <u>popcorn</u>.	popcorn pop-corn *popcorn* popc<u>or</u>n
This is a <u>poplar</u> tree. See how tall and thin it is. (poplars)	poplar pop-lar *poplar* popl<u>ar</u>
This flower is a <u>poppy</u>. <u>Poppies</u> are of many colors. (poppies)	poppy pop-py *poppy* poppy
Baby is on the <u>porch</u>. (porches)	porch *porch* p<u>or</u>ch

P
Q
R
S
T
U
V
W
X
Y
Z

pork *pork* p<u>o</u>rk	<u>Pork</u> is a kind of meat. <u>Pork</u> meat comes from pigs.
porridge por-ridge *porridge* p<u>o</u>rri<u>dge</u>	The three bears ate <u>porridge</u>. Goldenlocks ate up all the <u>porridge.</u> breakfast food.
porter por-ter *porter* p<u>o</u>rt<u>er</u>	This man is a <u>porter</u>. He carries people's bags for them. (porters)
possible pos-si-ble *possible* p<u>o</u>ssibl<u>e</u>.	I will go if <u>possible.</u> it can be done.

post
 	
post
 	
p<u>o</u>st
	The gate is fastened
	     to a <u>post</u>.
	
	I will <u>post</u>
	       mail
	
	grandma's letter.
	
	(posts posted posting)

Bob made this <u>poster</u>. He will hang it in the window. (posters)	poster post-er *poster* p<u>o</u>st<u>er</u>

The <u>postman</u> gave me
  a letter.
 	
The <u>postman</u> takes
  letters to people's
  homes.
 	
(postmen)
	postman
	post-man
	
	postman
	p<u>o</u>stman

I got some stamps at the <u>post office</u>. I mailed a letter at the <u>post office</u>. (post offices)	post office post of-fice *post office* p<u>o</u>st offic<u>e</u>₃
A flower <u>pot</u> a tea<u>pot</u> a kitchen <u>pot</u> These are pots. (pots)	pot *pot* pot
A white <u>potato</u> A sweet <u>potato</u> <u>Potatoes</u> grow in the ground. They are good to eat. (potatoes)	potato po-ta-to *potato* p<u>o</u>t<u>a</u>t<u>o</u>

P
Q
R
S
T
U
V
W
X
Y
Z

pound *pound* po͞und	Mother bought a <u>pound</u> of butter. A <u>pound</u> of butter is as heavy as a pint of milk. Father <u>pounded</u> the nails with a hammer. (pounds pounded pounding)
pour *pour* pou̇r	See Mary <u>pour</u> the milk into the glass. (pours poured pouring)
powder pow-der *powder* pow̲de̲r	Mother is putting <u>powder</u> on her face. <u>Powder</u> is fine like dust. (powders powdered powdering)
practice prac-tice *practice* practic̲e̲₃	Mary will | <u>practice</u> her music lesson. play it over and over. (practices practiced practicing)

P
Q
R
S
T
U
V
W
X
Y
Z

The teacher will | praise / speak well of | your work if you try hard.

(praises   praised   praising)

praise

praise

pr**a**is**e**s

Mary is saying her prayer.

(pray   prayed   praying)

prayer

pray-er

prayer

pr**a**y**e**r

Mary helps mother | prepare the dinner / get the dinner ready | every day.

(prepares   prepared   preparing)

prepare

pre-pare

prepare

pr**e**p**a**r**e**

Father had a birthday.

I gave him a | present. / gift. |

I was not in school yesterday but I am present today.

(presents   presented   presenting)

present

pres-ent

present

pr**e**s**e**nt

president pres-i-dent *president* president	In England the king is the leader. In the United States the <u>president</u> is the leader. (presidents)
press *press* press	Mother is <u>pressing</u> father's clothes. Bob is ⊡ <u>pressing</u> / pushing ⊡ the doorbell. (presses pressed pressing)
pretend pre-tend *pretend* pretend	Let us ⊡ <u>pretend</u> / make believe ⊡ we are fairies. (pretends pretended pretending)
pretty pret-ty *pretty* pretty	The rose is ⊡ <u>pretty.</u> / beautiful. ⊡ (prettier prettiest)
price *price* price	⊡ What <u>price</u> / How much money ⊡ did you pay for your dress? (prices)

We learn to read from a primer. first book. (primers)	primer prim-er *primer* prim<u>er</u>
The boy is a prince. son of a king. The <u>prince</u> ran after Cinderella. (princes)	prince *prince* prin<u>ce</u>₃
The girl is a princess. daughter of a king. A <u>princess</u> is the wife of the prince, too. (princesses)	princess prin-cess *princess* princess
These are foot<u>prints</u> in the snow. I can write my name and Mary can <u>print</u> her name. My father helps <u>print</u> the newspaper. (prints printed printing)	print *print* print

P
Q
R
S
T
U
V
W
X
Y
Z

prize *prize* prize	Tom won a <u>prize</u> for writing the best story. A <u>prize</u> is anything you win by doing better than anyone else. (prizes prized prizing)
promise prom-ise *promise* promises	Father always keeps his <u>promise</u>. does what he says he will do. (promises promised promising)
promote pro-mote *promote* promote	If you have good marks, your teacher will <u>promote</u> you. put you in a higher grade. (promotes promoted promoting)
prompt *prompt* prompt	Bob is always <u>prompt</u>. on time. (promptly) promptness)
pronounce pro-nounce *pronounce* pronounce	Baby cannot <u>pronounce</u> say plainly many words yet. (pronounces pronounced pronouncing)

P
Q
R
S
T
U
V
W
X
Y
Z

The <u>propeller</u>
on the airplane
goes around and around.

An airplane
<u>propeller</u>

(propellers)

propeller
pro-pel-ler

propeller

pr<u>o</u>pell<u>er</u>

It is │ <u>proper</u> / right │ to say,

"Excuse me," when you leave
the dinner table.   (properly)

proper
prop-er

proper

pr<u>o</u>p<u>er</u>

Bob will │ <u>protect</u> / See that nothing harms │

the baby.   (protection)

(protects   protected   protecting)

protect
pro-tect

protect

pr<u>o</u>tect

Baby │ is <u>proud</u> / thinks well │

of her new shoes.

(prouder   proudest)

proud

proud

pr<u>ou</u>d

I like <u>puddings.</u>

Mother made chocolate <u>pudding</u>
for dinner.

Sometimes she makes
cornstarch <u>pudding.</u>

(puddings)

pudding
pud-ding

pudding

pŭdding

P
Q
R
S
T
U
V
W
X
Y
Z

puff *puff* puff	This is a powder <u>puff</u>. Mother uses it to put powder on her face. The wolf huffed and he <u>puffed</u> / blew at little pig's house. (puffs puffed puffing)
pull *pull* pu̲ll	See the boy <u>pull</u> the wagon. The dentist <u>pulled</u> Bob's tooth. (pulls pulled pulling)
pumpkin pump-kin *pumpkin* pumpkin	I like <u>pumpkin</u> pie. We made a jack-o'-lantern out of a <u>pumpkin.</u> (pumpkins)
punish pun-ish *punish* puni̲s̲h	Bob's dog ran away. Bob will have to <u>punish</u> him. / whip or tie him up. (punishes punished punishing)

P
Q
R
S
T
U
V
W
X
Y
Z

In our grade there are ┌─────────────────────┐ │ twenty-five <u>pupils.</u> │ │ children. │ └─────────────────────┘ I am one <u>pupil</u> and Bob is another. (pupils)	pupil pu-pil *pupil* p<u>u</u>pil
A little dog is called a <u>puppy.</u> (puppies)	puppy pup-py *puppy* p<u>u</u>ppy
The water in this well is ┌─────────────────┐ │ <u>pure.</u> │ │ clear and clean. │ └─────────────────┘ (purer purest)	pure *pure* p<u>ure</u>
<u>Purple</u> is a color. We make <u>purple</u> by putting red and blue together.	purple pur-ple *purple* p<u>ur</u>pl<u>e</u>₄
Did you ever hear a cat <u>purr?</u> It sounds like a humming song. (purrs purred purring)	purr *purr* p<u>ur</u>r

P
Q
R
S
T
U
V
W
X
Y
Z

purse _purse_ p<u>ur</u>se₅	I keep my pennies in a <u>purse</u>. (purses)
push _push_ p<u>u</u>sh	See the man <u>push</u> the cart. I like to pull the cart better than to <u>push</u> it. (pushes pushed pushing)
pussy puss-y _pussy_ pŭssy	This is a |<u>pussy</u>. cat.|
pussy willow puss-y wil-low _pussy willow_ pŭssy will<u>o</u>w	This is a <u>pussy</u> <u>willow</u>. The buds along the stems are soft like a pussy's fur. (pussy willows)
put _put_ pŭt	I will |put / lay| the book on the table. <u>Put</u> means to place or set something, too. (puts putting)

2 q Q q   Q q

The turkey says, "Gobble, gobble." The duck says, "Quack, quack."	quack *quack* quack
Bob and Mary are good children. They never [quarrel. fight by saying things to each other.] (quarrels quarreled quarreling)	quarrel quar-rel *quarrel* quarrel
It takes two pints of milk to make a quart. (quarts)	quart *quart* quart
A whole pie A [quarter fourth] of a pie (quarters)	quarter quar-ter *quarter* quarter
This woman is a queen. She is the king's wife. (queens)	queen *queen* queen

Q
R
S
T
U
V
W
X
Y
Z

285

queer *queer* queer	The old woman is $\boxed{\begin{array}{l}\text{queer.}\\\text{strange.}\end{array}}$ She does the $\boxed{\begin{array}{c}\text{queerest}\\ \hline\text{strangest}\end{array}}$ things. (queerer queerest queerly)
question ques-tion *question* question	The teacher asked Tom a <u>question</u>. He could not answer the <u>question</u>. (questions)
quick *quick* quick	Mother said, "Be $\boxed{\begin{array}{c}\text{quick}\\ \hline\text{fast}\end{array}}$ about your work." (quicker quickly quickest)
quiet *quiet* quiet	The children were talking loudly. The teacher told them $\boxed{\begin{array}{l}\text{to be }\underline{\text{quiet}}.\\\text{to make no noise.}\end{array}}$ The children became very $\boxed{\begin{array}{l}\text{quiet.}\\\text{still.}\end{array}}$ (quieter quietest quietly)

Q
R
S
T
U
V
W
X
Y
Z

286

	quit
The men [quit / stop] working at 6 o'clock. It is [quitting time / time to stop] at 6 o'clock. (quits quitting)	*quit* q̲u̲it
The boy sang [quite / very] nicely. The house is q̲u̲i̲t̲e̲ warm.	quite *quite* q̲u̲i̲t̲e̲
Bob is not a q̲u̲i̲t̲t̲e̲r̲. Bob does not give up his work easily. (quitters)	quitter quit-ter *quitter* q̲u̲i̲t̲t̲e̲r̲

R
S
T
U
V
W
X
Y
Z

R r *R r R r*

rabbit rab-bit *rabbit* rabbit	This is a <u>rabbit</u>. See his long ears and short tail. He can jump fast. (rabbits)
race *race* r<u>a</u>c<u>e</u>	The boys ran a <u>race</u>. They <u>raced</u> to see who would win. (races raced racing)
radio ra-di-o *radio* r<u>a</u>di<u>o</u>	Bob likes to hear the <u>radio</u>. (radios)
radish rad-ish *radish* radi<u>sh</u>	Tom ate the <u>radish</u>. Some <u>radishes</u> are white, some are red. <u>Radishes</u> grow in the ground. (radishes)
rag *rag* rag	Mother washed the dishes with a dish $\boxed{\begin{array}{c}\text{rag.}\\ \text{cloth.}\end{array}}$ (rags)

R
S
T
U
V
W
X
Y
Z

There is a <u>rail</u>
around the porch
so baby will not
fall off.

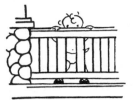

rail

rail

r<u>ai</u>l

The street car runs on <u>rails</u>.

(rails)

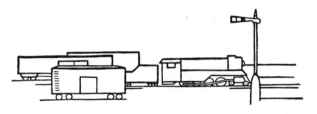

railroad

rail-road

railroad

r<u>ai</u>lr<u>oa</u>d

This is a <u>railroad</u>.

The train runs on the <u>railroad</u>.

(railroads)

rain

rain

r<u>ai</u>n

<u>Rain</u> is water that falls in drops.

The children are walking
in the <u>rain</u>.

It is <u>raining</u> hard.

(rains   rained   raining)
(rainy)

R
S
T
U
V
W
X
Y
Z

rainbow
rain-bow
rainbow
r<u>ai</u>nb<u>o</u>w

Mary sees the <u>rainbow</u> in the sky.

There are seven colors
in the <u>rainbow.</u>

When the sun shines through
the light rain, it makes
a <u>rainbow.</u>

(rainbows)

raincoat
rain-coat
raincoat
r<u>ai</u>nc<u>oa</u>t

Mary is wearing a <u>raincoat.</u>
It will keep her dry.

(raincoats)

rainstorm
rain-storm
rainstorm
r<u>ai</u>nst<u>o</u>rm

In winter it snows.

In summer it rains.

When it rains hard, we have a
<u>rainstorm.</u>

(rainstorms)

raise
raise
r<u>ai</u>s<u>e</u>

Mary can | raise
lift up | the window.

(raises   raised   raising)

A <u>raisin</u> is a dried grape. I like <u>raisins</u> on cookies. (raisins)	**raisin** rai-sin *raisin* r<u>a</u><u>i</u>s̆in

This is a <u>rake</u>.
 The farmer <u>rakes</u>
    his garden
    with the <u>rake</u>.
     (rakes   raked   raking)
	rake
	 rake
	 r<u>a</u>k<u>e</u>

The cat <u>ran</u> after the mouse. (run runs running)	**ran** *ran* ran
See Mary <u>rap / knock</u> on the window. (raps rapped rapping)	**rap** *rap* rap

<u>Raspberries</u> are good to eat.
       They are red, black,
          yellow, and purple.
 A <u>raspberry</u>
     (raspberries)
	raspberry
	 rasp-ber-ry
	 raspberry
	 rås̱pber'ry

rat *rat* rat	This is a <u>rat</u>. It is like a mouse but much larger. <u>Rats</u> are white, gray, black, and brown. <div align="right">(rats)</div>
rather rath-er *rather* ra<u>th</u>er	I want this doll <table><tr><td>rather</td></tr><tr><td>very much more</td></tr></table> than that one.
reach *reach* r<u>ea</u><u>ch</u>	Baby <table><tr><td>reached for</td></tr><tr><td>tried to get</td></tr></table> the bottle with her hand. She could not <table><tr><td>reach</td></tr><tr><td>get to touch</td></tr></table> the bottle. (reaches reached reaching)
read *read* r<u>ea</u>d	Betty has a book. She can <u>read</u> in it. She likes to <u>read</u> stories. (reads reading)

R
S
T
U
V
W
X
Y
Z

Jack could not go with us. His hands were not washed so he was not <u>ready</u>.	ready read-y *ready* rĕạdy
Baby had a candy cane but father had a <u>real</u> cane. <div align="right">(really)</div>	real *real* reạl
Bob came to school late. His teacher said, "What's the <u>reason</u> you are cause of your being late?" (reasons)	reason rea-son *reason* reạ̌son
This is Mary's birthday. She will <u>receive</u> get many gifts. (receives received receiving)	receive re-ceive *receive* rĕcĕivĕ
The colors of the American flag are <u>red</u>, white, and blue.	red *red* red

R
S
T
U
V
W
X
Y
Z

redbreast red-breast *redbreast* redbre͞ast	This bird is a | redbreast. robin.
reel *reel* re͞el	Father wound the hose on this | reel. frame that winds. (reels)
refrigerator re-frig-er-a-tor *refrigerator* re͡frige͡rato͡r	This is a <u>refrigerator.</u> Food keeps cold in the <u>refrigerator.</u> (refrigerators)
reindeer rein-deer *reindeer* re͞indee͞r	This is a <u>reindeer.</u> In some lands <u>reindeer</u> are used for work instead of horses. (reindeer)
remain re-main *remain* rema͞in	The children came but they did not | remain stay | long. I ate one apple and one | remained. was left. (remains remained remaining)

I can't $\boxed{\begin{array}{l}\text{remember}\\ \hline \text{call back to mind}\end{array}}$ your name. (remembers remembered remembering)	remember re-mem-ber *remember* r<u>e</u>memb<u>er</u>
Father is polite. He $\boxed{\begin{array}{l}\text{removes}\\ \hline \text{takes off}\end{array}}$ his hat when he comes into the house. All polite boys and men <u>remove</u> their hats in the house. (removes removed removing)	remove re-move *remove* r<u>e</u>móv<u>e</u>₂
We live in my uncle's house. We have to pay $\boxed{\begin{array}{l}\underline{\text{rent}}\text{ for it.}\\ \hline \text{money for using it.}\end{array}}$ (rents rented renting)	rent *rent* rent

Our teacher will $\boxed{\begin{array}{l}\underline{\text{repeat}}\\ \hline \text{say over again}\end{array}}$ the question.
 	
We <u>repeat</u> doing things,
   when we do them again and again.
 	
(repeats repeated repeating)
	repeat
	re-peat
	repeat
	r<u>e</u>p<u>ea</u>t

R
S
T
U
V
W
X
Y
Z

reply re-ply *reply* r<u>e</u>pl<del>y</del>	I wrote grandmother a letter. I did not get a <u>reply</u>. an answer. (replies replied replying)
report re-port *report* r<u>e</u>p<u>or</u>t	Mary gave a <u>report</u> of her visit told all <u>about</u> to the farm. (reports reported reporting)
resident res-i-dent *resident* rèsident	Jack's father is a <u>resident</u> in our town. person who lives (residents)
rest *rest* rest	Mother was tired. She sat down to <u>rest</u>. We ate the <u>rest</u> of the apples. apples that were left. (rests rested resting)

return
re-turn
return
r<u>e</u>t<u>ur</u>n
	The teacher gave Tom a book.
	
	He will <u>return</u> it tomorrow.
	        take it back
	
	I went to town but
	
	    <u>returned</u> home soon.
	    came back
	
	(returns returned returning)

R
S
T
U
V
W
X
Y
Z

	ribbon
  This is a bow of <u>ribbon</u> for Mary's hair. This is a package tied with <u>ribbon</u>. <u>Ribbon</u> is made of silk and velvet. (ribbons)	rib-bon *ribbon* ribbon
Chinese people eat much <u>rice</u>. Rice grows in very wet ground. Rice is something like wheat. Mother makes <u>rice</u> pudding.	rice *rice* r<u>i</u>c<u>e</u>
The man is <u>rich</u>. / has much money. (riches richer richest)	rich *rich* ri<u>ch</u>
The Pied Piper <u>rid</u> the town of rats. / took the rats from the town.	rid *rid* rid
The children were playing games. They were guessing <u>riddles</u>. (riddles)	riddle rid-dle *riddle* riddl<u>e</u>₄

R
S
T
U
V
W
X
Y
Z

297

ride *ride* r<u>i</u>d<u>e</u>	Bob <u>rides</u> a horse. Tom <u>rides</u> a bicycle. I <u>ride</u> in the car with father. (rides rode riding)
rider rid-er *rider* r<u>i</u>d<u>e</u>r	The man rides a horse. He is a good <u>rider</u>. (riders)
right *right* r<u>igh</u>t	Bob writes with his left hand. I write with my <u>right</u> hand. This picture This picture is wrong. is <u>right</u>.

rime
rime
r<u>i</u>m<u>e</u>
	This is a <u>rime</u>.
	    Old Mother Hubbard
	    Went to the cupboard.
	The words
	   cat and sat <u>rime</u>. / sound alike.
	
	(rimes)

R
S
T
U
V
W
X
Y
Z

The outside covering on an orange is called the <u>rind.</u> Lemons have <u>rinds,</u> too. (rinds)	rind *rind* r<u>i</u>nd
Jane has a <u>ring.</u> It is made of gold. See Bob <u>ring</u> the bell. It sounds loud. (rings rang rung ringing)	ring *ring* ri<u>ng</u>
The apple is | ripe. / ready to be eaten. | (riper ripest ripen ripened ripening)	ripe *ripe* r<u>i</u><u>p</u><u>e</u>
The boys watched the sun | rise. / come up. | We | rise / stand up | when we read aloud. (rises rose rising)	rise *rise* r<u>i</u><u>s</u><u>e</u>
The boat sails down the <u>river.</u> The water in the <u>river</u> moves along in one direction. (rivers)	river riv-er *river* riv<u>e</u>r

road *road* r<u>oa</u>d	We did not know the $\boxed{\begin{array}{c}\underline{road}\\ way\end{array}}$ to take to get to my grandmother's. The auto stood in the middle of the <u>road.</u> (roads)
roar *roar* r<u>oa</u>r	The dog barks but the lion $\boxed{\begin{array}{l}\underline{roars.}\\ \text{makes a big noise.}\end{array}}$ Did you ever hear a lion <u>roar</u>? (roars roared roaring)
roast *roast* r<u>oa</u>st	Mother put the meat in the oven to $\boxed{\begin{array}{l}\underline{roast.}\\ \text{cook.}\end{array}}$ (roasts roasted roasting)
rob *rob* rob	The bad dog $\boxed{\begin{array}{l}\underline{robbed}\text{ the cat of her supper.}\\ \text{stole the cat's supper.}\end{array}}$ (robs robbed robbing) (robber robbers)

This bird is a robin.

The robin's breast
is red.

(robins)

robin

rob-in

robin

robin

A rock or stone   See Mother rock
the baby.

(rocks   rocked   rocking)

rock

rock

rock

This is a fishing | rod. / pole.

(rods)

rod

rod

rod

The boys

roll the snowball.
turn the snowball over and over.

A roll is a kind of bread.

I like sweet rolls.

(rolls   rolled   rolling)

roll

roll

roll

rompers romp-ers *rompers* rompers	Baby wears <u>rompers</u> when she plays.
roof *roof* r<u>oo</u>f	The fireman is on the $\boxed{\begin{array}{c}\text{roof}\\\hline\text{top}\end{array}}$ of the house. <p align="right">(roofs)</p>
room *room* r<u>oo</u>m	How many <u>rooms</u> do you have in your house? We sleep in the bed<u>room</u>. We sit in the sitting <u>room</u>. We eat in the dining <u>room</u>. There is not enough <u>room</u> for everyone to play at one time. <p align="right">(rooms)</p>
rooster roost-er *rooster* r<u>oo</u>st<u>er</u>	This chicken is not a hen. He is a <u>rooster.</u> <p align="right">(roosters)</p>
root *root* r<u>oo</u>t	The <u>roots</u> of the plants are in the ground. <u>Roots</u> help plants get food and water from the ground. <p align="right">(roots)</p>

 Children like to jump the <u>rope</u>. We use a <u>rope</u> to tie up the dog. (ropes)	**rope** *rope* ro<u>p</u><u>e</u>
This flower is a <u>rose</u>. It grows on a bush. Some <u>roses</u> climb on frames. (roses) 	**rose** *rose* ro<u>s</u><u>e</u>
The rose grows on a bush. It is called a <u>rosebush</u>. (rosebushes)	**rosebush** rose-bush *rosebush* ro<u>s</u><u>e</u>bu<u>sh</u>
Paper is smooth. The sidewalk is <u>rough</u>.	**rough** *rough* ro<u>ug</u>h
A ball is <u>round</u>. A circle is <u>round</u>.	**round** *round* r<u>ou</u>nd

row

row

ro̲w̲²

The man plants his garden in rows.

See Bob row the boat.

(rows   rowed   rowing)

rub

rub

ru b

Did you ever rub your hands together to get warm?

Father rubbed his face with a towel.

My hands were not clean.

I rubbed them hard to get them clean.

(rubs   rubbed   rubbing)

rubber

rub-ber

rubber

ru b b er

Overshoes are made of rubber.

Tires are made of rubber.

Erasers are made of rubber.

Rubber is made from sap.

The sap comes from trees.

(rubbers)

	rude
The man	was rude. / had poor manners.	*rude*
	r**u**d**e**

ruffle
ruf-fle
ruffle
r u ff l **e** ₊

This is
a plain curtain.

This is
a curtain
with a ruffle
around it.

(ruffles)

rug
rug
rug

This is a | rug / cover | for the floor.

(rugs)

ruin
ru-in
ruin
r**u**in

If you get paint on your suit,

it will | ruin / spoil | it.

(ruins   ruined   ruining)

R
S
T
U
V
W
X
Y
Z

rule

rule

r<u>u</u>l<u>e</u>

This is a | rule. / ruler. |

The children wanted to play a new game.

The teacher read the <u>rules</u> which told them how to play it.

The King | rules / leads | his country.

(rules   ruled   ruling)

---

ruler

rul-er

ruler

r<u>u</u>l<u>e</u>r

This is a | ruler. / rule. |

The King is a | ruler / leader | of a country.

(rulers)

---

run

run

ru n

See the children <u>run</u>.

Some children can <u>run</u> fast.

(runs   ran   running)

R
S
T
U
V
W
X
Y
Z

Did you see the children [rush / hurry] out of the room? (rushes rushed rushing)	rush *rush* ru <u>sh</u>
Do you like <u>rye</u> bread? It is made from <u>rye</u> flour. <u>Rye</u> is something like wheat.	rye *rye* r<u>y</u><u>e</u>ₛ

R
S
T
U
V
W
X
Y
Z

sack *sack* sa ck	This is a $\boxed{\dfrac{\text{sack}}{\text{bag}}}$ of potatoes. (sacks)
sad *sad* sa d	Bob could not go to the party. This made him feel $\boxed{\dfrac{\text{sad.}}{\text{unhappy.}}}$ (sadder saddest sadly)
saddle sad-dle *saddle* sa d d l e₊	The horse has a $\boxed{\dfrac{\text{saddle}}{\text{seat}}}$ for the rider. (saddles)
safe *safe* sa fe	Cross the street when the light is green. You are $\boxed{\dfrac{\text{safe}}{\text{out of danger}}}$ then. (safely safety) (safer safest) This is a <u>safe</u> to keep money in. (safes)

Father asked me to help him. I <u>said</u>, "I will be glad to help you." (say says saying)	said *said* s<u>ai</u>d

This is a boat
     with a <u>sail</u> on it.
The wind blows against
    the <u>sail</u>.
The wind makes the boat go.
 	
Did you ever $\boxed{\begin{array}{c}\text{sail}\\\hline\text{travel}\end{array}}$ on a big boat?
 	
(sails sailed sailing)
	sail
	sail
	s<u>ai</u>l

This man is a <u>sailor</u>. He sails on big boats. (sailors)	sailor sail-or *sailor* s<u>ai</u>l<u>or</u>
Bob shoveled the snow $\boxed{\begin{array}{l}\text{for father's \underline{sake}.}\\\text{to help father.}\end{array}}$	sake *sake* s<u>a</u>k<u>e</u>

S
T
U
V
W
X
Y
Z

salad	I like pineapple salad.
sal-ad	Father likes lettuce salad.
salad	Salad has salad dressing on it.
salad	Salads are made from fruits, meats, and vegetables.
	(salads)

sale	Grandma's house is for sale. / is to be sold.
sale	Mother bought my dress at a sale.
sale	She did not pay much for it.
	(sales)

salmon	This fish is a salmon.
salm-on	We eat salmon.
salmon	Salmon is put into cans
salmon	and sold at the stores.

salt	We put salt in a salt shaker.
salt	We put salt on potatoes
salt	to make them taste good.
	A salt shaker
	(salty)

same	
same	Our books are just the same. / alike.
same	

The children like to play in the sand by the lake. Sand is tiny pieces of rock. (sandy)	sand *sand* sand
The sandman is a make-believe man. The sandman comes when we are sleepy.	sandman sand-man *sandman* sandman
A sandwich Mother put meat between the bread. This made a sandwich. Sometimes she makes jelly or lettuce sandwiches. (sandwiches)	sandwich sand-wich *sandwich* sandwich
The floor is | sandy. | covered with sand.	sandy sand-y *sandy* sandy
The boy sang a song. Do you like to sing? (sing sings singing)	sang *sang* sang

S
T
U
V
W
X
Y
Z

Santa Claus
San-ta Claus

Santa Claus
Santá Claus

Santa Claus comes
on Christmas Eve.

---

sap

sap
sap

Maple syrup is made from sap.

Sap is the juice of the maple tree.

Rubber is made from sap.

Rubber sap is the juice
of a rubber tree.

---

sardine
sar-dine

sardine
sardines

A sardine is a small fish.

They are put into cans.

Sardines are good to eat.

(sardines)

---

sash

sash
sash

Mary has a sash
around her waist.

The sash is made of ribbon.

(sashes)

Bill stood up. Mary <u>sat</u> in the chair. (sit sits sitting)	sat *sat* sat
Satin is a smooth silk cloth.	satin sat-in *satin* satin
We tried hard to <u>satisfy</u> / please our teacher. (satisfies satisfied satisfying)	satisfy sat-is-fy *satisfy* satisfy
We do not go to school on <u>Saturday</u> or Sunday.	Saturday Sat-ur-day *Saturday* Saturday
Do you like apple <u>sauce</u>? / apples cooked and sweetened? Grandmother put a sweet <u>sauce</u> over the pudding. I like tomato <u>sauce</u> on meat.	sauce *sauce* sauce,

S
T
U
V
W
X
Y
Z

saucer sau-cer *saucer* s<u>au</u>c<u>e</u>r	This is a cup and <u>saucer.</u> The cup is in the <u>saucer.</u> (saucers)
sauerkraut sauer-kraut *sauerkraut* s<u>au</u>erkr<u>au</u>t	<u>Sauerkraut</u> is made from cabbage. It is good to eat.
sausage sau-sage *sausage* s<u>au</u>s<u>a</u>g<u>e</u>	<u>Sausage</u> is made of chopped meat. (sausages)
save *save* s<u>a</u>v<u>e</u>	Mary put her money in a bank. She will $\boxed{\begin{array}{c}\underline{save}\\keep\end{array}}$ it to buy a doll. The boy $\boxed{\begin{array}{c}\underline{saved}\text{ the baby's life.}\\kept\text{ the baby from dying.}\end{array}}$ (saves saved savings)
saw *saw* s<u>aw</u>	This <u>saw</u> cuts wood. (saws) Yesterday I <u>saw</u> a black cat. (see seen seeing)

<u>Sawdust</u> is little bits of wood. When we saw a board it makes <u>sawdust</u>.	sawdust saw-dust *sawdust* s<u>aw</u>dust
I could not hear what you <u>said</u>. Please <u>say</u> it again. (says said saying)	say *say* s<u>ay</u>

Bob is standing
   on the <u>scale</u>.
 	
He is getting weighed.
 	
Chickens are covered with feathers.
Fishes are covered with <u>scales</u>.
 	
    (scales)
	scale
	scale
	sc<u>a</u>l<u>e</u>

The kitten has | scarcely / not quite | enough to eat. They had | scarcely / hardly | enough milk to drink.	scarcely scarce-ly *scarcely* sc<u>a</u>rc<u>e</u>ly
The dog barked at father but it did not | scare / frighten | him. (scares scared scaring)	scare *scare* sc<u>a</u>r<u>e</u>

scarecrow scare-crow *scarecrow* scạrẹcrŏw	 The farmer puts a scarecrow in his garden. A scarecrow scares the birds away. (scarecrows)
scarf *scarf* scạrf	 The boy has a woolen scarf around his neck. It will keep him warm. Mother put a long $\boxed{\frac{\text{scarf}}{\text{cover}}}$ on the table. (scarfs)
scatter scat-ter *scatter* scatter	Grandfather $\boxed{\begin{array}{l}\text{scattered the grass seeds.}\\\text{threw the seeds here and there.}\end{array}}$ (scatters scattered scattering)
scene *scene* scene	A scene is a part of a play. Each scene tells the time, the place, and what is happening. (scenes)

We go to <u>school</u> to learn.	school
In our <u>school</u> we have 20 teachers.	*school*
(schools)	scⁱhool

This is a <u>schoolhouse</u>.	schoolhouse
	school-house
We go to school in a <u>schoolhouse</u>.	*schoolhouse*
(schoolhouses)	scⁱhoolhouse₅

A <u>schoolroom</u> is a room in the schoolhouse where children are taught.	schoolroom
	school-room
	schoolroom
(schoolrooms)	scⁱhoolroom

These are <u>scissors</u>.	scissors
	scis-sors
We cut paper and cloth with <u>scissors</u>.	*scissors*
	scissors

Bob was a good boy in school.	scold
The teacher did not	*scold*
<u>scold</u> / find fault with him.	scold
(scolds scolded scolding)	

S
T
U
V
W
X
Y
Z

scoop *scoop* sc<u>oo</u>p	This is a <u>scoop</u>. Mother uses a <u>scoop</u> to take flour out of the can. Baby likes to <u>scoop</u> the sand into the pail. <center>(scoops scooped scooping)</center>
scooter scoo-ter *scooter* sc<u>oo</u>t<u>er</u>	This is a <u>scooter</u>. It goes very fast. <center>(scooters)</center>
scorch *scorch* sc<u>or</u>ch	When Mary ironed her doll's dress, she tried not to $\boxed{\dfrac{\text{scorch}}{\text{burn}}}$ it. <center>(scorches scorched scorching)</center>
score *score* sc<u>ore</u>₅	We played a ball game. Our side won because we had the biggest $\boxed{\dfrac{\text{score.}}{\text{number of points.}}}$ We $\boxed{\dfrac{\text{scored}}{\text{made a point}}}$ in the last minute of the game. <center>(scores scored scoring)</center>

S
T
U
V
W
X
Y
Z

The kitchen sink was dirty.

Mother had to $\boxed{\begin{array}{l}\text{scour it}\\ \text{rub it hard}\end{array}}$ to get it clean.

(scours   scoured   scouring)

scour

scour

scour

Tom's dog was hungry.

Tom gave him a $\boxed{\begin{array}{l}\text{scrap}\\ \text{small piece}\end{array}}$ of meat.

Mother saves $\boxed{\begin{array}{l}\text{scraps of food}\\ \text{bits of leftover food}\end{array}}$ for the chickens.

(scraps   scrapped   scrapping)

scrap

scrap

scrap

Mary cut out pictures and stories.
She pasted them in her

$\boxed{\begin{array}{l}\text{scrapbook.}\\ \text{book for pictures and stories.}\end{array}}$

(scrapbooks)

scrapbook

scrap-book

scrapbook

scrapbook

S
T
U
V
W
X
Y
Z

scrape *scrape* scr<u>a</u>p<u>e</u>	Bob got paint on his book. He tried to $\boxed{\begin{array}{c}\text{scrape} \\ \hline \text{rub}\end{array}}$ it off with a knife. <div align="center">(scrapes scraping scraped)</div>
scratch *scratch* scra<u>tch</u>	The cat tried to $\boxed{\begin{array}{c}\text{scratch} \\ \hline \text{dig}\end{array}}$ Bob with its claws. I have a $\boxed{\begin{array}{c}\text{scratch} \\ \hline \text{little cut}\end{array}}$ on my hand. When Mary's arm itches, she <u>scratches</u> it. <div align="center">(scratches scratched scratching)</div>
scream *scream* scr<u>ea</u>m	Mary burned her finger. Did you hear her $\boxed{\begin{array}{c}\text{scream?} \\ \hline \text{loud cry?}\end{array}}$ <div align="center">(screams screaming screaming)</div>

S
T
U
V
W
X
Y
Z

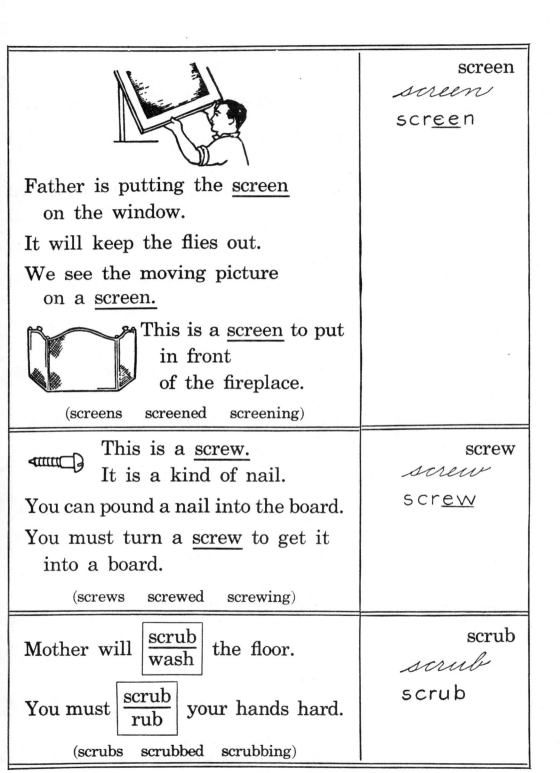

screen

screen

scr__ee__n

Father is putting the screen
on the window.

It will keep the flies out.

We see the moving picture
on a screen.

This is a screen to put
in front
of the fireplace.

(screens   screened   screening)

This is a screw.
It is a kind of nail.

You can pound a nail into the board.

You must turn a screw to get it
into a board.

(screws   screwed   screwing)

screw

screw

scr__ew__

Mother will | screw / wash | the floor.

You must | scrub / rub | your hands hard.

(scrubs   scrubbed   scrubbing)

scrub

scrub

scrub

S
T
U
V
W
X
Y
Z

sea *sea* s<u>ea</u>	The boat is on the <u>sea</u>. The <u>sea</u> is not as large as the ocean. The water in the <u>sea</u> is salty. (seas)
seal *seal* s<u>ea</u>l	These are <u>seals</u>. They live in the ocean. We use the <u>seal's</u> fur for coats. (seals)
seasick sea-sick *seasick* · s<u>ea</u>si<u>ck</u>	Some people get sick when they ride on a boat at sea. The rocking of the boat makes them <u>seasick</u>. (seasickness)
season sea-son *season* s<u>ea</u>s̆on	Winter and summer are $\boxed{\begin{array}{c} \text{seasons} \\ \hline \text{times} \end{array}}$ of the year. Spring and autumn are <u>seasons</u> of the year, too. Which <u>season</u> do you like best? (seasons)

S
T
U
V
W
X
Y
Z

322

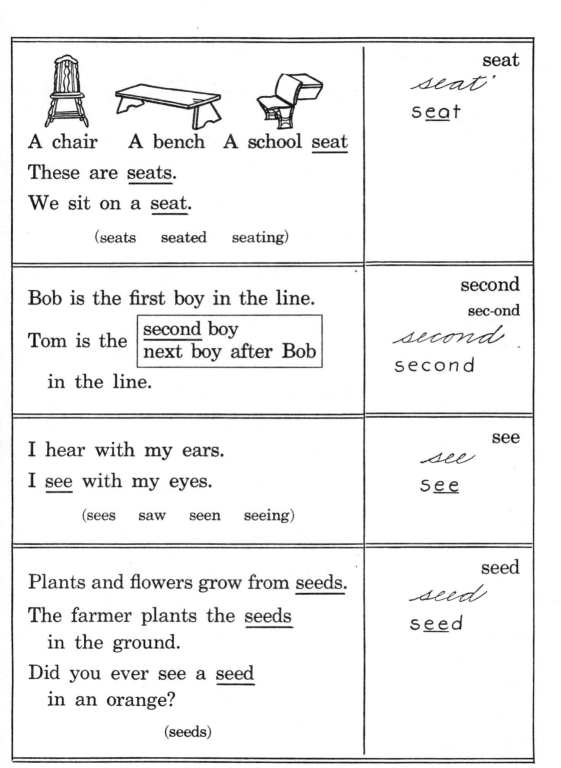

A chair   A bench A school seat

These are seats.

We sit on a seat.

(seats   seated   seating)

seat

seat'

s<u>ea</u>t

Bob is the first boy in the line.

Tom is the | second boy / next boy after Bob |

in the line.

second

sec-ond

second

second

I hear with my ears.

I see with my eyes.

(sees   saw   seen   seeing)

see

see

s<u>ee</u>

Plants and flowers grow from seeds.

The farmer plants the seeds
in the ground.

Did you ever see a seed
in an orange?

(seeds)

seed

seed

s<u>ee</u>d

S
T
U
V
W
X
Y
Z

seem *seem* s<u>ee</u>m	The cat did not $\boxed{\dfrac{\text{seem}}{\text{look to be}}}$ sick. (seems seemed seeming)
seen *seen* s<u>ee</u>n	Jack's dog ran away. Have you <u>seen</u> it anywhere? (see sees saw seeing)
seesaw see-saw *seesaw* s<u>ee</u>s<u>aw</u>	 The children are playing on the <u>seesaw.</u> The <u>seesaw</u> goes up and down.
seize *seize* s<u>ei</u>z<u>e</u>,	Did you see the dog $\boxed{\dfrac{\text{seize}}{\text{take hold of}}}$ the cat's tail? (seizes seized seizing)
seldom sel-dom *seldom* s<u>e</u>ld<u>o</u>m	$\boxed{\dfrac{\text{Seldom}}{\text{Not very often}}}$ does father scold me.

If you will ⌜select / pick out⌟ the dress you want, mother will buy it for you. (selects selected selecting)	**select** se-lect *select* s<u>e</u>lect
Tom had two apples. He gave one to me and kept one for himself. (sel<s>v</s>es)	**self** *self* self
<u>Selfish</u> children are those who think of themselves first. Do not be <u>selfish.</u> Think of other people first.	**selfish** self-ish *selfish* selfi<u>sh</u>
My father owns a store. He will <u>sell</u> you some oranges for a quarter. (sells sold selling)	**sell** *sell* sell
If mother needs bread from the store, she will ⌜send me / get me to go⌟ for it. Father <u>sent</u> mother some flowers. (sends sent sending)	**send** *send* send

S
T
U
V
W
X
Y
Z

sense *sense* sens<u>e</u>ₛ	I can think, see, hear, smell, and taste. These are called <u>senses.</u> Some people cannot smell. They have no <u>sense</u> of smell. <div align="center">(senses)</div>
sentence sen-tence *sentence* senten<u>ce</u>₃	Can you read the first ⌈sentence⌉ ⌊thought⌋ in the story? <u>Sentences</u> are words put together to tell or ask something. <div align="center">(sentences)</div>
separate sep-a-rate *separate* sep<u>a</u>r<u>a</u>t<u>e</u>	Bob will ⌈<u>separate</u>⌉ ⌊take away⌋ your books from mine. <div align="center">(separates separated separating)</div>
September Sep-tem-ber *September* Septemb<u>er</u>	<u>September</u> is the ninth month of the year. <u>September</u> is the first month of school. Labor Day is the first Monday in <u>September.</u>

S
T
U
V
W
X
Y
Z

A <u>servant</u> is a man or woman who is paid for working for someone else. Some <u>servants</u> take care of children. Some <u>servants</u> cook and <u>clean</u> house. <center>(servants)</center>	servant serv-ant *servant* s<u>e</u>rvant
If you want some ice cream, Mother will [<u>serve</u> / wait upon] you. I am happy to [<u>serve</u> / help] you. <center>(serves served serving)</center>	serve *serve* s<u>erve</u>₂
Mary [set / put] the cup on the table. <center>(sets setting)</center>	set *set* set
Here are [<u>seven</u> / 7] stars. Count them. (seventh)	seven sev-en *seven* seven
Bob has [<u>several</u> / a few] apples.	several sev-er-al *several* sev<u>e</u>ral

sew *sew* s<u>ew</u>	Mary is making a dress for her doll. She can <u>sew</u> with a needle and thread. Mother can <u>sew</u> on the <u>sewing</u> machine. (sews sewed sewing)
shade *shade* <u>sh</u>a<u>de</u>	Mother is pulling down the window <u>shade</u>. The sun cannot shine through the leaves. This makes shade / a darker place under the trees. It is cool in the <u>shade</u>. (shades shaded shading) (shady)
shadow shad-ow *shadow* <u>sh</u>a<u>dow</u>	This is a dog and his <u>shadow</u>. The <u>shadow</u> is the shade made by the dog. People, trees, and other things make <u>shadows</u>, too. (shadows)

The children | shake / rock | the tree to get the apples.

See these men <u>shake</u> hands.

(shakes   shook   shaking   shaken)

shake

shake

sh<u>a</u>k<u>e</u>

Tomorrow I <u>shall</u> give you some ice cream.

I <u>shall</u> go to town this afternoon.

shall

shall

sh<u>a</u>ll

The <u>shamrock</u> is a kind of clover.

It has three leaves.

(shamrocks)

shamrock

sham-rock

shamrock

sh<u>a</u>mro<u>ck</u>

The <u>shape</u> of a circle is round.

The <u>shape</u> of a pencil is round and long.

(shapes   shaped   shaping)

shape

shape

sh<u>a</u>p<u>e</u>

Mary did not have any pudding.

Bob gave her his | <u>share.</u> / part.

I will | <u>share</u> my lunch with you. / give you a part of my lunch.

(shares   shared   sharing)

share

share

sh<u>a</u>r<u>e</u>

sharp *sharp* <u>sh</u>arp	I cut my finger with the knife. The knife was very <u>sharp.</u> Father had just <u>sharpened</u> it. <center>(sharper sharpest)</center><center>(sharpen sharpened sharpening)</center>
shave · *shave* <u>sh</u>a<u>ve</u>	See father $\boxed{\begin{array}{c}\text{shave}\\ \hline \text{cut off}\end{array}}$ his whiskers. He looks nice after <u>shaving.</u> <center>(shaves shaved shaving)</center>
she *she* <u>sh</u>e	Betty is not home now. <u>She</u> will be back soon.
shears *shears* <u>sh</u>e<u>a</u>rs	These are $\boxed{\begin{array}{c}\text{shears.}\\ \hline \text{big scissors.}\end{array}}$ The farmer cuts the sheep's wool with <u>shears.</u>
shed *shed* <u>sh</u>ed	Grandfather keeps his wagon in a $\boxed{\begin{array}{c}\text{shed.}\\ \hline \text{low building.}\end{array}}$ Chickens $\boxed{\begin{array}{c}\text{shed}\\ \hline \text{lose}\end{array}}$ their feathers in spring. <center>(sheds shedding)</center>

S
T
U
V
W
X
Y
Z

This <u>sheep</u> has long wool. The farmer cuts his wool. It is made into cloth and yarn.		sheep *sheep* <u>sh</u><u>ee</u>p
I write on a $\boxed{\begin{array}{c}\text{sheet}\\\hline\text{piece}\end{array}}$ of paper. Mother put clean <u>sheets</u> and pillowcases on my bed. Bed <u>sheets</u> are made of white cloth. <center>(sheets)</center>		sheet *sheet* <u>sh</u><u>ee</u>t
Father put the vase of flowers on the <u>shelf.</u> The <u>shelf</u> is fastened to the wall. <center>(shelves)</center>		shelf *shelf* <u>sh</u>elf
The children found a <u>shell</u> on the seashore. Little animals live in <u>shells</u>. The outside of an egg is the <u>shell</u>. I $\boxed{\begin{array}{l}\text{shelled the peas.}\\\text{took the peas out of the pods.}\end{array}}$ <center>(shells shelled shelling)</center>		shell *shell* <u>sh</u>ell

shelter shel-ter *shelter* shelt<u>er</u>	The house <u>shelters</u> ━━━━━━ us from protects cold and rain. Umbrellas <u>shelter</u> us from the sun and rain. (shelters sheltered sheltering)
she's *she's* sh<u>e</u>'s	<u>She's</u> ━━━ going to school. She is
shine *shine* sh<u>i</u>n<u>e</u>	Tom likes to <u>shine</u> father's shoes. It makes them bright and clean. When the sun <u>shines,</u> it makes light. (shines shone shining shiny)
ship *ship* s<u>h</u>ip	This <u>ship</u> ━━ crosses the ocean. big boat People travel on <u>ships.</u> (ships)
shirt *shirt* s<u>h</u>i<u>r</u>t	Men wear <u>shirts.</u> This <u>shirt</u> has a collar on it. (shirts)

S
T
U
V
W
X
Y
Z

Bob was very cold. He began to **shiver / shake** with the cold. (shivers shivered shivering)	shiver shiv-er *shiver* sh<u>i</u>v<u>er</u>
This is a <u>shock</u> of corn. Farmers pile up wheat so it makes a <u>shock</u>, too. (shocks)	shock *shock* sh<u>o</u><u>ck</u>
One <u>shoe</u> has a high top. The other <u>shoe</u> is low. <u>Shoes</u> are made of leather. Some are made of cloth. (shoes)	shoe *shoe* sh<u>o</u>e_s
A man who makes shoes is a <u>shoemaker</u>. (shoemakers)	shoemaker (shoe-mak-er) *shoemaker* sh<u>o</u><u>e</u>m<u>a</u>k<u>er</u>
Mother <u>shook</u> the rug to get the dust out of it. (shake shakes shaking shaken)	shook *shook* sh<u>oo</u>k

S
T
U
V
W
X
Y
Z

shoot *shoot* sh<u>oo</u>t	The man will <u>shoot</u> the bear with his gun. (shoots shot shooting)
shop *shop* <u>sh</u>op	Mother went to the store to | <u>shop.</u> buy things. | A store is a <u>shop.</u> A place where things are made is a <u>shop.</u> (shops shopped shopping)
shore *shore* <u>shore</u>	The children like to play in the sand on the | <u>shore.</u> land near the sea. | (shores)
short *short* <u>sh</u>ort	Bob's pencil is long. Mary's pencil is | <u>short.</u> not long. | (shorter shortest)
shortcake short-cake *shortcake* <u>sh</u>ort<u>c</u>a<u>ke</u>	I like strawberry <u>shortcake.</u> It is made with biscuits and strawberries. (shortcakes)

S
T
U
V
W
X
Y
Z

Some children play in the street. They <u>should</u> play on the sidewalks.	should *should* s<u>h</u>o<u>ul</u>d
Father is carrying the baby on his <u>shoulders</u>. (shoulders)	shoulder shoul-der *shoulder* <u>sh</u>o<u>u</u>ld<u>er</u>
Mary was lost. Father did not hear her <u>shout.</u> / call loudly. (shouts shouted shouting)	shout *shout* <u>sh</u>o<u>u</u>t
We use a <u>shovel</u> to <u>shovel</u> the snow off the sidewalks. This is a steam <u>shovel</u>. It can lift heavy loads. (shovels shoveled shoveling)	shovel shov-el *shovel* <u>sh</u>ovel
Mother has a new coat. She will <u>show</u> it to you. / let you see it. We are going to a picture <u>show</u>. (shows showed showing shown showy)	show *show* <u>sh</u>o<u>w</u>

shower show-er *shower* <u>sh</u><u>ow</u><u>e</u>r	We were caught in a $\boxed{\begin{array}{l}\underline{\text{shower.}}\\ \text{light rain.}\end{array}}$ (showers)
shut *shut* <u>sh</u>ut	Bob will $\boxed{\begin{array}{l}\underline{\text{shut}}\\ \text{close}\end{array}}$ the door. (shuts shutting)

sick -
sick
si<u>ck</u>
	The doctor came
	  to see Mary.
	She was <u>sick</u>
	  in bed.
	
	(sicker sickest)

side *side* s<u>i</u><u>d</u><u>e</u>	 The cat is on one <u>side</u> of the fence. The dog is on the other <u>side</u>. (sides)
sidewalk side-walk *sidewalk* s<u>i</u>d<u>e</u>w<u>a</u>lk	Do not walk in the street. Walk on the $\boxed{\begin{array}{l}\underline{\text{sidewalk.}}\\ \text{walk at the side of the street.}\end{array}}$ (sidewalks)

S
T
U
V
W
X
Y
Z

The boy is blind.
 	
He | has no <u>sight.</u> |
    | cannot see. |
 	
Mother looked down the street.
 	
Father | was out of <u>sight.</u> |
      | could not be seen. |
	sight
	sight
	sight

The teacher told us to | <u>sign</u> our names to | | write our names on | the papers. I saw a <u>sign</u> on the telephone pole. It said, "This way to the zoo." (signs signed signing signal)	sign *sign* sign
The children were | <u>silent</u> | | quiet | while Mary was reading. (silently)	silent si-lent *silent* silent
Some thread is <u>silk.</u> Some cloth is <u>silk.</u> Mother's dress is made of <u>silk</u> cloth.	silk *silk* silk

S
T
U
V
W
X
Y
Z

silver sil-ver *silver* silv<u>er</u>	A dime is not made of gold. It is made of silver. Our knives and forks are made of silver.
since *since* sin<u>ce</u>₃	My kitty is lost. I have not seen her <table><tr><td>since morning.</td></tr><tr><td>from morning until now.</td></tr></table>
sing *sing* si<u>ng</u>	Mary plays the piano. Bob sings a song while Mary plays the piano. Singing is music. (sings sang sung singing singer)

sink
sink
sink
	If you throw a stone into the water,
	  it will <table><tr><td>sink.</td></tr><tr><td>go to the bottom.</td></tr></table>
	This is a kitchen sink.
	We wash dishes
	  in the sink.
	
	(sinks sank sunk sinking)

Bah, Bah, black sheep, Have you any wool? Yes, $\boxed{\frac{\text{sir,}}{\text{Mr.,}}}$ yes, $\boxed{\frac{\text{sir,}}{\text{Mr.,}}}$ Two bags full.	sir *sir* s<u>ir</u>

The girl is my <u>sister</u>.
 We have the same mother
     and father.
 	
         (sisters)
	sister
	 sis-ter
	 sister
	 sist<u>er</u>

When I am tired, I <u>sit</u> on a chair. (sits sat sitting)	sit *sit* sit
How many stars do you see? I see <u>six</u> stars. (sixth sixty)	six *six* six
Father will get you some shoes. Tell him $\boxed{\begin{array}{l} \text{what } \underline{\text{size}} \text{ shoes you wear.} \\ \text{how } \underline{\text{big}} \text{ your shoes should be.} \end{array}}$ My kite is $\boxed{\begin{array}{l} \text{the same } \underline{\text{size}} \\ \text{just as big} \end{array}}$ as yours. (sizes)	size *size* s<u>iz</u><u>e</u>

S
T
U
V
W
X
Y
Z

skate	
skate (cursive) sk<u>a</u>t<u>e</u>	This is a roller <u>skate</u>. We <u>skate</u> on the sidewalk with roller <u>skates</u>. This is an ice <u>skate</u>. We <u>skate</u> on the ice with ice <u>skates</u>. (skates skated skating)
skin *skin* (cursive) skin	The outside of an apple is the <u>skin</u>. The outside of your hand is the <u>skin</u>. Father [skinned / rubbed] the skin off his hand. (skins skinned skinning)
skip *skip* (cursive) skip	Can you [skip / jump] the rope? Mother [skipped / passed] over one page of the story. (skips skipped skipping)

S
T
U
V
W
X
Y
Z

This is a <u>skirt</u>.

It is a part of a dress.

(skirts)

skirt

skirt

skirt

The sun is in the <u>sky</u>.

The clouds are in the <u>sky</u>.

Stars are in the <u>sky</u> at night.

The sun makes pretty colors
in the <u>sky</u>.

(skies)

sky

sky

sky

This line stands   This is
straight up and   a <u>slant</u> line.
down.

Some houses have flat roofs.

Some houses have <u>slanting</u> roofs.

(slants   slanted   slanting)

slant

slant

slant

Do not | slap / hit | the dog

with your hand.

(slaps   slapped   slapping)

slap

slap

slap

S
T
U
V
W
X
Y
Z

sled *sled* sled	 The children like to slide down hill on a <u>sled</u>. <div align="right">(sleds)</div>
sleep *sleep* sl<u>ee</u>p	This baby is <u>sleeping.</u> I <u>sleep</u> at night. (sleeps slept sleeping sleepy)
sleet *sleet* sl<u>ee</u>t	Sometimes it rains. Sometimes tiny pieces of ice fall. This ice is called <u>sleet.</u> Sometimes rain and ice fall at the same time. This is <u>sleet,</u> too. <div align="center">(sleets sleeted sleeting)</div>

sleigh
sleigh
sl<u>eigh</u>
	
	This is a <u>sleigh.</u>
	It has runners to slide on
	  like a sled.
	Horses draw <u>sleighs</u>
	  over the ice and snow.
	<div align="center">(sleighs)</div>

S
T
U
V
W
X
Y
Z

Mary ate two | slices / flat pieces | of bread.

Mother | sliced / cut | it

for her.

Would you like a slice, too?

(slices   sliced   slicing)

slice

slice

slice

Did you ever
slide down a slide?

The slide is smooth
so you can go fast on it.

(slides   slid   slidden   sliding)

slide

slide

slide

Bob stepped on something smooth.

He slipped and fell down.
His feet went out from under him
and he fell down.

Did you ever slip on the ice?
Mary wrote her name

on a | slip / small piece | of paper.

Mother wears a slip
under her dress.

(slips   slipped   slipping)   A slip

slip

slip

slip

S
T
U
V
W
X
Y
Z

343

slipper slip-per *slipper* sl i pp <u>er</u>	This is a | slipper. low shoe. (slippers)
slow *slow* sl o͞w	Jack is | slow. not fast. He is always behind time. I write | slowly. not fast. (slower slowest) Father | slows down the car does not run the car so fast when we come to a railroad. (slows slowed slowing slowly)
sly *sly* sl y	The fox was | sly. tricky.
small *small* sm a͑ ll	I am big. Baby is | small. little. (smaller smallest)

S
T
U
V
W
X
Y
Z

Bob cut his finger. It made his finger <u>smart.</u> / <u>pain him.</u> Father is a <u>smart</u> man. He knows many things. (smarter smartest)	smart *smart* s m <u>a</u> r t
Mother knew the cake was burning. She could <u>smell</u> it. We <u>smell</u> with our noses. Flowers have a sweet <u>smell.</u> (smells smelled smelling)	smell *smell* s m e l l
Mother is pleased about something. She has a <u>smile</u> on her face. (smiles smiled smiling)	smile *smile* s m <u>i</u> l <u>e</u>
See the <u>smoke</u> come out of the chimney. Father <u>smokes</u> a pipe. (smoky) (smokes smoked smoking)	smoke *smoke* s m <u>o</u> k <u>e</u>

S
T
U
V
W
X
Y
Z

smooth *smooth* sm<u>oo</u>t͟h	The paper is not rough. It is <u>smooth</u>. Mother ironed the dress. to make it <u>smooth</u>. (smooths smoothed smoothing) (smoother smoothest)
snail *snail* sn<u>ai</u>l	A <u>snail</u> is a little soft animal. He lives in this shell. <u>Snails</u> move slowly. (snails)
snake *snake* sn<u>a</u>k<u>e</u>	This is a <u>snake</u>. He has no legs. He crawls fast. Some <u>snakes</u> make their nests in the ground. (snakes)
sneeze *sneeze* sn<u>ee</u>z<u>e</u>	Bob had a cold. Father said, "Put a handkerchief over your mouth when you <u>sneeze</u>." Sometimes pepper makes us <u>sneeze</u>. (sneezes sneezed sneezing)

In winter the <u>snow</u> falls
  on the trees.

<u>Snow</u> is white.

It has pretty shaped flakes.

(snows   snowed   snowing)

snow

snow

snŏw

The boys are rolling

a | <u>snowball.</u>
   | ball made of snow.

(snowballs)

snowball

snow-ball

snowball

snŏwbȧll

These are | <u>snowflakes.</u>
          | pieces of snow.

Each <u>snowflake</u> is different.

(snowflakes)

snowflake

snow-flake

snowflake

snŏwflakĕ

S
T
U
V
W
X
Y
Z

snow man snow man *snow man* snŏw mɑn	 The boys made a | **snow man.** | **man of snow.** (snow men)
snowstorm snow-storm *snowstorm* snŏwstŏrm	When the wind blows and the snow comes down fast, we have a <u>snowstorm</u>. (snowstorms)

so
so
sǫ
	Bob's dog ran away <u>so</u>
	    father tied him to the tree.
	
	I do not believe
	    what he told is | <u>so.</u> | true.
	
	Mother was <u>so</u> tired she couldn't
	    eat her supper.

soap *soap* sǫɑp	 This is a bar of <u>soap</u>. Tom washed his hands with <u>soap</u> and water. (soapy)
sob *sob* sob	The baby | <u>sobs</u> | cries | when he is hurt. (sobs sobbed sobbing)

S
T
U
V
W
X
Y
Z

These are <u>socks</u>. Socks are short. Stockings are long. (socks)	sock *sock* s o <u>ck</u>
The floor is hard. The pillow is <u>soft.</u> (softer softest softly)	soft *soft* s o ft

The farmer put the seeds
  in the <u>soil.</u> / ground.
If you play in the mud
  you will <u>soil</u> your dress. / get your dress dirty.
 	
    (soils   soiled   soiling)
	soil
	soil
	s<u>oi</u>l

I went to the store for an apple.
The grocer <u>sold</u> me an apple
  for two cents.
 	
    (sell   sells   selling)
	sold
	sold
	s<u>o</u>ld

This man is a <u>soldier</u>. He is in the army. (soldiers)	soldier sol-dier *soldier* s<u>o</u>l<u>di</u>er

some *some* some̲s	Father gave me ┌─────────────┐ │ some │ │ a number of │ └─────────────┘ apples. I had <u>some</u> soup for_ lunch.
somebody some-bod-y *somebody* some̲body	The mother bear said, ┌──────────────┐ │ "<u>Somebody</u> │ has been eating │ "Someone │ └──────────────┘ my soup."
someone some-one *someone* som<u>eo</u>ne	The father bear said, ┌──────────────┐ │ "<u>Someone</u> │ has been sitting │ "Some person │ └──────────────┘ in my chair."
something some-thing *something* some̲thing	Father has <u>something</u> for my birthday. I do not know what it is.
sometime some-time *sometime* som<u>eti</u>m<u>e</u>	I will see you ┌──────────────┐ │ <u>sometime</u>. │ │ at some time. │ └──────────────┘ (sometimes)
somewhere some-where *somewhere* som<u>ew</u>hére̲s	Grandmother lives ┌──────────────┐ │ <u>somewhere</u> │ │ some place │ └──────────────┘ on this street.

The man is the father. The woman is the mother. The boy is their <u>son</u>. (sons)	son *son* son
The boy is singing a <u>song</u>. The name of the <u>song</u> is "Mr. Turkey." (songs)	song *song* so<u>ng</u>
Father will be home | <u>soon.</u> | | in a short time. | (sooner soonest)	soon *soon* s<u>oo</u>n
Mary burned her hand. It made a <u>sore</u> on her hand. <u>Sores</u> sometimes hurt badly. (sores)	sore *sore* s<u>ore</u>
I was <u>sorry</u> for the man who was hurt. Bob treated Tom badly. Then he was <u>sorry</u>.	sorry sor-ry *sorry* só rry

S
T
U
V
W
X
Y
Z

sort *sort* s<u>o</u>rt	Bob helped │ <u>sort</u> separate │ the books. Mother <u>sorted</u> the clothes. She put all of baby's clothes together. She put all of father's clothes together. (sorts sorted sorting)
sound *sound* s<u>ou</u>nd	We heard the tinkling <u>sound</u> of a bell. Did you hear a │ <u>sound</u> noise │ at night? Mother's voice <u>sounds</u> as if she has a cold. (sounds sounded sounding)
soup *soup* s<u>ou</u>p	The little bear said, "Someone has been eating my <u>soup</u>." Mother made tomato <u>soup</u>. What kind of <u>soup</u> do you like?
sour *sour* s<u>ou</u>r	Sugar is sweet. Lemons are <u>sour</u>. (sourer sourest)

S
T
U
V
W
X
Y
Z

In winter birds go <u>south</u> where it is warm. I live north of our school. Tom lives <u>south</u> of our school. <center>(southern)</center>	south *south* s<u>ou</u>th
The farmer <u>sows</u> / plants his grain. <center>(sows sowed sowing)</center>	sow *sow* s<u>ow</u>
Mary put the books on the shelf. She did not leave any <u>space</u> / room between them. <center>(spaces spaced spacing)</center>	space *space* sp<u>a</u><u>ce</u>
This is a <u>spade.</u> We dig with a <u>spade.</u> <center>(spades spaded spading)</center>	spade *spade* sp<u>a</u><u>de</u>
This bird is a <u>sparrow.</u> The <u>sparrow</u> is brown and gray. <center>(sparrows)</center>	sparrow spar-row *sparrow* spárro<u>w</u>

S
T
U
V
W
X
Y
Z

353

speak *speak* sp<u>ea</u>k	Father does not <table><tr><td>speak</td></tr><tr><td>talk</td></tr></table> very loudly. I will <u>speak</u> to mother about the party. (speaks spoke speaking **spoken)**
speck *speck* spe<u>ck</u>	Mary got a <table><tr><td>speck</td></tr><tr><td>little spot</td></tr></table> of dirt on her dress. (specks)
speckled speck-led *speckled* spe<u>ck</u>l<u>e</u>d	This is a <u>speckled</u> egg. It has little <table><tr><td>speckles</td></tr><tr><td>spots</td></tr></table> all over it.
speed *speed* sp<u>ee</u>d	<table><tr><td>At what <u>speed</u></td></tr><tr><td>How fast</td></tr></table> does your father drive? It is not safe to <table><tr><td>speed.</td></tr><tr><td>go fast.</td></tr></table> The car <u>speeded</u> down the street. (speeds sped speeded speeding)

S
T
U
V
W
X
Y
Z

Mary can <u>spell</u> the word dog. She can put the letters ⎡ so they <u>spell</u> dog. ⎣ in the right order. (spells spelled spelling)	spell *spell* s p e l l
I can ⎡ **spend** ⎣ pay out ⎤ ten cents for fruit. Yesterday I ⎡ **spent** ⎣ paid out ⎤ a nickel at the grocery. (spends spent spending)	spend *spend* s p e n d
This is a <u>spider</u> and its web. <u>Spiders</u> crawl. A <u>spider</u> has eight legs. This is a ⎡ spider ⎣ skillet ⎤ to cook in. (spiders)	spider spi-der *spider* s p<u>i</u>d <u>er</u>
Baby ⎡ spilled the milk ⎣ let the milk fall ⎤ on the floor. (spills spilled spilling)	spill *spill* s p i l l

S
T
U
V
W
X
Y
Z

355

spin *spin* spin	Tom has a top. He will ┌ <u>spin</u> it. └ make the top go around and around. Spiders ┌ <u>spin</u> ┐ webs. └ make ┘ (spins spun spinning)
spinach spin-ach *spinach* spin<u>ach</u>	<u>Spinach</u> is a green leaf. It is good to eat when cooked. Pop-eye, the sailor, eats <u>spinach</u>.
splash *splash* spla<u>sh</u>	The children like to ┌ <u>splash</u> ┐ water └ toss ┘ on each other. (splashes splashed splashing)
spoil *spoil* sp<u>oi</u>l	Do not get ink on your dress. It will <u>spoil</u> it. Mother put the milk in the icebox so it would not <u>spoil</u>. (spoils spoiled spoiling)

Father [**spoke** / said something] to mother. (speak speaks speaking spoken)	spoke *spoke* s p o k e
One [**spoke** / bar] on the wheel is broken. (spokes)	spoke *spoke* s p o k e
This is a <u>spool</u> with thread on it. (spools)	spool *spool* s p o o l

Baby eats with a <u>spoon</u>.
 	
We eat some things
  with <u>spoons</u>.
 	
Mother mixed the cake
  with a <u>spoon</u>.
 	
(spoons)
	spoon
	spoon
	s p o o n

Playing ball is [<u>sport.</u> / fun.] Games are <u>sports</u>. (sports)	sport *sport* s p o r t

S
T
U
V
W
X
Y
Z

spot *spot* spot	Mary got a $\boxed{\begin{array}{c}\text{spot}\\\hline\text{speck}\end{array}}$ of ink on her dress. This cloth $\boxed{\begin{array}{l}\text{is spotted.}\\\text{has spots on it.}\end{array}}$ (spots spotted spotting)
spray *spray* spr<u>a</u>y	Mary likes to $\boxed{\begin{array}{c}\text{spray}\\\text{sprinkle}\end{array}}$ the flowers. (sprays sprayed spraying)
spread *spread* spre͟a d	Mother $\boxed{\begin{array}{l}\underline{\text{spread}}\text{ the butter on the bread.}\\\text{covered the bread with butter.}\end{array}}$ Mary put a $\boxed{\begin{array}{l}\text{bedspread}\\\text{cover}\end{array}}$ on her bed. (spreads spreading)
spring *spring* spri<u>ng</u>	These <u>springs</u> make the bed soft. The farmer plants seeds in the <u>spring.</u> Trees become green in the <u>spring.</u> (springs)

S
T
U
V
W
X
Y
Z

It is
sprinkling
raining a little
today.

Mother will
sprinkle
put drops of water on
the clothes, so they
will iron nicely.

Father sprinkles the garden
every day.

(sprinkles   sprinkled   sprinkling)

sprinkle

sprin-kle

sprinkle

sprinkl̲e̲₄

The children played, "I spy."

Someone hid a thimble.

The first to see it said, "I
spy."
see."

(spies   spied   spying)

spy

spy

sp̲y̲

This is a square.

All the sides are
the same size.

(squares)

square

square

squ̲a̲r̲e̲

These are squashes.

They are red, yellow,
and white.

Squashes are good to eat.

Squash pie tastes like
pumpkin pie.

(squashes)

squash

squash

squ̲a̲sh̲

S
T
U
V
W
X
Y
Z

squeeze

squeeze

s**quee**z**e**₅

See Mother | squeeze / press | the water out of the dish cloth.

Mary | squeezed / pressed | the juice out of the orange.

(squeezes   squeezed   squeezing)

---

squirrel

squir-rel

squirrel

s**qui**rrel

Squirrels have bushy tails.

There are red, gray, and black squirrels.

They like to eat nuts and grain.

(squirrels)

---

squirt

squirt

s**qui**rt

See the water | squirt / rush |

out of the hole in the pipe.

(squirts   squirted   squirting)

---

stable

sta-ble

stable

st**a**ble₄

This is a stable.

It is like a barn.

The farmer keeps his horses and cows in the stable.

(stables)

S
T
U
V
W
X
Y
Z

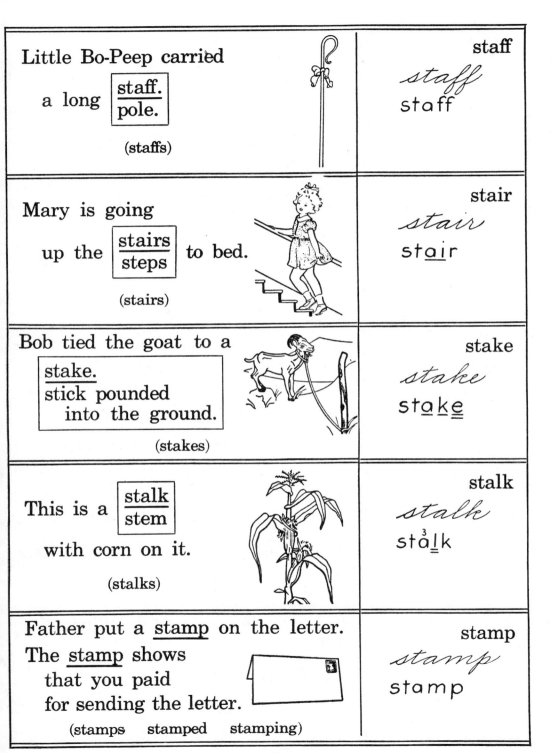

Little Bo-Peep carried

a long | staff.
pole.

(staffs)

staff

staff

staff

Mary is going

up the | stairs
steps | to bed.

(stairs)

stair

stair

st<u>ai</u>r

Bob tied the goat to a

stake.
stick pounded
into the ground.

(stakes)

stake

stake

st<u>a</u>k<u>e</u>

This is a | stalk
stem

with corn on it.

(stalks)

stalk

stalk

st<u>a</u>lk

Father put a <u>stamp</u> on the letter.
The <u>stamp</u> shows
that you paid
for sending the letter.

(stamps   stamped   stamping)

stamp

stamp

stamp

stand *stand* stand	 This boy is sitting down. This boy is <u>standing</u> up. (stands stood standing)
star *star* st<u>a</u>r	We watched the <u>stars</u> in the sky at night. (stars)
starch *starch* st<u>ar</u>ch	Mother put some <u>starch</u> in my dress when she washed it. <u>Starch</u> makes clothes stiff. (starches starched starching)
start *start* st<u>a</u>rt	The show will start / begin soon. Mother will start / begin to go home now. (starts started starting)
state *state* st<u>a</u>t<u>e</u>	I live in the <u>state</u> of Michigan. In which <u>state</u> do you live? There are 48 <u>states</u> in the United <u>States</u>. (states)

S
T
U
V
W
X
Y
Z

The train stopped at the railroad <u>station</u>. People wait in the <u>station</u> for trains to come and go. We buy gasoline at a gasoline <u>station</u>. (stations)	station sta-tion *station* sta<u>tio</u>n
This is the <u>Statue</u> of Liberty. Some <u>statues</u> are made of stone and marble. <u>Statues</u> are made to look like people or the objects they stand for. (statues)	statue stat-ue *statue* statu<u>e</u>,
Bob went to see Tom. Mother wanted him to hurry. He did not <u>stay</u> long. (stays stayed staying)	stay *stay* st<u>ay</u>
The dog tried to <u>steal</u> / take away the cat's supper. <u>Stealing</u> is taking things that do not belong to you. (steals stole stealing)	steal *steal* st<u>ea</u>l

S
T
U
V
W
X
Y
Z

steam *steam* steam	The water in the teakettle is boiling. See the <u>steam</u> come out. <u>Steam</u> makes the engine go. In winter <u>steam</u> gathers on the cold window glass. (steams steamed steaming)
steep *steep* steep	Bob and Mary climbed a <u>steep</u> hill. It was almost straight up and down. (steeper steepest)
stem *stem* stem	This is a flower fastened to a <u>stem</u>. This apple has a <u>stem</u>. The <u>stem</u> held it to the tree. (stems)
step *step* step	The baby took a long <u>step</u>. Bob went up the <u>steps</u>. (steps stepped stepping)

This is a <u>stepladder</u>.

Mother stands
on a <u>stepladder</u>
to wash the windows.

(stepladders)

stepladder

step-lad-der

stepladder

stepladd<u>er</u>

This is a <u>stick</u> of candy.

We gathered | <u>sticks</u> |
| pieces of wood |

to make a fire.

We use paste

to | <u>stick</u> | things together.
| fasten |

(sticks   stuck   sticking   sticky)

stick

stick

sti<u>ck</u>

A pencil is <u>stiff</u>.

It will not bend.

(stiffer   stiffest)

stiff

stiff

stiff

The baby is sleeping.

We must be | <u>still</u>. |
| quiet. |

The car is | standing <u>still</u>. |
| not moving. |

still

still

still

S
T
U
V
W
X
Y
Z

sting *sting* sti<u>ng</u>	Did a bee ever <u>sting</u> you? A <u>sting</u> is like a bite. It hurts to be <u>stung</u> by a bee. (stings stung stinging)
stir *stir* st<u>ir</u>	Mother $\boxed{\begin{array}{c}\text{stirs}\\\hline\text{mixes}\end{array}}$ the cake with a spoon. (stirs stirred stirring)
stocking stock-ing *stocking* sto<u>ck</u>i<u>ng</u>	These are silk <u>stockings</u>. I had a hole in one <u>stocking.</u> (stockings)
stone *stone* st<u>o</u>n<u>e</u>	This is a big $\boxed{\begin{array}{c}\text{stone.}\\\hline\text{rock.}\end{array}}$ Diamonds are <u>stones</u> that are cut and polished. (stones)
stood *stood* st<u>oo</u>d	Sam sat down. Bob <u>stood</u> up. (stand stands standing)

S
T
U
V
W
X
Y
Z

Mother has a <u>stool</u> in the kitchen. Father puts his feet on a <u>stool</u>. The farmer sits on a <u>stool</u> while milking the cows. (stools)	stool *stool* st<u>oo</u>l
The children did not go. The policeman said <u>stop</u>. (stops stopped stopping)	stop *stop* stop
The girls wanted some cookies. They went to the <u>store</u> for them. We buy things at a <u>store</u>. (stores)	store *store* st<u>ore</u>
The man who owns the store is the <u>storekeeper</u>. (storekeepers)	storekeeper store-keep-er *storekeeper* st<u>ore</u>k<u>ee</u>p<u>er</u>

S
T
U
V
W
X
Y
Z

stork *stork* st**o**rk	The <u>stork</u> has long legs and a long bill. He can walk in deep water. A <u>stork</u> (storks)
storm *storm* st**o**rm	We had a bad <u>storm</u>. Rain fell and the wind blew hard. (storms stormed storming)
story sto-ry *story* st**o**ry	The teacher read a <u>story</u> to us. I do not know the name of the <u>story</u>. (stories)
storybook sto-ry-book *storybook* st**o**ryb**oo**k	The teacher read a story from the <u>storybook</u>. (storybooks)
stove *stove* st**o**v**e**	The fire in this <u>stove</u> keeps us warm. Mother cooks on this <u>stove</u>. (stoves)

S
T
U
V
W
X
Y
Z

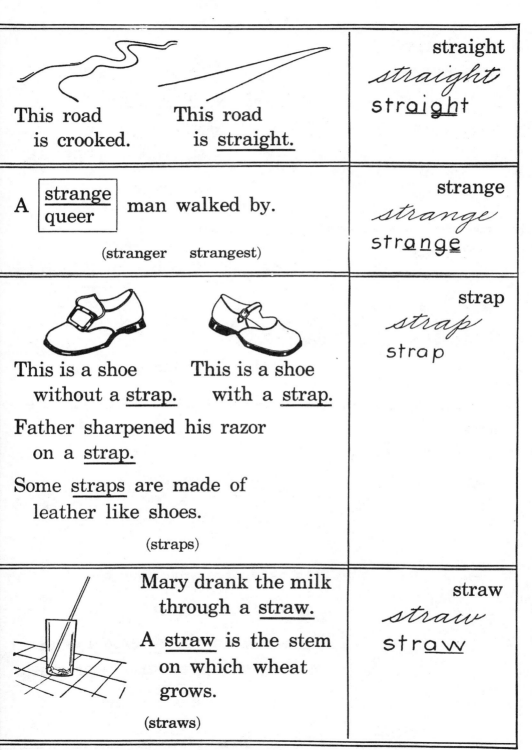

This road is crooked.

This road is straight.

straight

straight

straight

A strange / queer man walked by.

(stranger   strangest)

strange

strange

strange

This is a shoe without a strap.

This is a shoe with a strap.

Father sharpened his razor on a strap.

Some straps are made of leather like shoes.

(straps)

strap

strap

strap

Mary drank the milk through a straw.

A straw is the stem on which wheat grows.

(straws)

straw

straw

straw

S
T
U
V
W
X
Y
Z

strawberry straw-ber-ry *strawberry* stra<u>w</u>bérry	 This is a <u>strawberry</u>. <u>Strawberries</u> are red. Mother made a <u>strawberry</u> shortcake. (strawberries)
strawstack straw-stack *strawstack* stra<u>w</u>sta<u>ck</u>	 The boy is asleep by the $\begin{array}{\|c\|}\hline \text{strawstack.} \\ \hline \text{pile of straw.} \\ \hline \end{array}$ (strawstacks)
stream *stream* str<u>ea</u>m	 This is a <u>stream</u> of water. A <u>stream</u> is a river. The water in the <u>stream</u> moves toward a bigger <u>stream</u> or a sea. (streams)

S
T
U
V
W
X
Y
Z

We drive the auto in the <u>street</u>.
Stop! Look! and Listen! before
you cross the <u>street</u>.

(streets)

street

street

str<u>ee</u>t

Rubber will | **stretch** / get longer |

if you pull it.

(stretches   stretched   stretching)

stretch

stretch

stre<u>tch</u>   ,

Mother said, "Do not | **strike** / hit | the dog."

I heard the clock | **strike** / sound | ten times.

(strikes   striking   struck)

strike

strike

str<u>ike</u>

These children can

| **string** beads. / put beads on <u>string</u>. |

The <u>string</u>
is tied
to the kite.

(strings   stringing   strung)

string

string

stri<u>ng</u>

S
T
U
V
W
X
Y
Z

strip *strip* strip	 Mary put a $\boxed{\begin{array}{c}\text{strip}\\ \hline \text{long narrow piece}\end{array}}$ of paper in her book. (strips)
stripe *stripe* stri<u>p</u><u>e</u>	This is an American flag. It has thirteen <u>stripes</u>. The <u>stripes</u> are red and white. (stripes striped striping)
strong *strong* stro<u>ng</u>	Tom could not roll the big stone. He was not <u>strong</u> enough. (stronger strongest)
stuck *stuck* stu<u>ck</u>	The paper had paste on it, so it <u>stuck</u> to my book. (stick sticks sticking)

S
T
U
V
W
X
Y
Z

I will | study / read and try to learn | from a book.

We <u>study</u> in school.

(studies   studied   studying)

study

stud-y

study

study

Mary is making a cat of cloth for the baby.

She will | stuff it with / fill it full of | cotton.

(stuffs   stuffed   stuffing)

stuff

stuff

stuff

The bee | stung / bit | Bob.

It hurts to be <u>stung</u> by a bee.

(sting   stings   stinging)

stung

stung

stu<u>ng</u>

If you work hard,

you will | succeed. / do well. |

(succeeds   succeeded   succeeding)

succeed

suc-ceed

succeed

succ<u>ee</u>d

Our baby is <u>such</u> a nice baby.

We never saw | such a storm. / a storm like that. |

such

such

su<u>ch</u>

suddenly sud-den-ly *suddenly* suddenly	<u>Suddenly</u> When we were not looking for it, it started to rain. Suddenly / All at once the door opened. (sudden)
sugar sug-ar *sugar* sŭgạr	Candy is sweet. It is made of <u>sugar</u>.
suggestion sug-ges-tion *suggestion* suggestion	Bob could not make the box. Father said, "Maybe I can give you a <u>suggestion</u> / an idea about making it." Perhaps Father's <u>suggestion</u> / plan will work. (suggestions)
suit *suit* sŭit	 This is father's new <u>suit</u> of clothes. The teacher liked Mary's pictures and said, "They <u>suit</u> / please me." (suits suited suiting)

S
T
U
V
W
X
Y
Z

The snow falls in winter. The flowers grow in <u>summer</u>. (summers)	**summer** sum-mer *summer* summ<u>er</u>
  The <u>sun</u> is in the sky. We see the <u>sun</u> in the daytime. The <u>sun</u> makes us warm. (suns sunny)	**sun** *sun* sun
We do not go to school on <u>Sunday</u>. We go to church on <u>Sunday</u>.	**Sunday** Sun-day *Sunday* Sund<u>ay</u>
The <u>sunflower</u> is tall. The center is brown. The outside is yellow. Birds like the seeds from a <u>sunflower</u>. (sunflowers)	**sunflower** sun-flow-er *sunflower* sunfl<u>ow</u><u>er</u>

S
T
U
V
W
X
Y
Z

sunlight sun-light *sunlight* sunl<u>igh</u>t	At night there is no	sunlight. light from the sun.	
sunset sun-set *sunset* . sunset	In the evening we sat by the lake. We watched the	sunset. going down of the sun.	 (sunsets)
sunshine sun-shine *sunshine* sun<u>shine</u>	The	sunshine sunlight	came through the window.
supper sup-per *supper* supp<u>er</u>	In the morning we eat breakfast. At night we eat <u>supper</u>. (suppers)
suppose sup-pose *suppose* supp<u>ose</u>	I	suppose think	I can go. (supposes supposed supposing)
sure *sure* <u>sure</u>	Jack wanted to go to the party. He was not <u>sure</u> that his mother would let him. (surely)

Mary has a birthday today.

We are having a <u>surprise</u> party
for her.

Mary does not know
about the party.

(surprises   surprised   surprising)

surprise
sur-prise
surprise
s<u>u</u>rpri<u>s</u><u>e</u>

The boy put too much bread
into his mouth at one time.

He could not <u>swallow</u> it.

This bird is a <u>swallow</u>.

Some <u>swallows</u> build
nests in barns.

Some build nests
in the sides of
hills.

(swallows   swallowing   swallowed)

swallow
swal-low
swallow
sw<u>a</u>ll<u>ow</u>

Can you swim in the water?

This boy <u>swam</u> across the river.

(swim   swims   swimming)

swam
swam
swam

S
T
U
V
W
X
Y
Z

sweater

sweat-er

sweater

sweater

This is a <u>sweater</u> to wear.

It will keep you warm.

(sweaters)

---

sweep

sweep

sweep

Mother can <u>sweep</u> with
  a broom.

It will make the floor clean.

(sweeps   sweeping   swept)

---

sweeper

sweep-er

sweeper

sweeper

This man is a street <u>sweeper</u>.

He sweeps the streets clean.

(sweepers)

---

sweet

sweet

sweet

Candy is not sour.
It is <u>sweet.</u>

(sweeter   sweetest)
(sweetly   sweetened)

Baby bumped her arm.

Her arm began to | swell. / get larger. |

(swells   swelled   swelling   swollen)

swell

swell

swell

The boy is | swift / fast | with his work.

The dog runs swiftly.

(swifter   swiftest   swiftly)

swift

swift

swift

See this boy swim in the water.

Fish swim in the water, too.

(swims   swimming   swam)

swim

swim

swim

This is a swing.

Mary swings in the swing.

It goes back and forth.

(swings   swinging   swung)

swing

swing

swing

S
T
U
V
W
X
Y
Z

sword
sword
s<u>w</u><u>o</u>rd
	This <u>sword</u> has
	    sharp edges.
	Men used to fight with <u>swords</u>.
	       (swords)

syrup
syr-up
syrup
syrup
	<u>Syrup</u> is made with sugar and
	    water or juices.
	Do you like maple <u>syrup</u>
	    on pancakes for your breakfast?

S
T
U
V
W
X
Y
Z

This is a <u>table</u>. We sit at a <u>table</u> when we eat. (tables)	table ta-ble *table* ta<u>b</u>le <u>4</u>
Mary needs a new \boxed{\text{tablet} \\ \text{book of paper}} to write in. Some medicine is round pills and some is flat <u>tablets</u>. (tablets)	tablet tab-let *tablet* ta blet
The man put a <u>tag</u> on the dog's collar. The <u>tag</u> had the dog's name on it. The children played <u>tag</u>. Bob \boxed{\text{tagged} \\ \text{touched}} Tom, then Tom chased the other children. (tags tagged tagging)	tag *tag* tag
The horse has a long <u>tail</u>. The rabbit has a short <u>tail</u>. (tails)	tail *tail* tail

T
U
V
W
X
Y
Z

tailor
tai-lor
tailor
t<u>ai</u>l<u>or</u>
	The man who makes
	    father's clothes is called a <u>tailor.</u>
	
	    (tailors)

take *take* t<u>a</u> k<u>e</u>	Mother said she would $\boxed{\begin{array}{c}\text{take}\\\hline\text{go with}\end{array}}$ us for a ride. (takes taking took taken)
tale *tale* t<u>a</u> l<u>e</u>	Our teacher tells us a $\boxed{\begin{array}{c}\text{tale}\\\hline\text{story}\end{array}}$ each morning. (tales)
talk *talk* tả<u>l</u>k	Bob wanted to $\boxed{\begin{array}{c}\text{talk.}\\\hline\text{say something.}\end{array}}$ (talks talking talked)
tall *tall* tả<u>l</u>l	One girl is short. The other is <u>tall.</u> (taller tallest)

T
U
V
W
X
Y
Z

Jane is wearing her | tam-o'shanter. / cap. |

(tam-o'shanters)

tam-o'shanter
tam-o'shan-ter

tam-o' shanter

tam-o'shanter

Jane's hat was a | tan / light brown | color.

tan

tan

tan

Mary's hair gets | tangled / twisted together | at night.

Does your hair tangle when you sleep?

(tangles   tangled   tangling)

tangle
tan-gle

tangle

tangle.

This is a tank for bath water.

Father put gasoline in the tank of our automobile.

(tanks)

tank

tank

tank

We heard a | tap / light knock | on the window.

I tapped on mother's door.

(taps   tapped   tapping)

tap

tap

tap

T
U
V
W
X
Y
Z

tardy tar-dy *tardy* t<u>a</u>rdy	Mary has never been tardy / late for school. (tardier tardiest)
tart *tart* t<u>a</u>rt	A <u>tart</u> is a small pie with jelly or jam in it. (tarts)
tassel tas-sel *tassel* tassel	This is a hat with a <u>tassel</u> on it. Stalks of corn have <u>tassels</u> too. (tassels)
taste *taste* t<u>a</u>s<u>te</u>	Baby put the medicine in her mouth. She didn't like the bitter <u>taste</u> of it. (tastes tasted tasting)
taught *taught* t<u>au</u>ght	Bob's father <u>taught</u> him / helped him learn to skate. (teach teaches teaching)

T
U
V
W
X
Y
Z

We pay ┌ **taxes** ┐ to the city. └ **money** ┘
 	
Tax money is used to pay
  policemen, firemen,
  and other helpers.
 	
(taxes   taxed   taxing)
	tax
	tax
	tax

Milk is good for children to drink. Coffee and tea are not good for them. Tea is made from dried tea leaves.	tea *tea* tea
Can you make a kite? I will ┌ **teach you** ┐ how. └ **help you learn** ┘ (teaches teaching taught)	teach *teach* teach
We go to school. Our teacher helps us learn to read. (teachers)	teacher teach-er *teacher* teacher
Our school has a baseball team. A baseball team is nine boys who play ball together. (teams)	team *team* team

T
U
V
W
X
Y
Z

tear *tear* te͞ar	Jane will <u>tear</u> the paper in two. Mother said, "Do not │ <u>tear</u> │ make a hole in your dress." (tears tearing tore torn)
tear *tear* te͞ar	Mary is crying. She has │ <u>tears</u> │ drops of water in her eyes. (tears)
teaspoon tea-spoon *teaspoon* te͞asp͞o͞on	A <u>teaspoon</u> is a small spoon. We eat ice cream with a <u>teaspoon</u>. (teaspoons teaspoonful)
Teddy bear Ted-dy bear *Teddy bear* Teddy be͞ar	This is the baby's toy <u>Teddy bear</u>. She likes to play with it. (Teddy bears)
teeth *teeth* te͞eth	Baby opened his mouth. He had two white <u>teeth</u>. (tooth)

Mother had a ⎡telegram / message⎤ from father. **Telegrams** are news sent by electricity. (telegrams)	telegram tel-e-gram *telegram* tel<u>e</u>gram
  These are **telephones**. We talk through **telephones**. Did you ever talk through a **telephone?** (telephones)	telephone tel-e-phone *telephone* tel<u>e</u>ph<u>o</u>n<u>e</u>
The children asked the teacher to **tell** a story. (tells telling told)	tell *tell* tell
 How many stars do you see? I see ⎡ten / 10⎤ stars. (tenth)	ten *ten* ten
Mother will ⎡tend / take care of⎤ the baby. (tends tended tending)	tend *tend* tend

T
U
V
W
X
Y
Z

tender ten-der *tender* tend<u>er</u>	Some meat is tough and hard to chew. Some meat is $\boxed{\dfrac{\text{tender}}{\text{soft}}}$ and easy to chew. (tenderer tenderest)
tent *tent* tent	 This is a <u>tent</u>. It is fun to live in a <u>tent</u> in summer. (tents)
terrible ter-ri-ble *terrible* t́erribl<u>e</u>₄	Mother had a $\boxed{\dfrac{\text{terrible}}{\text{very bad}}}$ cold.
terrier ter-ri-er *terrier* t́erri<u>er</u>	This dog is a <u>terrier</u>. (terriers)
test *test* test	Our teacher gave us a $\boxed{\dfrac{\text{test}}{\text{try out}}}$ to see how well we could read. (tests)

I am older <u>than</u> you. I am bigger <u>than</u> you.	than *than* <u>th</u>an

The woman gave me an apple.
I said, "<u>Thank</u> you."
 	
     (thanks   thanking   thanked)
     (thankful)
	thank
	thank
	<u>th</u>ank

On <u>Thanksgiving</u> Day
   we say thanks to God
   for all he has done for us.
	Thanksgiving
	Thanks-giv-ing
	Thanksgiving
	<u>Th</u>anksgivi<u>ng</u>

Mary wants this book, but I want <u>that</u> one over there.	that *that* <u>th</u>at
<u>That's</u> the last apple I have. That is	that's *that's* <u>th</u>at's
This story is about <u>the</u> three bears.	the *the* <u>the</u>

T
U
V
W
X
Y
Z

their *their* th**ĕ**ir	Three little kittens Lost <u>their</u> mittens. <center>(theirs)</center>
them *them* th**e**m	The goats were in the turnip field. "One, two, I will get <u>them</u> out for you," said the wolf.
themselves them-selves *themselves* themselv**es**	The girls kept the apples for <u>themselves</u>.
then *then* th**e**n	"I will come to the party <u>then.</u>" at that time."
there *there* th**é**r**e**ₛ	Father said, "Put the book <u>there.</u>" in that place."
therefore there-fore *therefore* th**é**r**e**f**or**e	Baby is sick, <u>therefore,</u> for that reason, we can't go.
there's *there's* th**é**r**e**'s	<u>There's</u> one more flower in bloom. There is

This book is mine. These books are mine, too.	these *these* th̬ėsȩ
The children were running. They are very tired.	they *they* th̬ey
They're They are going to the party.	they're *they're* th̬ey'rȩ,

Baby has much hair.
Her hair is thick.
One book is thin, but the other
   is thick.
 	
    (thicker   thickest)
	thick
	thick
	thịck

A thief is a person who takes things
   that do not belong to him.
 	
      (thieves)
	thief
	thief
	thịef

This is a thimble.
 	
Mother puts it
   on her finger
   when she sews.
 	
    (thimbles)
	thimble
	thim-ble
	thimble
	thịmblȩ,

thin	
thin th in	This book is ⌈thin. not thick.⌋ This boy is ⌈thin. not fat.⌋ (thinner thinnest)
thing	
thing th ing	Baby puts <u>things</u> in her mouth. Mary didn't have a <u>thing</u> to play with. (things)
think	

think
th ink
	I ⌈think
	believe⌋ it is colder today.
	
	Mary knew where the book was but
	   she could not <u>think</u> when
	   I asked her.
	
	(thinks thinking thought)

third	
third th ird	The first time is one time. The second time is two times. The <u>third</u> time is three times. (thirds)

T
U
V
W
X
Y
Z

Billy drank some water. He was <u>thirsty</u>. (thirstier thirstiest)	thirsty thirst-y *thirsty* <u>th</u><u>ir</u>sty
Ten apples and three apples make	thirteen / 13	apples.	thirteen thir-teen *thirteen* <u>th</u><u>ir</u>t<u>ee</u>n
Ten, Twenty,	Thirty	 10 20 30 <u>Thirty</u> cents is a quarter and a nickel.	thirty thir-ty *thirty* <u>th</u><u>ir</u>ty
Twenty marbles and fifteen marbles make	thirty-five / 35	marbles.	thirty-five thir-ty-five *thirty-five* <u>th</u><u>ir</u>ty-f<u>iv</u><u>e</u>
That book is mine. <u>This</u> one is yours.	this *this* <u>th</u>is

T
U
V
W
X
Y
Z

393

thistle this-tle *thistle* th͟i͟s͟t͟l͟e͟₄	 This plant is a <u>thistle</u>. Some <u>thistles</u> have purple flowers. The <u>thistle</u> has sharp stickers on the stems. (thistles)
thorn *thorn* th͟o͟rn	Some plants have $\boxed{\begin{array}{l}\text{thorns}\\\hline\text{sharp points}\end{array}}$ on them. Roses have <u>thorns</u>. <u>Thorns</u> will stick you. (thorns)
those *those* th͟o͟s͟e͟	These books are mine. <u>Those</u> books over there are yours.
though *though* th͟o͟u͟g͟h͟	Bob went home $\boxed{\begin{array}{l}\text{though}\\\hline\text{even if}\end{array}}$ he did not want to go.

I | thought |
   | believed | I could go.

The things you __think__ about
    are your __thoughts.__

      (think   thinks   thinking)
      (thoughts)

thought

thought

thought

This is a spool of __thread.__

We sew our clothes
    with __thread.__

Grandma could not see to

| thread |
| put a __thread__ through | her needle.

    (threads   threading   threaded)

thread

thread

thread

☆ ☆ ☆

Here are | three |
         | 3 | stars.

three

three

three

Did you ever see a farmer

| thresh |
| take the seeds from | wheat?

    (threshes   threshed   threshing)

thresh

thresh

thresh

T
U
V
W
X
Y
Z

| throat *throat* <u>thr**oa**t</u> | The boy has his hand on his \| throat. / the front of his neck. \| (throats) |

| throne *throne* <u>thr**o**n**e**</u> | This is the \| throne / seat \| where the king or queen sits. (thrones) |

| through *through* <u>thr**ou**gh</u> | Father looked <u>through</u> the book for a picture. I put the thread <u>through</u> the eye of the needle. We went <u>through</u> the tunnel. We are \| through / finished \| with our work. |

| throw *throw* <u>thr**ow**</u> | See Jack <u>throw</u> the ball. (throws   throwing   threw) (thrown) |

This hand has four fingers and one <u>thumb</u>. (thumbs)	thumb *thumb* <u>th</u>um<u>b</u>
The man | thumped / pounded | the drum. (thump thumps thumping)	thumped *thumped* <u>th</u>ump<u>ĕd</u>
I saw the lightning and heard the | thunder / loud noise | when it rained. (thunders thundered thundering)	thunder thun-der *thunder* <u>th</u>und<u>er</u>
<u>Thursday</u> is the fifth day of the week.	Thursday Thurs-day *Thursday* <u>Th</u>ur<u>s</u>d<u>ay</u>
Listen to the clock. It says, <u>tick</u>, tock. (ticks ticked ticking)	tick *tick* ti<u>ck</u>
Bob gave the conductor his <u>ticket</u>. He paid money for the <u>ticket</u>. The conductor will let him ride if he has a <u>ticket</u>. (tickets)	ticket tick-et *ticket* ti<u>ck</u>et

T
U
V
W
X
Y
Z

tickled
tick-led
 	
tickled
tick̆le̊d
	The dog licked my hand
	with his tongue.
	
	It | tickled
	       made funny little feelings on |
	my hand.
	
	I was | tickled
	       pleased | to get new shoes.
	
	(tickle tickles tickling)

tidy ti-dy *tidy* tĭdy	Mother is very | tidy. neat. | She puts things where they belong. (tidier tidiest)

tie
 	
tie
tíe
	This is father's <u>tie</u>.
	
	                      (ties)
	
	Billy tried to | tie
	           fasten |
	the strings together.
	
	Father <u>tied</u> the dog to the post.
	
	(ties tying tied)

T
U
V
W
X
Y
Z

This is a <u>tiger</u>.
 	
His fur has yellow and
   black stripes.
 	
<u>Tigers</u> are wild.
 	
       (tigers)
	tiger
	ti-ger
	tiger
	t<u>ige</u>r

The ring is <u>tight</u>
     not loose
 	
on my finger.
 	
  (tighter   tightest   tightly)
	tight
	tight
	t<u>ig</u>ht

He ran <u>till</u> he saw a fox. until	till *till* till

John looked at the clock to see
   what <u>time</u> it was.
 	
Once upon a <u>time</u> I saw a bear.
 	
       (times)
	time
	time
	t<u>ime</u>

She put the gingerbread boy in a <u>tin</u> pan to bake. Mother bought a <u>tin</u> can of corn.	tin *tin* tin
I heard the <u>tinkle</u> of the bells. sound (tinkles tinkled tinkling)	tinkle tin-kle *tinkle* tinkl<u>e</u>

T
U
V
W
X
Y
Z

tiny ti-ny *tiny* t<u>i</u>ny	The baby is | tiny. / very small. | (tinier tiniest)
tip *tip* tip	Baby will | tip / upset | the glass of milk. (tips tipped tipping)
tiptoe tip-toe *tiptoe* tipt<u>oe</u>	Baby is trying to reach the glass pitcher. She is standing on | her tiptoes. / the ends of her toes. | (tiptoes)
tire *tire* t<u>ire</u>	Father put a new <u>tire</u> on the car. Hard work will | <u>tire</u> you. / make you <u>tired</u>. | (tires tired tiring)
tired *tired* t<u>ire</u>d	I worked hard. I am too <u>tired</u> to play. (tire tires tiring)

What is the ⎡title / name⎤ of the story

you are reading?

Books have titles, too.

(titles)

title
ti-tle

title

t͟i͟tl͟e͟₄

Jack threw

the ball ⎡to me. / in my direction.⎤

Mary likes to help mother.

to

to

tŏ

This is a toad.

He looks like a frog.

He has no tail.

He eats bugs and worms.

(toads)

toad

toad

to͟a͟d

I eat toasted bread for breakfast.

We make toast

in a toaster.

I do not like toast

that is too brown.

(toasts   toasted   toasting)

toast

toast

to͟a͟st

T
U
V
W
X
Y
Z

tobacco to-bac-co *tobacco* tobacco	Father smokes <u>tobacco</u> in his pipe.
today to-day *today* today	I am going to school <u>today.</u> / on this day.
toes *toes* toes	We have five <u>toes</u> on each foot. (toe)
together to-geth-er *together* together	The children sat <u>together.</u> / with each other.
told *told* told	Bob could not read to us so he <u>told</u> us a story. (tell tells telling)
tomato to-ma-to *tomato* tomato	This is a <u>tomato.</u> <u>Tomatoes</u> grow on vines. <u>Tomatoes</u> are red. They are good to eat. (tomatoes)

T
U
V
W
X
Y
Z

I am going to school	**tomorrow**
tomorrow.	to-mor-row
on the day after today.	*tomorrow*
	tomorrow
Father bought a <u>ton</u> of coal.	**ton**
There are 2000 pounds in a <u>ton</u>.	*ton*
(tons)	ton
The dog's mouth is open.	**tongue**
We can see his <u>tongue</u>.	*tongue*
Our <u>tongues</u> are in our mouths.	tongue
You could not talk if you had no <u>tongue</u>.	
(tongues)	
You can see the stars if you look	**tonight**
into the sky tonight. / this evening.	to-night
	tonight
	tonight
Father went to the store.	**too**
Bob went to the store, too. / also.	*too*
	too

T
U
V
W
X
Y
Z

took *took* t$\overset{2}{oo}$k	The cow wanted a drink. I <u>took</u> some water to her. (take takes taking taken)

tools
 	
tools
 	
t$\underline{oo}$l$\overset{2}{s}$
	
	When a man makes a house,
	   he uses these <u>tools</u>.
	
	A <u>tool</u> is anything you use
	   when you work.
	
	(tool)

tooth *tooth* t$\underline{oo}$<u>th</u>	When baby opened her mouth, I saw one <u>tooth</u>. (teeth)
toothache tooth-ache *toothache* t$\underline{oo}$th$\overset{2}{\underline{a}}$<u>che</u>	Did you ever have a [toothache? pain in a tooth?]
toothbrush tooth-brush *toothbrush* t$\underline{oo}$<u>th</u>bru$\underline{sh}$	 This is a <u>toothbrush</u>. We clean our teeth with a <u>toothbrush</u>. (toothbrushes)

T
U
V
W
X
Y
Z

Bob likes to spin his <u>top</u>.

The roof is the <u>top</u> of the house.

Mother put the can

on the | <u>top</u>
highest | shelf.

(tops)

top

top

top

Mary and Spot were playing.

Her dress was <u>torn</u> by the dog.

(tear   tears   tore   tearing)

torn

torn

t<u>o</u>rn

This is a <u>tortoise</u>.

We call him a turtle.

He has a shell on his back.

He lives on land.

(tortoises)

tortoise

tor-toise

tortoise

t<u>o</u>rt<u>oi</u>s<u>e</u>s

T
U
V
W
X
Y
Z

toss *toss* toss	The boys like to $\boxed{\begin{array}{c}\text{toss}\\\text{throw}\end{array}}$ the ball up in the air. (tosses tossing tossed)
touch *touch* t<u>ou</u>ch	Baby burned her hand on the stove. She will not $\boxed{\begin{array}{c}\text{touch}\\\text{feel}\end{array}}$ the stove again. (touches touching touched)
tough *tough* t<u>ou</u>gh	Some meat is tender and some meat is <u>tough</u>. Tough meat is hard to chew. (tougher toughest)
toward to-ward *toward* t<u>ow</u>ard	The auto was going $\boxed{\begin{array}{c}\underline{\text{toward}}\\\text{in the direction of}\end{array}}$ the city. (towards)
towel tow-el *towel* t<u>ow</u>el	This is a bath <u>towel</u>. Mary wiped her face dry on a clean <u>towel</u>. (towels)

T
U
V
W
X
Y
Z

town

town

t<u>ow</u>n

Some children live in the country.

We live in a

| town. |
| place where many people live. |

(towns)

toys

toys

t<u>oy</u>s

Santa Claus brought

many | toys. |
| playthings. |

I like to play with <u>toys</u>.

(toy)

track

track

tra<u>ck</u>

This is a track for a <u>train</u>.

We saw a rabbit's | tracks |
| footprints |

in the snow.

(tracks)

trade *trade* tr<u>a</u>d<u>e</u>	Mary and Betty will **trade** **exchange** papers. My father's **trade** **business** is building houses. He is a carpenter by <u>trade</u>. (trades traded trading)
traffic traf-fic *traffic* traffic	There is much <u>traffic</u> today. Many people and cars are going by.
trailer trail-er *trailer* tr<u>ai</u>l<u>e</u>r	Many people live in a <u>trailer</u> in summer. Men use this <u>trailer</u> to move things from place to place. (trailers)
train *train* tr<u>ai</u>n	 The <u>train</u> is on the track. This <u>train</u> carries people and mail. (trains)

T
U
V
W
X
Y
Z

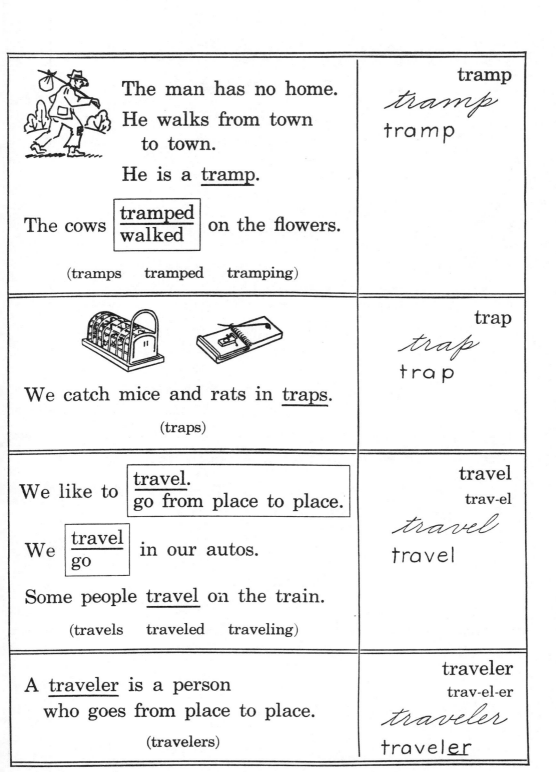

The man has no home.

He walks from town
 to town.

He is a tramp.

The cows $\boxed{\begin{array}{c}\underline{\text{tramped}}\\ \text{walked}\end{array}}$ on the flowers.

(tramps   tramped   tramping)

tramp

tramp

tramp

We catch mice and rats in traps.

(traps)

trap

trap

trap

We like to $\boxed{\begin{array}{l}\underline{\text{travel.}}\\ \text{go from place to place.}\end{array}}$

We $\boxed{\begin{array}{c}\underline{\text{travel}}\\ \text{go}\end{array}}$ in our autos.

Some people travel on the train.

(travels   traveled   traveling)

travel

trav-el

travel

travel

A traveler is a person
 who goes from place to place.

(travelers)

traveler

trav-el-er

traveler

traveler

T
U
V
W
X
Y
Z

tray
tray
tray
	This is a <u>tray</u>.
	When I was sick,
	   Mother brought me my dinner
	   on a <u>tray</u>.
	                 (trays)

treat
treat
tr<u>ea</u>t
	The children
	    <u>treat</u> mother kindly.
	    act kindly toward mother.
	
	Bob <u>treated</u> Tom to
	       gave Tom
	   an ice cream cone.
	   (treats treated treating)

tree
tree
tr<u>ee</u>
	This is a <u>tree</u>.
	Most <u>trees</u> lose their leaves
	    in the winter.
	The pine <u>tree</u> is green
	   all the time.
	             (trees)

tremble
trem-ble
tremble
tremb<u>le</u>₄
	The dog was so cold that
	   he <u>trembled</u>.
	       shook all over.
	   (trembles trembled trembling)

T
U
V
W
X
Y
Z

Father is giving his new car a ⬚trial / try out⬚ to see how it runs. The teacher gave Bill another ⬚trial. / chance.⬚ (trials)	trial tri-al *trial* tri͟al
The Indian was the chief of his ⬚tribe. / group.⬚ (tribes)	tribe *tribe* tri͟b͟e
Bob's dog can stand up and beg. He can do other <u>tricks,</u> too. (tricks)	trick *trick* tri͟ck
  A <u>tricycle</u> has three wheels. Can you ride a <u>tricycle?</u> (tricycles)	tricycle tri-cy-cle *tricycle* tri͟cycl͟e₄
Baby fell into the water. I <u>tried</u> to get her out. (try tries trying)	tried *tried* tri͟e̅d

T
U
V
W
X
Y
Z

trim *trim* trim	See the children <u>trim</u> the Christmas tree. They are putting colored balls on it. Mary's new dress is <u>trimmed</u> with buttons. (trims trimmed trimming)
trip *trip* trip	Baby $\boxed{\begin{array}{l}\text{tripped}\\ \hline \text{caught her foot on something}\end{array}}$ and nearly fell. Be careful not to <u>trip</u> on the rug. We went for a long $\boxed{\begin{array}{l}\text{trip}\\ \hline \text{journey}\end{array}}$ in the car. (trips tripped tripping)
trouble trou-ble *trouble* trouble	It isn't any $\boxed{\begin{array}{l}\text{trouble}\\ \hline \text{extra work}\end{array}}$ to stop for you. Bad boys get into <u>trouble</u>. Some children make <u>trouble</u> for their mother. (troubles troubled troubling)
trousers trou-sers *trousers* trousers	This is a pair of men's $\boxed{\begin{array}{l}\text{trousers.}\\ \hline \text{pants.}\end{array}}$

T
U
V
W
X
Y
Z

This is a big <u>truck</u>. **Trucks** carry heavy loads. (trucks)	truck *truck* tru<u>ck</u>
The story is not | true. correct. | (truer truest truly)	true *true* tru<u>e</u>
  We put our clothes Elephants have in the <u>trunk</u>. long <u>trunks</u>. (trunks)	trunk *trunk* trunk
I | trust believe | Bob, because he tells the truth. (trusts trusted trusting)	trust *trust* trust
Tom told | the <u>truth</u>. what was right. | It pays to tell the <u>truth</u>. (truthful truthfully)	truth *truth* tr<u>ut</u>h

T
U
V
W
X
Y
Z

413

try *try* tr̶y	If you │ **try** hard / do your best │ you will get the picture finished. (tries tried trying)
tub *tub* tu b	 Mother put the clothes in the <u>tub</u>. (tubs)
tube *tube* t<u>u</u>b<u>e</u>	This is a <u>tube</u> of tooth paste. We drink lemonade through a <u>tube</u>. (tubes)
Tuesday Tues-day *Tuesday* Tu<u>e</u>šday	The third day of the week is <u>Tuesday</u>.
tulip tu-lip *tulip* t<u>u</u>lip	These flowers are <u>tulips</u>. They are of many bright colors. (tulips)

T
U
V
W
X
Y
Z

Clowns $\boxed{\begin{array}{c}\text{tumble}\\\hline\text{roll}\end{array}}$ on the grass. The baby $\boxed{\begin{array}{c}\text{tumbled}\\\hline\text{fell}\end{array}}$ off the bed. <div align="center">(tumbles tumbled tumbling)</div>	<div align="right">tumble tum-ble</div> *tumble* tumble₄
This is a glass <u>tumbler</u>. We drink from a <u>tumbler</u>. <div align="center">(tumblers)</div>	<div align="right">tumbler tum-bler</div> *tumbler* tumbler
Men dig $\boxed{\begin{array}{c}\text{tunnels}\\\hline\text{roadways}\end{array}}$ through hills. Trains can go through <u>tunnels</u>. <div align="center">(tunnels)</div>	<div align="right">tunnel tun-nel</div> *tunnel* tunnel
<div align="right">This is a <u>turkey</u>. <u>Turkeys</u> are good to eat. (turkeys)</div>	<div align="right">turkey tur-key</div> *turkey* t<u>ur</u>ke<u>y</u>

We can't all get
   a drink at once.
 	
We wait our <u>turn</u>.
 	
     The car <u>turned</u>
     the corner.
<div align="center">(turns   turned   turning)</div>
	<div align="right">turn</div>
	turn
	t<u>ur</u>n

T
U
V
W
X
Y
Z

turnip tur-nip *turnip* t<u>ur</u>nip	This is a <u>turnip</u>. <u>Turnips</u> grow in the ground. <u>Turnips</u> are good to eat. (turnips)
turtle tur-tle *turtle* t<u>ur</u>tl<u>e</u>₄	This is a <u>turtle</u>. He has a shell on his back. He swims in the water. (turtles)
tusks *tusks* tusks	The elephant has two ⎰ tusks. ⎱ ⎰ outside teeth. ⎱ (tusk)
twelve *twelve* twel<u>ve</u>₂	☆☆☆☆☆☆☆☆☆☆☆☆ Here are <u>twelve</u> stars. Count them. (twelfth)
twenty twen-ty *twenty* twenty	1 2 3 4 5 6 7 8 9 10 11 12 13 14 15 16 17 18 19 20 These are the numbers from one to ⎰ twenty. ⎱ ⎰ 20. ⎱
twice *twice* tw<u>ice</u>	Mother called Mary ⎰ twice. ⎱ ⎰ two times. ⎱

T
U
V
W
X
Y
Z

The boys gathered	**twig**
twigs small branches from trees	*twig*
to make a fire.	twig
(twigs)	

These boys are **twins.** They are brothers. They were born on the same day. (twins)	**twin**
	twin
	twin

See the stars **twinkle.** Sometimes they are very bright and sometimes they are not. (twinkled twinkles twinkling)	**twinkle** twin-kle
	twinkle
	twinkle

These wires are twisted / wound together. (twists twisted twisting)	**twist**
	twist
	twist

How many stars do you see? I see **two** stars. (two's)	**two**
	two
	two

This is a **typewriter.** We write on a **typewriter.** (typewriters)	**typewriter** type-writ-er
	typewriter
	typewriter

T
U
V
W
X
Y
Z

417

U u   *U u* U u

ugly
ug-ly
 	
ugly
ugly
	The witch that the fairy saw
	
	was ┌─────────────────┐
	     │ ugly. │
	     │ not nice to look at. │
	     └─────────────────┘
	
	Our teacher read the story
	   about "The Ugly Duckling."
	
	(uglier ugliest)

umbrella
um-brel-la
 	
umbrella
umbrella
	Mary has
	   a big umbrella.
	It keeps the rain
	   off Mary.
	
	(umbrellas)

uncle un-cle *uncle* uncle	The man is father's brother. He is my uncle. (uncles)
under un-der *under* under	 The dish is on the table. The shoes are under the table.

The shoes are [underneath / under] the table.	underneath un-der-neath *underneath* und<u>er</u>n<u>ea</u>th
Baby does not talk plainly. It is hard to <u>understand</u> her. I don't [understand / know] how to spell. I do not [<u>understand</u> you. / know what you mean.] (understands understood) (understanding)	understand un-der-stand *understand* und<u>er</u>stand
We wear [underwear / underclothes] to keep us warm.	underwear un-der-wear *underwear* und<u>er</u>w<u>ea</u>r
Mother will [<u>undress</u> the baby. / take <u>off</u> the baby's clothes.] (undresses undressed undressing)	undress un-dress *undress* undress

U
W
X
Y
Z

unfold un-fold *unfold* (cursive) unf<u>o</u>ld	Mary [**unfolded** / opened out] her handkerchief and put it in her pocket. (unfolds unfolded unfolding)
unhappy un-hap-py *unhappy* (cursive) unhappy	When Tom is bad, mother is [**unhappy.** / sad.] (unhappily)
United States U-nit-ed States *United States* (cursive) <u>U</u>nit<u>e</u>d St<u>a</u>tes	We are Americans. We live in the <u>United States</u>.
unkind un-kind *unkind* (cursive) unk<u>i</u>nd	Some boys are [**unkind** / not kind] to their dogs.
unknown un-known *unknown* (cursive) unkn<u>ow</u>n	The name of the man is [**unknown.** / **not known.**]
unless un-less *unless* (cursive) unless	You cannot go <u>unless</u> you get your work done.

U
V
W
X
Y
Z

Mary tied her ribbon in a hard knot. She pulled one end of the ribbon but could not <u>untie</u> the bow. (unties untying untied)	untie un-tie *untie* unti͟e
Bob came for me. I could not go <u>until</u> I washed my face and hands.	until un-til *until* until
One kite is high $\boxed{\begin{array}{c}\text{up}\\\hline\text{above}\end{array}}$ in the sky. The other is down on the ground.	up *up* up
Mother set the dish $\boxed{\begin{array}{c}\text{upon}\\\hline\text{on}\end{array}}$ the table.	upon up-on *upon* upon
Write your name in the $\boxed{\begin{array}{c}\text{upper}\\\hline\text{higher}\end{array}}$ right corner of the paper.	upper up-per *upper* upp͟er

U
V
W
X
Y
Z

upstairs up-stairs *upstairs* upst<u>ai</u>rs	I go $\boxed{\dfrac{\text{upstairs}}{\text{up the stairs}}}$ to bed. The <u>upstairs</u> is the higher part of the house.
upward up-ward *upward* upw<u>ar</u>d	The children looked $\boxed{\dfrac{\text{upward.}}{\text{above.}}}$
us *us* us	We are going to the party. Will you go with <u>us</u>?
use *use* <u>u</u><u>s</u><u>e</u>	Mary did not have a book. "You may <u>use</u> mine," said Bob. (uses using used)
useful use-ful *useful* <u>us</u>eful	A hammer $\boxed{\begin{array}{l}\text{is } \underline{\text{useful.}}\\ \text{can be used for many things.}\end{array}}$

U
V
W
X
Y
Z

V v

When school is out, we are going to have [a vacation. / time for play and rest.] (vacations)	vacation va-ca-tion *vacation* vacation
This is a <u>valentine</u>. St. Valentine's Day is on February 14. (valentines)	valentine val-en-tine *valentine* valentine
Mother's diamond ring is [valuable. / worth much money.]	valuable val-u-a-ble *valuable* valuable
What is the [value / price] of mother's ring? How much is it worth? (values valued valuing)	value val-ue *value* value
This is a moving <u>van</u>. Men move furniture in moving <u>vans</u>. (vans)	van *van* van

V
W
X
Y
Z

423

vase *vase* v<u>a</u><u>s</u><u>e</u>	 The flowers are in a <u>vase</u>. (vases)
vegetable veg-e-ta-ble *vegetable* veg<u>e</u>t<u>a</u>ble₄	 Corn, potatoes, cabbage and carrots are <u>vegetables</u>. We eat <u>vegetables</u> to keep us well. Do you know other <u>vegetables</u>? (vegetables)
velvet vel-vet *velvet* velvet	<u>Velvet</u> is a soft silk cloth. Dresses are made of <u>velvet</u>.
verse *verse* v<u>e</u>rs<u>e</u>₅	Bob knows only one $\boxed{\dfrac{\text{verse}}{\text{line}}}$ of the poem. (verses)
very ver-y *very* vĕry	It is a <u>very</u> warm day. Dick is a <u>very</u> small boy.

V
W
X
Y
Z

A <u>vest</u> has no sleeves. Father wears a <u>vest</u> under his coat. (vests)	vest *vest* vest
We saw a beautiful $\boxed{\begin{array}{c}\text{view}\\\hline\text{scene}\end{array}}$ of the river. We $\boxed{\begin{array}{c}\text{viewed}\\\hline\text{saw}\end{array}}$ the river from the train. (views viewed viewing)	view *view* vi͞ew
A <u>village</u> is a small group of houses. Towns are bigger than <u>villages.</u> (villages)	village vil-lage *village* villa͟g͟e͟
A <u>vine</u> is a plant that climbs or crawls. Watermelons grow on <u>vines.</u> Grapes grow on a <u>vine,</u> too. (vines)	vine *vine* vi͟n͟e͟
Mother puts <u>vinegar</u> on pickles. <u>Vinegar</u> makes the pickles sour.	vinegar vin-e-gar *vinegar* vin͟e͟g͟a͟r͟

V
W
X
Y
Z

violet vi-o-let *violet* v<u>io</u>let	This flower is a <u>violet</u>. <u>Violets</u> are purple, yellow or white. (violets)
violin vi-o-lin *violin* v<u>io</u>lin	This is a <u>violin</u>. I like the music of a <u>violin</u>. (violins)
visit vis-it *visit* višit	We are going $\boxed{\begin{array}{c} \text{to } \underline{\text{visit}} \\ \text{to see} \end{array}}$ our aunt. (visits visiting visited)
visitor vis-i-tor *visitor* višit<u>or</u>	Several $\boxed{\begin{array}{c} \underline{\text{visitors}} \\ \text{people} \end{array}}$ came to see us. (visitors)

voice
voice
v<u>oi</u>c<u>e</u>₃
	When you talk or sing,
	    a sound comes through your
	    mouth.
	This sound is your <u>voice</u>.
	(voices)

V
W
X
Y
Z

I wanted Bob for our captain. I <u>voted</u> for him. Bob had fifteen <u>votes</u>. (votes voted voting)	vote *vote* v<u>o</u>t<u>e</u>
Father and mother are going on a long │voyage. │trip across the sea. They are going on a big boat. (voyages)	voyage voy-age *voyage* v<u>o</u>y<u>a</u>g<u>e</u>

V
W
X
Y
Z

Ww *Ww*Ww

wade *wade* wa<u>d</u><u>e</u>	 See these children |<u>wade</u> / walk| in the water. (wades waded wading)
wag *wag* wag	My dog likes me. See him |<u>wag</u> his tail. / move his tail from side to side.| (wags wagged wagging)
wages wag-es *wages* wa<u>g</u>e<u>s</u>	Father's |<u>wages</u> are / pay is| $25.00 a week. We work to earn our |wages. / money.|
wagon wag-on *wagon* wagon	This is Bob's <u>wagon</u>. He will take the baby for a ride in his <u>wagon</u>. (wagons)

W
X
Y
Z

This is Bob's [waist. / shirt.] Bob put his belt around his <u>waist</u>. (waists)	waist *waist* w<u>ai</u>st
The door was not open. I had to <u>wait</u> for someone to open it. The groceryman said, "May I [wait on / serve] you?" (waits waited waiting)	wait *wait* w<u>ai</u>t
This man is a <u>waiter</u>. He waits on us. He puts food on the table for us to eat. (waiters)	waiter wait-er *waiter* w<u>ai</u>t<u>er</u>
Little Boy Blue is fast asleep. Will you <u>wake</u> him? (wakes waking waked woke)	wake *wake* w<u>a</u>k<u>e</u>

W
X
Y
Z

walk *walk* wålk	I do not like to run,
	   but I like to <u>walk</u>.
	
	Will you <u>walk</u> with me?
	
	Do not play in the street.
	
	Play on the side<u>walk</u>.
	
	         (walks walked walking)

wall *wall* wåll	Mother hung the picture
	   on the <u>wall</u>.
	
	           (walls)

wallpaper
wall-pa-per
wallpaper
wållpaper
	The man
	   put the <u>wallpaper</u>
	   on the wall.

walnut wal-nut *walnut* wålnut	<u>Walnuts</u> grow on trees. They are good to eat. Furniture is made from <u>walnut</u> trees. (walnuts)

W
X
Y
Z

	walrus
This animal is a <u>walrus</u>. He lives in the water. See his long tusks. His skin is made into leather.	wal-rus *walrus* wắlrus

	wander
Bob and his dog like to ┌─────────────┐ │ <u>wander</u> │ through the woods. │ walk slowly │ └─────────────┘ (wanders wandered wandering)	wan-der *wander* wắnd<u>er</u>

	want
Baby saw Tom's cookies. She <u>wanted</u> some, too. ┌──────────────────┐ I │ <u>want</u> │ one, too. │ should like to have │ └──────────────────┘ (wants wanted wanting)	*want* wặnt

	war
The soldiers went to <u>war</u> to fight for their country. (wars)	*war* w<u>ar</u>

W

X

Y

Z

warm *warm* w**a**rm	The sun makes us <u>warm.</u> The snow makes us cold. (warmer warmest)
warned *warned* w**a**rn**e**d	Before we started to school, mother <u>warned</u> us about told us of the danger of crossing the street when the light was red. (warns warn warning)
was *was* w**a**s	There <u>was</u> an old woman, Who lived in a shoe. It <u>was</u> raining when I came home.
washboard wash-board *washboard* w**a**<u>sh</u>b**oa**rd	This is a <u>washboard.</u> You rub clothes on a <u>washboard</u> to get them clean. (washboards)

W
X
Y
Z

This is a <u>washbowl</u>.

We wash our hands
   in the <u>washbowl</u>.

(washbowls)

washbowl

wash-bowl

washbowl

wȧ<u>sh</u>b<u>ow</u>l

Mary is
   <u>washing</u> her face.

Mary likes
   to <u>wash</u> her face.

Mother <u>washes</u> our clothes
   on Monday.

(wash   washes   washed)

washing

wash-ing

washing

wȧ<u>sh</u>ing

washing machine

wash-ing ma-chine

washing machine

wȧ<u>sh</u>ing ma<u>ch</u>ine

This is a <u>washing machine</u>.

We wash clothes
   in a <u>washing machine</u>.

(washing machines)

This is a picture
   of George <u>Washington</u>.

He was the first president
   of the United States.

Washington

Wash-ing-ton

Washington

Wȧ<u>sh</u>ington

W

X

Y

Z

wasn't *wasnt* wȧ̇s̆n't	It $\boxed{\begin{array}{c}\text{wasn't}\\ \hline \text{was not}\end{array}}$ very warm today.
wasp *wasp* wȧsp	This is a <u>wasp</u>. It stings like a bee. (wasps)
waste *waste* wa̲s̲t̲e̲	 We put paper that has been used in the <u>waste</u> basket. The boy $\boxed{\begin{array}{l}\underline{\text{wastes}}\text{ his paste.}\\ \text{uses more paste than he needs.}\end{array}}$ (wastes wasted wasting wasteful)
watch *watch* wȧt̲c̲h̲	This is grandpa's <u>watch</u>. He will tell you what time it is by his <u>watch</u>. Mary likes to $\boxed{\begin{array}{c}\text{watch}\\ \hline \text{look after}\end{array}}$ the baby. (watches watched watching)

W
X
Y
Z

We drink <u>water</u>.

Mother filled the pitcher
  with <u>water</u>.

Bob | watered / put water on | the flowers.

Boats sail on <u>water</u>.

(waters   watered   watering)

water
wa-ter
water
wa<u>te</u>r

The <u>water</u> <u>lily</u> grows in the water.

Its flat leaves float on the top
  of the water.

(water lilies)

water lily
wa-ter lil-y
water lily
wa<u>te</u>r lily

This is a <u>watermelon</u>.

It is red inside and
  green outside.

<u>Watermelons</u> grow on a vine.

The vine is on the ground.

<u>Watermelons</u> are good to eat.

(watermelons)

watermelon
wa-ter-mel-on
watermelon
wa<u>te</u>rmelon

W

X

Y

Z

435

wave
wave
w<u>a</u>v<u>e</u>
	Mother has a <u>wave</u>
	   in her hair.
	
	See father <u>wave</u> his hand
	   at the children.
	
	We sat by the lake and
	   watched the <u>waves</u> in the water.
	
	   (waves waved waving)

wax *wax* wax	Some candles are made of <u>wax</u>. Father	waxed put wax on	the floors. It made them smooth.

way
way
w<u>ay</u>
	Mary did not know
	   which <u>way</u> to go.
	
	Bob said,
	
	   "I will show you the
		<u>way</u>."
		road."
			
			   (ways)

we *we* w<u>e</u>		We You and I	will go. | We The children and I	will go.

Grandmother has been sick. She is ⎡**weak**⎤ yet. 　　　⎣not strong⎦ 　　　(weaker　weakest)	weak *weak* w<u>ea</u>k
Betty put on her new dress. She likes to <u>wear</u> her new dress. (wears　wore　worn　wearing)	wear *wear* wĕăr
We played so hard that we were ⎡**weary.**⎤ 　　　　　　⎣tired.⎦	weary wea-ry *weary* w<u>ea</u>ry
Sometimes it is warm and 　sometimes it is cold. I like warm <u>weather</u> best. I do not like rainy <u>weather</u>. I like sunshiny <u>weather</u>.	weather weath-er *weather* w<u>ĕă</u>th<u>er</u>
This Indian is <u>weaving</u> a rug. She goes under and over, 　under and over each thread. (weaves　wove　weaving)	weave *weave* w<u>ea</u>v<u>e</u>

W
X
Y
Z

web	
web web	 This is a spider's <u>web</u>. The spider spins his own <u>web</u>. He catches flies in his <u>web</u>. <center>(webs)</center>
webbed *webbed* webb<u>ĕd</u>	The feet of a goose are <u>webbed</u>. The toes are fastened together with a web. <u>Webbed</u> feet help geese to swim.
wed *wed* wed	Father and mother were ⎧ wed ⎫ ⎩ married ⎭ a long time ago.
Wednesday Wednes-day *Wednesday* Wednesd<u>a</u>y	The fourth day of the week is <u>Wednesday</u>. Monday, Tuesday, <u>Wednesday</u>. 2nd day, 3rd day, 4th day.
wee *wee* w<u>ee</u>	I have a ⎧ wee ⎫ kitten. ⎩ very little ⎭

W
X
Y
Z

Some plants grow where they are not wanted.	weed
These plants are <u>weeds</u>.	*weed*
Dandelions are <u>weeds</u>.	w<u>ee</u>d
(weeds)	

There are seven days in a <u>week</u>.	week
Monday, Tuesday, Wednesday, Thursday, Friday, Saturday, and Sunday are the days of the <u>week</u>.	*week*
	w<u>ee</u>k
(weeks)	

Mary broke her doll.	weep
She started to <u>weep</u>. / cry.	*weep*
	w<u>ee</u>p
(weeps wept weeping)	

Bob is seeing	weighs
how much he <u>weighs</u>. / heavy he is.	*weighs*
He <u>weighs</u> 40 pounds.	w<u>eigh</u>s
(weigh weighed weighing)	

W
X
Y
Z

welcome wel-come *welcome* welcome	Mary thanked Bob for the book. Bob said, "You are <u>welcome</u>." We are <u>welcome</u> at grandma's. She is always glad to see us. (welcomes welcomed welcoming)

well
well
well
	I am not sick.
	I am <u>well</u>.
	The farmer can get
	    water from the <u>well</u>.
	A <u>well</u> is a deep hole
	    in the ground
	    with good water in it.

we'll *we'll* we'll	We'll / We will play with you.
went *went* went	I go to school. One day I was sick. I <u>went</u> home early.

W
X
Y
Z

Mary [wept / cried] when she broke her doll. (weep weeps weeping)	wept *wept* wept
The ponies <u>were</u> afraid to go over the bridge yesterday.	were *were* w<u>ere</u>$_s$
[We're / We are] making a kite.	we're *we're* w<u>e're</u>$_s$
The sun comes up in the east. The sun goes down in the <u>west</u>. (western)	west *west* west
Water makes the grass <u>wet</u>. The sunshine makes the grass dry. (wets wetting)	wet *wet* wet
   This big animal is a whale. He lives in the sea. (whales)	whale *whale* <u>whale</u>

W
X
Y
Z

what *what* <u>wh</u>å<u>t</u>	There was an old woman Who lived in a shoe. She had so many children She didn't know <u>what</u> to do. <u>What</u> are you making?
what's *what's* <u>wh</u>å<u>t's</u>	My name is John. $\boxed{\begin{array}{c} \underline{\text{What's}} \\ \text{What is} \end{array}}$ your name?
wheat *wheat* <u>wh</u>e<u>at</u>	This is <u>wheat.</u> Wheat is a grain. We make flour from <u>wheat.</u> Bread is made from flour.
wheel *wheel* <u>wh</u>e<u>el</u>	The <u>wheel</u> is round. The <u>wheel</u> has spokes to make it strong. (wheels)

W
X
Y
Z

wheelbarrow

wheel-bar-row

wheelbarrow

wheelbárrow

The farmer can carry corn
for his pigs in a <u>wheelbarrow</u>.

(wheelbarrows)

We are going for a ride

when
at the time

father comes home.

when

when

when

We will come

whenever
any time

you want us to come.

whenever

when-ev-er

whenever

whenever

Bob saw Tom.

He asked,

"Where
"To what place

are you going, Tom?"

where

where

whéres

I will go with you

wherever
any place

you go.

wherever

wher-ev-er

wherever

whérever

W
X
Y
Z

whether wheth-er *whether* <u>whether</u>	Bob doesn't know <u>whether</u> he can go or not. <u>Whether</u> it rains or snows, we must go to school.
which *which* <u>which</u>	I want this apple. <u>Which</u> one do you want?
while *while* <u>while</u>	I will read $\boxed{\begin{array}{c}\text{while}\\\hline\text{at the time}\end{array}}$ you write.
whine *whine* <u>whine</u>	Bob would not let his dog into the house. The dog started to $\boxed{\begin{array}{c}\text{whine.}\\\hline\text{cry\ softly.}\end{array}}$ (whines whined whining)
whip *whip* <u>whip</u>	Grandfather is good to his horses. He does not $\boxed{\begin{array}{c}\text{whip}\\\hline\text{hit}\end{array}}$ them. I like <u>whipped</u> cream on jello. <u>Whipped</u> cream is white and fluffy. (whips whipped whipping)

W
X
Y
Z

444

Father is shaving off his <u>whiskers.</u>
 	
Whiskers are stiff hairs
   that grow on a man's face.
 	
Our cat has <u>whiskers.</u>
 	
     (whiskers)
	whisker
	whisk-er
	whisker
	<u>wh</u>is<u>ker</u>

Baby likes to ⌐whisper⌐
              └speak in a low voice┘
 	
  in mother's ear.
 	
I like to talk out loud.
 	
(whispers whispered whispering)
	whisper
	whis-per
	whisper
	<u>wh</u>is<u>per</u>

 This is a <u>whistle.</u>
    The <u>whistle</u> makes a
      noise when you blow
      through it.
 	
Bob can <u>whistle</u> through his lips.
 	
(whistles whistled whistling)
	whistle
	whis-tle
	whistle
	<u>wh</u>is<u>tle</u>

Coal is black. The snowman is <u>white.</u>	white *white* <u>wh</u>i<u>te</u>

who	There was an old woman
who	Who lived in a shoe.
wh**o**̇̈	Who is ringing the door bell?

whole	
whole	This is $\begin{array}{l} \text{a } \underline{\text{whole}} \text{ apple.} \\ \text{all of the apple.} \end{array}$
wh**o**l**e**	This $\begin{array}{l} \text{is not a } \underline{\text{whole}} \\ \text{is part of an} \end{array}$ apple.

whooping cough	Tom could not go to school.
whoop-ing cough	He had whooping cough.
whooping cough	He coughs very hard.
wh**oo**pi**ng** co**u**gh	The other children might get it if he went to school.

whose	The black hat is mine.
whose	Whose hat is this one?
wh**o**̇̈**se**ₛ	To whom does this one belong?

Jack did not come to school Monday. The teacher asked, | "Why did you "What is the reason you did | not come, Jack?"	why *why* w<u>h</u>y

Wicked people do bad things. It is wicked to steal.	wicked wick-ed *wicked* wi<u>ck</u>ed

One book will not go into the box. The book is too wide. (wider widest)	wide *wide* w<u>ide</u>

The farmer makes the garden. The farmer's wife washes the dishes. Father is the husband. Mother is the wife. (wives)	wife *wife* w<u>ife</u>

W
X
Y
Z

wig *wig* wig	This is a <u>wig</u> of long curly hair. Mary is going to wear it in the play. (wigs)
wigwam wig-wam *wigwam* wigwăm	 This is the Indian's | <u>wigwam</u>. | tent. | The Indian lives in a <u>wigwăm</u>. (wigwams)
wild *wild* w<u>i</u>ld	The dog is a tame animal. The lion is | a <u>wild</u> | not a tame | animal. (wilder wildest)
will *will* will	He <u>will</u> be ready when you come. He <u>will</u> see you after school.
willing will-ing *willing* willin<u>g</u>	The boy was | willing | ready and wanted | to work.

W
X
Y
Z

448

win

win

win

The boys ran a race to the fence.

Bob did not [win the race. / get to the fence first.]

(wins winning won)

---

wind

wind

wind

The wind is blowing the flag.

I closed the window
to keep out the cold wind.

(winds windy)

---

wind

wind

wind

See grandma [wind / turn] the yarn into a ball.

(winds winding wound)

---

windmill

wind-mill

windmill

windmill

The farmer has a windmill to pump water for his horses.

This is a windmill you would see in Holland.

The wind makes the windmill pump the water.

(windmills)

W

X

Y

Z

window win-dow *window* wind**o͞w**²	The glass in this <u>window</u> is broken. Put up your <u>windows</u> at night to let in the air. (windows)
window sill win-dow sill *window sill* wind**o͞w**² sill	The flower stands on the |<u>window</u> <u>sill</u>. |<u>bottom</u> of the window. (window sills)
wing *wing* wi**ng**	The bird has two <u>wings</u>. He flies with his <u>wings</u>. The airplane has two <u>wings</u>. (wings)
winter win-ter *winter* wint**er**	In summer it is warm. In <u>winter</u> it is cold. It snows in <u>winter</u>. (winters)

W
x
y
z

See the boy <u>wipe</u> his face dry with a towel. (wipes wiped wiping)	**wipe** *wipe* wipe
This is a <u>wire</u> fence. The telephone <u>wires</u> are fastened to the poles. (wires)	**wire** *wire* wire
The man is very <u>wise.</u> / smart. (wiser wisest)	**wise** *wise* wise
The fairy told the old man to make a <u>wish.</u> / to ask for what he wanted most. I <u>wish</u> you / hope you have a Merry Christmas. (wishes wished wishing)	**wish** *wish* wish

W
X
Y
Z

witch *witch* wi<u>tch</u>	This is the <u>witch</u> the fairy told us about. <div align="center">(witches)</div>
with *with* wi<u>th</u>	This is a boy $\boxed{\begin{array}{c}\text{with}\\\hline\text{by the side of}\end{array}}$ his cat. We live <u>with</u> our father and mother.
within with-in *within* wi<u>th</u>in	Father will be there $\boxed{\begin{array}{c}\text{within}\\\hline\text{sometime in}\end{array}}$ the next hour.
without with-out *without* wi<u>th</u><u>ou</u>t	This is a pan $\boxed{\begin{array}{c}\text{without}\\\hline\text{with no}\end{array}}$ handles.
woke *woke* w<u>o</u>k<u>e</u>	Baby was asleep. She <u>woke</u> up when the bell rang. <div align="center">(wake wakes waking)</div>

W
X
Y
Z

The <u>wolf</u> looks like a dog. He eats the farmer's lambs. (wolves)	wolf *wolf* w<u>o</u>lf
This is a <u>woman</u>. This is a man. (women)	woman **wom-an** *woman* w<u>o</u>man
Here are two <u>women</u>. (woman)	women **wom-en** *women* w<u>o</u>men
The boys ran a race to the fence. Bob <u>won</u> the race. got to the fence first. (win wins winning)	won *won* won
I <u>won't</u> / will not be here long.	won't *won't* w<u>o</u>n't
Furniture is made of <u>wood</u>. Some houses are made of <u>wood</u>. The woodman cuts down the trees in the <u>woods</u>. This is the <u>woods</u> where trees and flowers grow. (woods)	wood *wood* w<u>oo</u>d

W
X
Y
Z

453

woodcutter wood-cut-ter *woodcutter* w**oo**dcutt**er**	A <u>woodcutter</u> is a man who cuts down trees. (woodcutters)
wooden wood-en *wooden* w**oo**den	Baby plays with a $\boxed{\begin{array}{l}\underline{\text{wooden}}\text{ doll.}\\\text{doll made of wood.}\end{array}}$
woodman wood-man *woodman* w**oo**dman	This man cuts down trees in the woods. He is a <u>woodman.</u> (woodmen)
woodpecker wood-peck-er *woodpecker* w**oo**dpe**ck**e**r**	This bird is a <u>woodpecker.</u> He has a red head. His tail helps him in climbing. His bill is strong. He picks through the bark of the tree to get bugs to eat. (woodpeckers)
wool *wool* w**oo**l	We get $\boxed{\begin{array}{l}\underline{\text{wool}}\\\text{short soft hair}\end{array}}$ from sheep. Sheep's <u>wool</u> is made into yarn and cloth. (woolen woolly)

dog　ran　shop　cat These are <u>words.</u> Baby cannot say the <u>word</u> dog. 　　　(words)	word *word* w<u>or</u>d
I put on my blue dress yesterday. I <u>wore</u> it all day. 　(wear　wears　wearing)	wore *wore* w<u>ore</u>_s
I like to play. I do not like to <u>work.</u> Father <u>works</u> in a store. Mother does the <u>work</u> 　about the house. 　(works　worked　working)	work *work* w<u>or</u>k
 This is father's <u>workbench.</u> He keeps his tools on the 　<u>workbench.</u> 　　(workbenches)	workbench work-bench *workbench* w<u>or</u>kben<u>ch</u>
This is the picture 　of the | world. 　　　　 earth. | 　　(worlds)	world *world* w<u>or</u>ld

W
X
Y
Z

worm *worm* w<u>o</u>rm	This is a <u>worm</u>. Birds eat <u>worms</u>. (worms)
worn *worn* w<u>o</u>rn	Mary likes to wear her pink dress. She has <u>worn</u> it two times. (wear wears wore wearing)
worse *worse* w<u>o</u>rs<u>e</u>s	Bill is sick. He is \[worse / not so well \] today. I write \[worse / more poorly \] than Bob does.
worst *worst* w<u>o</u>rst	Jim is a bad boy, but Henry is the <u>worst</u> boy in school.
worth *worth* w<u>o</u>r<u>th</u>	I cannot sell you my marbles. I do not know how much money they are <u>worth</u>.
would *would* w<u>ou</u>ld	I am going to school. <u>Would</u> you like to go, too?
wouldn't *wouldn't* w<u>ou</u>ldn't	Jack \[wouldn't / would not \] drink milk.

W
x
y
z

Grandma <u>wound</u> the yarn into a ball. Grandpa <u>wound</u> the clock so it would run. (wind winds winding)	wound *wound* w<u>ou</u>nd
Mother will | <u>wrap</u> up / put a paper around | my lunch for me. (wraps wrapped wrapping)	wrap *wrap* <u>wr</u>ap
The teacher made a <u>wreath</u> of flowers to put on Mary's head. (wreaths)	wreath *wreath* <u>wr</u>ea<u>th</u>
The <u>wren</u> is a very small bird. The <u>wren</u> has a sweet song. <u>Wrens</u> build nests in bushes or birdhouses that children build for them. (wrens)	wren *wren* <u>wr</u>en

W
X
Y
Z

wrench *wrench* wre̱nc̱h	This tool is a <u>wrench</u>. Father uses a <u>wrench</u> when he changes a tire on the car. (wrenches) 
wringer wring-er *wringer* wri̱nge̱r	Mother puts the clothes through the <u>wringer</u> to get the water out of them. (wringers)
write *write* wri̱te̲	 See Mary <u>write</u> on the blackboard. She <u>writes</u> with her right hand. (writes writing wrote written)
wrong *wrong* wro̱ng	Mary spelled three words right and two <table><tr><td>wrong.</td></tr><tr><td>not right.</td></tr></table>
wrote *wrote* wro̱te̲	Mary <u>wrote</u> her name on the blackboard. (write writes writing)

<u>Xmas</u> means the same as
   Christmas.

Xmas
Xmas
X̲mås

This is a <u>xylophone</u>.

It makes sweet music.

You play on a <u>xylophone</u>
   with hammers.

(xylophones)

xylophone
xy-lo-phone
xylophone
x̲y̲l̲o̲p̲h̲o̲n̲e̲

X

Y

Z

Y y

yard
yard
y<u>a</u>rd

The children do not play
 in the street.

They play

 in the | yard.
 | place around the house.

Mother bought a <u>yard</u> of ribbon.

A <u>yard</u> is 36 inches or 3 feet.

(yards)

yarn
yarn
y<u>a</u>rn

Sweaters are made of <u>yarn.</u>

Mother made baby's bonnet of <u>yarn.</u>

<u>Yarn</u> is like a heavy thread.

Woolen <u>yarn</u> is warm.

yawn
yawn
y<u>aw</u>n

When baby is sleepy

 she <u>yawns.</u>
 she opens her mouth wide.

When I am sleepy I <u>yawn,</u> too.

(yawns   yawning   yawned)

Y
z

How old are you? "I am six <u>years</u> old," said Betty. <div align="center">(years)</div>	<div align="right">year</div> *year* y<u>e</u>ar
The boys <u>yell</u> | cry out when their team wins. <div align="center">(yells yelled yelling)</div>	<div align="right">yell</div> *yell* yell
Dandelions are <u>yellow</u>. Butter is <u>yellow</u>. Lemons are <u>yellow</u>. (yellowish)	yellow yel-low *yellow* yell<u>o</u>w
I wanted to go. Mother said, "<u>Yes,</u> you may go."	yes *yes* yes
Today is Monday. Yesterday | The day before today was Sunday.	yesterday yes-ter-day *yesterday* yest<u>e</u>rd<u>a</u>y
Father has not come home yet. | as soon as now.	yet *yet* yet

Y

Z

yolk
 	
yolk
yo̲l̲k
	The yellow part of the egg
	   is the <u>yolk.</u>
	
	      (yolks)

you *you* yo̲u	Mother was going for a ride. "I want to go with <u>you,</u>" said Fred. The pencil does not belong to me. It belongs to <u>you.</u>
young *young* yo̲u̲ng	This is a <u>young</u> man. He is 18 years old. This is an old man. He is 80 years old. (younger youngest)
your *your* yo̲u̲r	This is my ball. Is that <u>your</u> ball? (yours)
you're *you're* yo̲u̲r̲e̲,	You're / You are a big boy now.

Is this ball <u>yours</u>?
Does this ball belong to you?

(your)

yours

yours

y<u>ou</u>rs

I do not like to play by myself.

Do you like to play by <u>yourself</u>?

(yourselves)

yourself

your-self

yourself

y<u>ou</u>rself

Y

Z

z z Z z

zebra

ze-bra

zebra

z<u>e</u>brȧ

This animal is a <u>zebra.</u>

I saw him at the zoo.

He has dark stripes.

(zebras)

zero

ze-ro

zero

z<u>e</u>r<u>o</u>

It is very cold today.

It is 5 below | zero.
| 0.

Bob missed all the words.

The teacher put a <u>zero</u> on his paper.

A <u>zero</u> means nothing.

(zeros)

zinnia

zin-ni-a

zinnia

z<u>i</u>nn<u>i</u>ȧ

These flowers are <u>zinnias.</u>

They are of many colors.

<u>Zinnias</u> last a long time.

(zinnias)

When you wait for a street car,	zone
stand in the **safety zone.** place marked off for people to stand in.	*zone* z<u>o</u>n<u>e</u>
(zones)	
We saw all kinds of animals at the <u>zoo</u>.	zoo
(zoos)	*zoo* Z<u>OO</u>

Z

Things You Will Want To Know

Days of the Week—

Sunday—Sun.	Thursday—Thurs.
Monday—Mon.	Friday—Fri.
Tuesday—Tues.	Saturday—Sat.
Wednesday—Wed.	

Months of the Year—

January—Jan.	July
February—Feb.	August—Aug.
March—Mar.	September—Sept.
April—Apr.	October—Oct.
May	November—Nov.
June	December—Dec.

Special Days—

New Year's Day—Jan. 1
Lincoln's Birthday—Feb. 12
Valentine's Day—Feb. 14
Washington's Birthday—Feb. 22
Easter Sunday
Memorial Day—May 30
Flag Day—June 14
Fourth of July—July 4
Labor Day—First Monday in September
Columbus Day—October 12
Armistice Day—November 11
Thanksgiving Day—Last Thursday in November
Christmas Day—December 25

EXPLANATION OF
PICTURE WORD BOOK

A CHILD'S DICTIONARY

A dictionary is an indispensable element in the equipment of every educated adult, but it is a formidable and discouraging obstacle to beginning readers. Yet the needs of the children in the early grades for the assistance a dictionary renders in language activities are as real and as pressing as those of their parents. It is surprising that the world has had to wait until the twentieth century for a dictionary written to meet the needs of little children.

The PICTURE WORD BOOK is both less and more than a children's dictionary: less, in that the pronunciation, derivations, and much of the other intricate machinery that constitute the dictionary of the adult is unsuited to the immaturity of beginning readers, and has been omitted; more, in that special care has been taken to present words by pictures, comparisons, context, print, and script in ways that make it possible for very, very young readers to find meanings for unfamiliar symbols, to discover new words related in meaning and spelling to known words, and to adventure on their own initiative in all the activities of language comprised in the conventional school subjects of reading, writing and spelling.

This is a child's own book. The words have been selected with children's needs in mind, and the illustrations, type and arrangement have been adjusted to childish levels of development. Every detail of preparation has been planned for the purpose of *helping* little children who use this book. Here is a children's text which is not designed to be "taught" but "used," and whose use will automatically contribute to worthwhile growth.

Progressive teachers into whose hands this volume falls will welcome a new instrument for developing self-direction, self-appraisal and self-control in children. The average teacher who gives it a trial with her classes will quickly be convinced of its value. Traditionally-minded teachers will find little difficulty in fitting the book into the conventional scheme of memorization and drill. Fortunately, today, all of us are coming to recognize more and more that true growth arises only from self-directed purposeful activity, and that for real learning a child must teach himself. Purpose proves to be the key to educational efficiency, and the intelligent teacher will make plain to the children the potentialities for self-help which the volume offers, practice them in the techniques of its use, and then leave

467

the rest to the children and the book. Any child in the first or second grade who has the desire to read a story, who knows "how" to use this PICTURE WORD BOOK and who has the will to put his knowledge to practical use, can study out by himself the meanings in most books up to a high third grade level. In spelling and language work the book is no less effective. By its help all language activities may be transformed from formal, subject matter, teacher-directed *acquisitions* into natural life-like activities, productive of growth in personality and power.

In selecting the words for this PICTURE WORD BOOK, it was necessary to determine the range of words required to serve adequately the needs and purposes of children in the primary grades. Words were gathered from written work, oral conversation and an analysis of forty-six readers for the primary grades.

For the purpose of determining the relative importance of the words, a composite list was made and checked against Gates "Reading Vocabulary for Primary Grades," the "Horn-Packer List" and Thorndike's "Teachers' Word Book."

The final list of words used for the PICTURE WORD BOOK contains 91.4 per cent of all the words from the forty-six readers. The words selected were common to three or more readers. The list further contains all but five of the Horn-Packer List and all but ten of the Gates List (1926 Edition). The latter ten words consist of words like *ho, ow, hey,* etc. Thirty-nine of the words selected are not found in Thorndike's "Teachers' Word Book." Thirty-two of these words are words like *moving picture,* which are used together frequently as one word but are written as two words. Seventy-two per cent of the words are found in the first and second thousands of the "Teachers' Word Book."

Altogether there are 2154 basic words and 2678 variants. All the variants are not explained. They are placed in parentheses with the basic word to help the child in spelling them. If the child knows the meaning of the basic word, it will be easy for him to interpret the meaning of the variant.

A WORD TO TEACHERS

A book may be used in a great variety of ways, each appropriate for a different purpose, but the *most effective* way to use it is in accordance with the purpose which prompted its formulation. The Picture Word Book may be used as any ordinary textbook is used by teachers who are interested in teaching reading, writing, spelling, and similar language skills. Children will enjoy looking at the pictures, reading the short stories about the words they know, puzzling out the meanings of words they do not know, learning the alphabet, and so on. However, the book was designed specifically for use by those teachers who believe that educational development is best achieved when it occurs spontaneously and incidentally as a by-product of self-directed, purposeful activity.

For the guidance of teachers who are in the process of shifting from traditional to progressive methods, the following suggestions are offered:

1. AIM • In using this Picture Word Book let your goal be "to help children to help themselves." Do nothing for them that they can be stimulated to do for themselves. Remember that each individual is different from every other individual and has the right to follow his own best path of development, choosing in terms of his own taste, growing at his own rate and by his own choice of method.

Let your responsibility be presenting situations, stimulating purposes, helping children plan, act, judge, generalize, conserve and appraise the results of their purposing. Have no fear if the children fail to learn to read, to spell, etc., as rapidly as you had anticipated. Mastery of these skills will result from purposeful activity. Eventually each child will acquire ability mature enough to deal successfully with situations which involve the use of the language arts, but his growth as a person, his integrity as an individual, demands he shall have freedom to develop in terms of his own nature.

2. MEANS • The Picture Word Book is **a tool**; it should always be used **as a means to an end**, never as an end in itself. The teacher should create situations in which need is apparent to the child before putting the means of satisfying that need in his hands. Always have in mind a purpose beyond the means which will predetermine the use of the means itself. The child must have the desire to achieve some purpose and must have met some obstacle to the achievement of that goal that the Picture Word Book can help remove, **before** he is given the book itself. For instance, if a child finds a story about a dog in his reader and really desires to enjoy the story but comes upon words like "excited," or "rushed," the meaning of which he does not know, his enjoyment of the story is blocked. The teacher might say, "Here is a book that will help you. I can show you how to find words you do not know in this book. It will tell you what the words mean. When you know how to use this Picture Word Book you can read any story." The child will appreciate that the dictionary is a tool which he can use to help him achieve his own purpose of enjoying printed stories.

3. PREREQUISITES • The Picture Word Book is a supplementary book. As soon as beginning readers have grasped the concept of words as symbols for experiences and ideas, the use of the dictionary may be begun. Its use should continue until the maturity of the reader has led him into vocabularies beyond the five thousand words in the Picture Word Book (about third grade development). By this time he will be ready to change from the simple Picture Word Book to some more advanced dictionary for children.

4. USES • As soon as little first graders have learned to recognize any words as symbols for objects, they will enjoy searching through the Picture Word Book for words that they can identify by the pictures. This is probably the simplest use of the Picture Word Book.

The next step is more difficult but equally enjoyable: searching through the Picture Word Book for the names of objects. If a teacher puts a series of drawings on the board—a cat, dog, or cow—and the child who first finds the corresponding picture and name in his book comes and prints the name of the object on the board, copying it from his dictionary, the game is one which gives the child a sense of delightful power. The next step is easy. The teacher prints unknown words like "rabbit" or "tree" on the board and the child looks them up to discover their meanings from their pictures. This of course is the true use of the dictionary.

A child does not need to know his alphabet to look up words; he has to be able only to match letters, and with very immature beginning readers this matching activity can well be carried on as a game Note that although a child may not know the alphabet when he first begins to use the dictionary, he soon learns it through continuous use. When the children become fairly free in using the alphabet, there comes a time when the slower children will profit by drills designed to give the child systematic and conscious control over the alphabet as such. It is better to let the children grow into a knowledge of the alphabet before drill than to attempt to teach the alphabet specifically first. The same thing is true of phonics. Help the child **generalize** the sounds of the letters from his experiences with words rather than try to teach him the sounds as an aid **to** reading words.

Before very long first graders will begin of themselves to enjoy reading the short stories (definitions) under the pictures in the Picture Word Book, an activity which should be encouraged. The Picture Word Book is essentially a series of stimuli to self-help in "puzzling things out for one's self" and as soon as this activity makes its appearance, it should be highly praised and rejoiced over. Once a child gets the idea that self-help is possible, he will use his dictionary to tackle any reading. Indeed the danger is that he will expect **too** much of his tool.

It is only a **first** dictionary and is most valuable to readers on the levels found in the first three grades. When a child first finds a word in his reading that is not presented in the Picture Word Book, it will be necessary for the teacher to tell him what the word means, but as soon as the demands on the teacher begin to multiply, it is time to introduce the children to a dictionary on a higher level. The transition should be gradual; occurring more and more frequently until at last the child himself abandons the Picture Word Book for a more advanced dictionary.

A teacher will do well to have two kinds **of** learning experiences in her class. At first the children will spend most of their time in formal reading exercises directed by the teacher, with occasional games in the use of the Picture Word Book to break the monotony and to serve the purposes of review and stimulation. Then, as some children progress faster than others, they can be set free for self-directed reading involving self-help use of the dictionary. The teacher's group will gradually become smaller and smaller so that she can focus her attention on the more difficult cases. From time to time the whole class will be brought together for testing and review, but for the most part the Picture Word Book makes it possible for a teacher soon to **individualize completely** her work and let each child progress at his own rate, and read in terms of his own tastes and choices.

A wise teacher will grade her books and supplementary reading materials and see that each child reads material at his own reading level. If a child must look up **every** word in the Picture Word Book he gets little pleasure from his activity, but if he knows most of the words in a book, it is a pleasure to master those he does not know. By arranging a carefully graded series of readers a teacher can insure both continuous progress on the part of the child and continuous enjoyment of his reading.

5. USES OTHER THAN READING • The use of the Picture Word Book should not be restricted to the reading class. In his English work, if a child is in doubt about the spelling of a word. he should be encouraged to look it up in his dictionary Similarly, the dictionary furnishes script models for the writing class, and print models for children who have not yet learned to write or who prefer manuscript. A child meets unknown words in arithmetic and other classes and the use of the dictionary should be encouraged in these classes also. In other words the wise teacher takes care to develop the "dictionary habit" from the very first grade.

6. APPRAISAL • The Picture Word Book may be used for testing purposes in reading, writing spelling, etc. Sentences involving new words may be put on the board and the whole class tested as to the rate at which the children are able to read and write their interpretations. Words which they are able to recognize may be classified and written in alphabetical lists. There is scarcely any phase of the language arts for which the ingenious and resourceful teacher cannot use the Picture Word Book as a test booklet.

By far the most significant appraisal, however is the child's own spontaneous use of the Picture Word Book for his own purposes. The child who of his own volition takes out the dictionary and pores over its pages, reading and rereading the words and stories he knows, puzzling out ever more of those he does not know is making satisfactory progress and learning to love to read. The child who insists on having his dictionary handy whenever he tries to read and who is adventurous and courageous in tackling by means of his dictionary any printed matter to which he has access has acquired ideas and powers far more valuable than any mere reading skill. It is to be hoped that all teachers into whose hands the Picture Word Book comes, will capitalize its many opportunities for the development of self-direction, self-appraisal and self-control as well as those for the development of the narrower language purposes and skills.

7. HOW TO USE THE INDEX • The index (pages 471-478), which contains both the defined and undefined words included in this dictionary, was compiled to aid teachers, not children. It will help them in determining quickly whether a word sought appears in the dictionary and it will serve those engaged in word study research. All defined words are next to the margin and all the variants included but not defined are indented.

WHERE TO FIND WORDS IN THIS PICTURE WORD BOOK
A CHILD'S DICTIONARY

All defined words are next to the margin and all variants included but not defined are indented.